Organised Crime, Criminal Procedure, and Prisons

This book explores a range of topics relating to the prosecution and trial of organised crime and the punishment, especially imprisonment, of members of organised criminal groups. Organised crime poses particular challenges to the criminal justice system. While much of the attention of policy-makers, legislators, law enforcement, and the media is on criminalisation and investigation, much less attention, including academic analysis, has been devoted to the unique problems posed by organised crime to criminal procedure and to the prison system. This book gives particular attention to the role and powers of prosecutors and the judiciary, measures relating to criminal proceedings, international cooperation, sentencing, and the situations in prisons. The book is intended to be a valuable guide for academics, researchers and policy-makers working in the areas of organised crime, international criminal justice, criminal procedures, and prisons.

Andreas Schloenhardt (PhD, Adelaide; chief editor) is Professor of Criminal Law at The University of Queensland and Honorary Professor of Foreign and International Criminal Law at the University of Vienna.

Bettina Weisser (Dr jur, University of Konstanz) is Professor of Criminal Law and Director of the Institute for Comparative Criminal Law at the University of Cologne.

Monika Stempkowski (Dr ius, University of Vienna) is a postgraduate researcher in the Department of Criminal Law and Criminology at the University of Vienna. She is also a trained clinical psychologist and practices as a mediator.

Gian Ege (Dr ius, University of Zurich) is Assistant Professor of Criminal Law and Criminal Procedure at the University of Zurich.

Transnational Criminal Justice

The concept of 'transnational criminal justice' has frequently been interpreted in the academic literature as 'international criminal justice' or 'global criminal justice'. Many publications that use the term 'transnational' therefore discuss international criminal justice and international legal frameworks. Another form of studies that has developed under the umbrella of transnationality in the field of criminal law is comparative. There has hence been a move from the terminology of 'international', 'global' and 'comparative' criminal justice towards 'transnational' criminal justice.

This series considers these developments, but focuses primarily on publications that adhere to a more literal interpretation of the term 'transnational'. The aim of the series is to provide a forum for discussion of bilateral and multilateral relationships between nations in the field of criminal justice. International law influences these relationships, but is not the focus here. Equally, to explain transnational relationships, comparative analyses are required. While incorporating comparative studies in this series, their aim is the explanation of challenges to criminal justice cooperation in bilateral or multilateral relationships.

Series Editor
Saskia Hufnagel, Queen Mary University of London, UK

Titles in this series:

Cultural Property Crime and the Law
Legal Approaches to Protection, Repatriation, and Countering Illicit Trade
Michelle Fabiani, Kate Melody Burmon and Saskia Hufnagel

Extradition and Political Crimes
The Use of the Political Offence Exception in Europe
Sibel Top

Organised Crime, Criminal Procedure, and Prisons
Prosecuting and Punishing Organised Criminal Groups
Edited by Andreas Schloenhardt, Bettina Weisser, Monika Stempkowski, and Gian Ege

For more information about this series, please visit:
https://www.routledge.com/Transnational-Criminal-Justice/book-series/TRANSCJ

Organised Crime, Criminal Procedure, and Prisons

Prosecuting and Punishing Organised Criminal Groups

Edited by Andreas Schloenhardt, Bettina Weisser, Monika Stempkowski, and Gian Ege

Routledge
Taylor & Francis Group
LONDON AND NEW YORK

First published 2025
by Routledge
4 Park Square, Milton Park, Abingdon, Oxon OX14 4RN

and by Routledge
605 Third Avenue, New York, NY 10158

Routledge is an imprint of the Taylor & Francis Group, an informa business

British Library Cataloguing-in-Publication Data
A catalogue record for this book is available from the British Library

Library of Congress Cataloging-in-Publication Data
Names: Schloenhardt, Andreas, editor. | Weisser, Bettina, editor. | Stempkowski, Monika, editor. | Ege, Gian, editor.
Title: Organised crime, criminal procedure, and prisons : prosecuting and punishing organised criminal groups / [edited by] Andreas Schloenhardt, Bettina Weisser, Monika Stempkowski, Gian Ege.
Other titles: Organized crime, criminal procedure, and prisons
Description: Abingdon, Oxon [UK] ; New York, NY : Routledge, 2025. | Series: Transnational criminal justice | Includes bibliographical references and index.
Identifiers: LCCN 2025003069 | ISBN 9781032852102 (hardback) | ISBN 9781032856674 (paperback) | ISBN 9781003519317 (ebook)
Subjects: LCSH: Organized crime--Law and legislation. | Transnational crime--Law and legislation. | Criminal procedure. | Prisons--Law and legislation. | Human trafficking--Law and legislation. | Obstruction of justice | Prosecution.
Classification: LCC K5240 .O74 2025 | DDC 345/.05--dc23/eng/20250128
LC record available at https://lccn.loc.gov/2025003069

ISBN: 978-1-032-85210-2 (hbk)
ISBN: 978-1-032-85667-4 (pbk)
ISBN: 978-1-003-51931-7 (ebk)

DOI: 10.4324/9781003519317

Typeset in Sabon
by Deanta Global Publishing Services, Chennai, India

Contents

About the editors and authors

Andreas Schloenhardt (PhD, Adelaide; chief editor) is Professor of Criminal Law at The University of Queensland and Honorary Professor of Foreign and International Criminal Law at the University of Vienna.

Bettina Weisser (Dr jur, University of Konstanz) is Professor of Criminal Law and Director of the Institute for Comparative Criminal Law at the University of Cologne.

Monika Stempkowski (Dr ius, University of Vienna) is a postgraduate researcher in the Department of Criminal Law and Criminology at the University of Vienna. She is also a trained clinical psychologist and practices as a mediator.

Gian Ege (Dr ius, University of Zurich) is Assistant Professor of Criminal Law and Criminal Procedure at the University of Zurich.

Contributors

Gianmarco Bondi (PhD) is a postdoctoral researcher at the University of Ferrara.

Benedikt Grünert (Mag iur) is a research assistant and doctoral candidate at the Department of Constitutional and Administrative Law at the University of Vienna.

Joseph Lelliott (PhD) is a senior lecturer at The University of Queensland in Brisbane.

Jonathan Macziola is a research associate and PhD candidate at the Institute for Comparative Criminal Law at the University of Cologne.

Marilù Porchia (PhD) is a postdoctoral researcher at the University of Tuscia and a PhD graduate from the University of Ferrara.

Genevieve Rule (LLB/BA Int'l Relations, Econ) is a Judge's Associate at the Supreme Court of Queensland.

Lena Wasser is a research associate and PhD candidate at the Institute for Comparative Criminal Law at the University of Cologne.

Abbreviations

ASEAN	Association of South-East Asian Nations
BGH	Bundesgerichtshof [Federal Court of Justice (Germany)]
cf.	compare
CDPP	Commonwealth Director of Public Prosecutions
CJEU	Court of Justice of the European Union
Cth	Commonwealth of Australia
EAW	European Arrest Warrant
ECHR	European Convention on Human Rights
ECtHR	European Court of Human Rights
e.g.	for example
EPPO	European Public Prosecutor's Office
esp.	especially
EU	European Union
EUR	Euro
Eurojust	European Union Agency for Criminal Justice Cooperation
Europol	European Union Agency for Law Enforcement Cooperation
ICCPR	International Covenant for Civil and Political Rights
JIT	Joint Investigation Team
LED	[European Union] Law Enforcement Directive
MLAT	Mutual Legal Assistance Treaty
MoU	Memorandum of Understanding
OAS	Organization of American States
OHCHR	Office of the United Nations High Commissioner for Human Rights
StGB	Strafgesetzbuch [*Criminal Code* (Germany)]
StPO	Strafprozessordnung [*Code of Criminal Procedure* (Germany)]
UNCAC	United Nations Convention against Corruption
UNODC	United Nations Office on Drugs and Crime
UNTOC	United Nations Convention against Transnational Organized Crime
US	United States
USD	United States Dollar

1 Introduction

Andreas Schloenhardt

Organised crime poses particular challenges to the criminal justice system. The influence and power, assets and other resources, geographical and personal networks of organised criminal groups not only make it difficult to detect their crimes, disrupt their operations, and penetrate them; through coercion and corruption, such groups can pervert the course of justice, frustrate prosecutions, disrupt criminal proceedings, and, even if convicted, continue their activities from behind prison walls.

Much has been said and written about the need to criminalise organised criminal groups and enhance laws and law enforcement. The *United Nations Convention against Transnational Organized Crime*,[1] which celebrates its 25th anniversary in the year this book is published, marks a milestone in global efforts to prevent and suppress organised crime. Despite its many flaws, this Convention has established a universal framework that has found widespread adoption around the world and has achieved a level of synergy and harmonisation of the vocabulary, criminal offences, and investigative measures used to fight organised crime in different jurisdictions.

But while much of the attention of policymakers, legislators, law enforcement, international organisations, and the media has been on the criminalisation and investigation of organised crime, much less attention, including academic analysis, has been devoted to the unique problems posed by organised criminal groups to criminal procedure and the prison system. This book seeks to be a starting point to close this gap, to draw attention to the many ways in which organised criminal groups can interfere with and exert influence over criminal justice authorities, and to provide insight into the challenges faced by prosecutors, the judiciary, and correctional services when confronting organised crime.

Specifically, this book on *Organised Crime, Criminal Procedure, and Prisons: Prosecuting and Punishing Organised Criminal Groups* aims to identify and document the unique challenges associated with the prosecution,

1 Opened for signature 15 November 2000, 2225 UNTS 209 (entered into force 29 September 2003).

DOI: 10.4324/9781003519317-1

judicial proceedings, and detention of organised criminal groups and their members; illustrate these problems using international and national examples; outline and critically analyse legislative and practical measures adopted at the international level to address these problems; examine selected national responses to address challenges faced by prosecutors, the judiciary, and correctional services; and, insofar as possible, identify existing weaknesses and gaps and develop recommendations to address these deficiencies.

It is acknowledged from the outset that there are many limitations to this quest. For reasons of time and space, a book of this size can merely capture a small selection of examples and solutions. Wherever possible, the book prioritises global perspectives over regional approaches and national experiences. Such approaches and examples are included, where relevant, to highlight specific problems or to showcase notable responses.

The editors are well aware that there are many facets of organised criminal groups and many 'weapons' used in the so-called 'war on organised crime' that find no or only marginal mention in this book. While every effort has been made to comprehensively explore the problems posed by organised crime to criminal procedure and prisons, this book is—and is intended to be—merely a first step to canvass the issues, raise critical questions, and flag promising practices. The editors hope that this provides inspiration and encouragement to the authors of the present chapters as well as other scholars to critically examine the myriad of challenges and countermeasures developed at national, regional, and global levels in greater detail than a book of this size and scope can deliver.

This book is a product of the joint Transnational Organised Crime programme, a research and learning network first established in 2018 by the University of Queensland (Brisbane, Australia), the University of Vienna (Austria), and the University of Zurich (Switzerland). In 2022, the University of Cologne (Germany) and the University of Ferrara (Italy) joined this programme. Bringing together a global network of established and emerging scholars to work collaboratively within a structured research and learning framework, this programme aims to produce high-quality research outcomes on topics relating to transnational organised crime. The programme involves some of the best-known scholars on organised crime and transnational criminal law and three directors of university centres in Austria, Germany, and Italy devoted to research on organised crime, law enforcement, criminal justice, and international criminal law. The programme also provides an opportunity for doctoral candidates, postgraduate and undergraduate students to conduct in-depth research under the guidance of senior staff and to work closely with international organisations, national authorities, and other experts on topics of concern to policymakers, legislators, and criminal justice authorities. The present volume is a product of this unique teaching and research collaboration, and it is testimony to the enthusiasm that carries the Transnational Organised Crime programme. This book follows the publication of previous edited collections on wildlife trafficking (2020), arms trafficking (2022), and the legalisation and decriminalisation of narcotic drugs and psychotropic substances (2023). For further information about the programme, its people, and publications visit www.toc.jura.uni-koeln.de.

This book is divided into three parts: (1) procedure, (2) international cooperation, and (3) prisons.

Part 1—Organised crime and criminal procedure

Chapter 2 provides an overview of the challenges posed by organised crime to criminal justice proceedings. Since the driving force behind such crimes is the organisation itself, it does not suffice to investigate individual crimes that have already been committed. Instead, law enforcement authorities must target the organisation itself in order to dismantle its business structures and thus effectively prevent it from initiating crimes in the future. After a brief description of the specific difficulties in combating organised crime, a variety of procedural countermeasures are presented.

Organised criminal groups frequently intimidate and bribe witnesses, threaten police officers, and sometimes even kill prosecutors and judges. Obstruction of justice is one of the most powerful tools in achieving impunity, constituting a considerable threat to the criminal justice system and those involved in it. Chapter 3 examines obstruction of justice in the context of organised crime from a criminological perspective, analyses relevant international frameworks regarding criminalisation, and highlights different approaches to implementing obstruction of justice as a statutory offence throughout various jurisdictions.

Chapter 4 explores the role of confiscation in relation to organised crime on national and international levels. It outlines strengths and shortcomings, in particular the difficulties in linking specific assets to specific crimes. The concept of non-conviction-based confiscation, that is confiscation without a conviction by a criminal court, is explored as a possible remedy for long-standing problems. A closer look is taken at the German legislation on non-conviction-based confiscation in organised crime cases, and how the challenges in implementing such laws may be addressed.

Victims of trafficking in persons are commonly required to appear as witnesses in criminal proceedings against their traffickers. While often necessary to secure convictions of perpetrators, this entails potentially serious risks for victims. In addition to the threats generally faced by witnesses, trafficked persons have particular vulnerabilities as victims of crime. They may also face re-traumatisation in the process of giving evidence. Chapter 5 examines the protection of victim-witnesses of trafficking in persons, including international obligations and best practices, as well as approaches to the protection of such persons in Australia. It concludes with several suggestions to improve the treatment of victim-witnesses in criminal proceedings.

Part 2—International cooperation

Comprehensive international cooperation is essential to ensure the appropriate investigation and prosecution of transnational organised crime. Chapter 6 presents and outlines the main mechanisms in international law which enable and enhance cross-border prosecution and judicial cooperation in organised crime cases. The main focus is on the provisions on extradition, mutual legal assistance, transfer of proceedings, and transfer of sentenced persons under the *United Nations Convention against Transnational Organized Crime* (UNTOC). Relevant frameworks established by regional organisations are also considered where relevant.

Chapter 7 explores the question of whether the European Arrest Warrant could serve as a possible model for global extradition agreements in order to fight transnational organised crime. After comparing the European Arrest Warrant with traditional extradition law and the existing extradition regime in the UNTOC, the chapter investigates whether and how the concept of the European Arrest Warrant could be transferred to the global level.

Chapter 8 explores the role of Joint Investigation Teams (JITs) set up under Article 19 of the UNTOC in cases involving transnational organised crime and the impact JITs could have on internationally protected human rights. The chapter introduces the structure, content, and scope of Article 19. It then examines potential human rights issues arising in connection with the operation of a JIT. The chapter's conclusion outlines strategies to find a balance between the prosecution's needs in organised crime cases and human rights safeguards, putting forward recommendations to States.

Part 3—Organised crime and prisons

The detention of members of organised criminal groups poses unique challenges to the prison system, with members continuing their criminal activities, recruiting new members, and fighting rival groups in prison. International legal frameworks and regional prison standards provide almost no guidance to States on how best to address these issues. The purpose of Chapter 9 is to identify the relevant challenges for the criminal justice system as well as to explore the (limited) international frameworks setting out detention parameters. The chapter analyses a range of legal and practical measures adopted by national correctional systems and highlights their advantages and disadvantages.

The '41 bis' Italian prison regime (named after the article in the *Prison Administration Act*) is designed to limit interaction between those deemed dangerous for their ties to organised criminal groups to other inmates and the outside. Chapter 10 discusses the rationale and criticism concerning the purposes and contents of this regime and its compatibility with the *Italian Constitution* and the *European Convention for the Protection of Human Rights and Fundamental Freedoms.*[2] It examines the special prison regime (including its 'reserved areas') by analysing the case law of the European Court of Human Rights. Furthermore, potential future trends are assessed with reference to international detention standards. Finally, the issue of proportionality is discussed, and reform proposals are offered.

2 Opened for signature 4 November 1950, ETS No 5 (entered into force 3 September 1953).

Part 1

Organised crime and criminal procedure

2 The challenge of organised crime to criminal proceedings

Bettina Weisser

2.1 Introduction

In June 2024, 300 kilogrammes of cannabis were stolen from a warehouse in Cologne, Germany. Since then, the State of North-Rhine Westphalia has seen a series of mysterious explosions, shots fired at private homes, and abductions at more than 20 different crime scenes in and around Cologne. More than 40 investigations are currently ongoing.[1] The *modus operandi* of the perpetrators—more than 30 suspects are in custody—is similar, and the odds are high that the crimes are connected. The key suspect is in custody in France, and extradition has been requested by German investigative bodies. Law enforcement authorities also suspect links to Dutch and Belgian organised crime structures, mainly active in the field of drug crimes. Since the origin of the drugs is in the Netherlands, a connection to the Dutch so-called 'Mocro Mafia' is very likely. Against this backdrop, it seems that a turf war among drug crime syndicates that has been taking place in the Netherlands for years is now spilling over to Germany after the German legislator partially legalised the use of cannabis in July 2024.

This is only one very recent and dramatic example of organised crime, yet it already illustrates the challenges that the combat of organised crime entails for law enforcement authorities. Some of the hurdles standing in the way of effective law enforcement and the procedural remedies for overcoming them will be outlined below. However, an in-depth analysis would require a broad comparative perspective of numerous national procedural systems, which cannot be provided here due to the limited space of this chapter. The main perspective of this chapter is that of the European Union.

2.2 Defining organised crime

It is obvious and undisputed that the specific character of organised crime causes unique challenges for criminal proceedings. However, as widely as this

1 This text dates to October 2024.

DOI: 10.4324/9781003519317-3

fact is agreed upon in the literature, as well as in judicial practice, as vague and unclear is the actual definition of what the term organised crime encompasses.[2] Neither the *United Nations Convention on Transnational Organised Crime* (UNTOC)[3] nor any legal instrument of the European Union entails a legally binding, comprehensive definition of organised crime.

This chapter is certainly not the place for an extensive debate on the various concepts of the phenomenon of organised crime as such.[4] Instead, the following outline concentrates on the most pertinent aspects of organised crime and on specific features of organised crime that are particularly linked to investigative and procedural challenges. The cause for most procedural challenges is the commission of crimes by a multitude of accomplices over a certain period and in the framework of an organisational structure. In that regard, the UNTOC defines the crucial term 'organised criminal group' to mean

> a structured group of three or more persons, existing for a period of time and acting in concert with the aim of committing one or more serious crimes or offences … in order to obtain, directly or indirectly, a financial or other material benefit.[5]

In general, such criminal groups are engaged in a wide range of crimes directed at gaining profits. The classic examples are trafficking in persons, drugs, and

2 Liz Campbell, *Organised Crime and the Law. A Comparative Analysis* (Hart, 2013) 13–20.

3 Opened for signature on 15 November 2000, 2225 UNTS 209 (entered into force on 29 September 2003). See, on the lack of a definition of organised crime in the UNTOC, Neil Boister, *An Introduction to Transnational Criminal Law* (Oxford University Press, 2nd ed 2018) 132–135; Neil Boister, 'The UN Convention Against Transnational Organised Crime 2000' in Pierre Hauck and Sven Peterke (eds), *International Law and Transnational Organised Crime* (Oxford University Press, 2016) 126, 134–135.

4 See for an overview of definitions provided in academic literature and in judicial practice: Klaus von Lampe, *Organized Crime. Analysing Illegal Activities, Criminal Structures, and Extra-Legal Governance* (Sage, 2016) 26–30; Arndt Sinn, 'Transnational Organised Crime: Concepts and Critics' in Pierre Hauck and Sven Peterke (eds), *International Law and Transnational Organised Crime* (Oxford University Press, 2016) 24, 29–33. The problem of according more intrusive procedural powers to law enforcement in the area of organised crime while at the same time relying on an unclear definition of this crime phenomenon is addressed by Stefania Carnevale, 'The Notion of Organised Crime as a Justification for Special Rules of Criminal Procedure: The Derogations from the Ordinary Model and their Rationale' in Stefania Carnevale, Serena Forlati and Orsetta Giolo (eds), *Redefining Organised Crime: A Challenge for the European Union?* (Hart, 2017) 359, 359–361.

5 UNTOC, Article 2(a). Similarly, Article 1 of the *Council Framework Decision 2008/841/JHA of 24 October 2008 on the Fight Against Organised Crime* defines the term 'criminal organisation' to mean 'a structured association, established over a period of time, of more than two persons acting in concert with a view to committing offences which are punishable by deprivation of liberty or a detention order of a maximum of at least four years or a more serious penalty, to obtain, directly or indirectly, a financial or other material benefit', OJ L 300/42, 43.

firearms; (online) fraud; organised property crime; corruption; counterfeiting and cyberattacks; extortion and racketeering.[6]

The root of these crimes lies in the criminal organisation which coordinates the array of accomplices and provides the infrastructure for sustained activity in certain fields of crime. As long as the organisation persists, the commission of crimes will continue even if individual actors are prosecuted. Therefore, effective law enforcement must target the organisation as such rather than single members or supporters (see 2.3.2).

Criminal organisations and their *modi operandi* can take many different forms, requiring increasingly sophisticated responses to combat them. The classic Mafia-like organised criminal group[7] is perceived as a hierarchically structured criminal organisation, specialising in one field of crime and directed by one leading figure positioned at the organisation's top management level. However, nowadays such clearly structured 'traditional' organisations, which are also defined by strong personal (family) ties between their members, are complemented by more modern networks lacking a strictly hierarchical structure with only one figurehead. Instead, these organisations are structured more loosely and often consist of a number of cells cooperating in a fragmented manner.[8] Things are further complicated by organised groups working together for certain crimes and then separating again for others. Finally, sometimes criminal networks also collaborate sporadically with individual 'outsiders' (for example, persons with specific expert knowledge needed for the commission of certain crimes).[9]

6 Europol, *Decoding the EU's Most Threatening Criminal Networks* (2024) <https://www.europol.europa.eu/cms/sites/default/files/documents/Europol%20report%20on%20Decoding%20the%20EU-s%20most%20threatening%20criminal%20networks.pdf> 27. See also Fulvia Staiano, *Transnational Organized Crime. Challenging International Law Principles on State Jurisdiction* (Edward Elgar, 2022) 10–12; Philip B Heymann and Stephen P Heymann, *Challenging Organized Crime in the Western Hemisphere: A Game of Moves and Countermoves* (Routledge, 2019) 40.

7 On the history of this 'prototype' of a criminal organisation, see Boister, *An Introduction to Transnational Criminal Law* (n 3) 126–128.

8 Europol (n 6) 6: 'network environment where cooperation between criminals is fluid, systematic and profit-driven'; see also Europol, *European Union Serious and Organised Crime Threat Assessment. A Corrupting Influence: The Infiltration and Undermining of Europe's Economy and Society by Organised Crime* (2021) <https://www.europol.europa.eu/publications-events/main-reports/socta-report> 50; and European Commission, *Communication from the Commission to the European Parliament, the Council, the European Economic and Social Committee and the Committee of the Regions on the EU Strategy to Tackle Organised Crime 2021–2025*, COM(2021) 170 final (14 April 2021) 11 ('COM(2021) 170 final').

9 Europol (n 6) 6.

2.3 Four reasons for the difficulties in combating organised crime

Many investigative and prosecutorial problems are caused by these organisational peculiarities and complex cooperation structures behind the crimes committed, but also by the specific nature of the crimes themselves.

2.3.1 The lack of immediate victims and/or witnesses due to the 'cooperative' character of crimes

The prosecution targets individuals responsible for specific crimes, in most cases after a victim and/or witnesses report the crime—like a car theft or a bodily assault—to the police. However, the crimes committed in the framework of criminal organisations—for example, drug trafficking and dealing or corruption—are very often committed cooperatively on both sides of the crime. Therefore, there is no victim interested in filing charges or alerting the police. Hence, law enforcement must actively look out for crimes like drug trafficking or trafficking in firearms to bring the perpetrators to justice. Consequently, from the outset, this type of criminal investigation requires a significantly greater investigative effort than cases of ordinary crimes.[10]

2.3.2 The division of labour among a multitude of accomplices

The most pressing challenges in investigating and prosecuting organised criminal activities are caused by the organisational structure of the crimes. Naturally, it is easier to apprehend a single perpetrator than to uncover the multi-faceted links between the criminal masterminds devising a plan, the primary perpetrators carrying out the crime, the aiders and abettors supporting its commission, and finally those who launder the illicit profits, usually by running legal businesses. Investigation and prosecution must move away from concentrating on individual participants of specific crimes and strive for the bigger picture of the organisation's activities as a whole.[11] Merely taking a single suspect out of the picture by prosecuting him or her does not necessarily mean that the organisation or even the network of organisational cells is in any way hampered. In a criminal organisation, a single actor can usually easily be replaced by another. Moreover, an immense downside of apprehending one of the accomplices could be the organisation or whole network being alerted and strengthening their efforts in covering up their criminal activities. This could jeopardise the investigation of the organisation itself, for example, if its members start looking for and identifying whistleblowers or undercover

10 Cf. von Lampe (n 4) 383.

11 Cf. European Commission, *Communication from the Commission to the European Parliament and the Council on the EU Roadmap to Fight Drug Trafficking and Organised Crime*, COM(2023) 641 final (18 October 2023) 11 ('COM(2023) 641 final').

agents, intimidating them, and, in the worst case, 'turning' them, thereby setting back the entire investigation.

Furthermore, even if an apprehended member is one of the organisation's leaders, their detention and/or successful prosecution and conviction does not necessarily stop or even affect the business activities of the network. In some cases, figureheads continue their work behind bars and find ways to effectively direct criminal networks from there.[12] To prevent this, some countries, such as Italy, have introduced very rigid prison conditions for organised crime leaders to prevent their continuing activities.[13]

Accordingly, the second difficulty presents itself in that not only a single crime must be investigated and solved, but numerous different crimes forming part of the organisation's various legal and illegal activities. The investigation is thus directed at a whole tapestry of undertakings consisting of numerous people with numerous different roles in the organisation or the organisational network. In some cases, investigations will also extend to supporting third parties, such as straw men or minors, who are misused for criminal activities such as scouting out buildings or stealing property.

2.3.3 The element of time in organised criminal activity

The third problem results from organised crime not occurring at a defined point in time but stretching over a longer period and, in most cases, continuing while investigations are underway. The interwoven criminal network not only leads to the necessity of investigating multiple people, but also requires that the focus of the investigation not be solely on crimes committed in the past. If law enforcement aims to stop the criminal activities of the network

12 Europol (n 6) 26: 'Leaders often continue to coordinate criminal operations from prison ... some networks also demonstrate a high degree of resilience and agility with multiple key network members imprisoned'.

13 Article 41 bis of the Italian *Prison Administration Act* entails very harsh communication restrictions – see for details including restrictive decisions of the Italian Constitutional Court: Carnevale (n 4) 370, 377–379; cf. also 'Italy's "41 bis" Special Prison Regime for Leading Organised Crime Figures', Chapter 10 in this volume. A similar so-called *incommunicado* provision was introduced in Germany (§ 31 *Introductory Act to the Courts Constitution Act*) in the heyday of terrorist attacks committed by the so-called Red Army Faction in the 1970s exclusively for incarcerated terrorists. However, since then, the measure has never again been practised—and it has been partly abandoned since the formerly possible prohibition of contact even with the (defence) counsel was abolished in 2017; see *Zweites Gesetz zur Stärkung der Verfahrensrechte von Beschuldigten im Strafverfahren und zur Änderung des Schöffenrechts vom 27. August 2017* [Second Law to Strengthen the Procedural Rights of Defendants in Criminal Proceedings and to Amend the Law on Jurors of 27 August 2017], Bundesgesetzblatt ['BGBl'] I, 2017, 3295; Cf. in detail Bettina Weisser, 'Confidentiality of Correspondence with Counsel as a Requirement of a Fair Trial: The Situation in Germany' in Lorena Bachmaier Winter, Stephen C Thaman and Veronica Lynn (eds), *The Right to Counsel and the Protection of Attorney-Client Privilege in Criminal Proceedings. A Comparative View* (Springer, 2020) 105, 122.

altogether, simply bringing the participants of certain past crimes to justice does not suffice. Instead, the network as a whole needs to be studied to put an end to its detrimental activities. Hence, the focus of law enforcement must extend beyond the mere detection of past crimes to the prevention of future crimes envisaged in furtherance of the organisation's criminal endeavours.[14]

2.3.4 *The spatial element of organised crime*

The fourth issue is the commission of organised crimes not being concentrated at a defined location but usually spread across many locations, including across borders.[15] Therefore, suspects as well as evidence are located at various places. This leads to local law enforcement seeing only limited parts of the whole picture. The problem of transnational commission of crimes is exacerbated by the fact that crimes (esp. fraud) are increasingly committed over the internet[16] and are therefore borderless by nature.

2.4 Procedural remedies

To identify and apprehend as many of the involved individuals as possible, one must examine multiple facets of the criminal organisation over an extended period of time. Factors to be considered include organisational structures, the interplay between numerous actors, the *modus operandi* in the commission of serious crimes, as well as business conduct and the relationship between legal and illegal business structures. Forceful responses to organised crime must take all the above-mentioned aspects into consideration and can thus only be achieved through a holistic effort.[17] This also means that investigations must not only focus on the past but must also take on a preventive approach.[18] The main effort must be to stop criminal organisations' activities for the future by

14 Cf. Heymann and Heymann (n 6) 43.

15 In the area of freedom, security and justice of the European Union, the most threatening criminal networks extend not only over all of the 27 EU Member States and neighbouring countries participating in the Schengen agreement but also over all global regions, see Europol (n 6) 44.

16 Cf. Europol, *Internet Organised Crime Threat Assessment (IOCTA)* (2024) <https://www.europol.europa.eu/publications-events/main-reports/iocta-report>.

17 COM(2023) 641 final (n 11) 6: '... it is vital to increase law enforcement and judicial authorities' capabilities to dismantle criminal networks, disrupt their business models and confiscate their profits'.

18 Ibid.: 'A strong focus on prevention is ... necessary: to prevent people and businesses from being exploited by criminal networks, we need to tackle the root causes of organised crime and take action against criminal activities as a permanent solution. This requires not only efforts of law enforcement authorities but also of municipalities and local communities'. See also von Lampe (n 4) 383.

disrupting their organisational structures, taking away their knowledge, manpower, and, above all, their illegal profits.[19]

2.4.1 *Access to information*

To effectively combat organised crime, it is salient to shed light on the interplay of collaborating accomplices in and among criminal organisations and/or criminally organised networks. Information on the structure of criminal organisations, the division of labour, the interplay of members and supporters, as well as the different fields of engagement, is key for an effective fight against their criminal activities. All these factors must be studied closely over a length of time. To this end, the covert monitoring of members and supporters of criminal organisations is necessary.[20] This can be achieved by covert investigative measures such as the surveillance of communication and the conduct of criminals, both in public and in private.[21] The more intrusive the investigative measures are and the more they move away from observing conduct in public to actually encroaching on a group of suspects' private lives, the more procedural safeguards are needed. In most jurisdictions, a court order is necessary for intrusive covert investigative measures directed at individuals.[22]

The use of informants on the inside of an organisation or of undercover agents acting within organised structures can be even more effective than investigative measures targeting individuals from the outside.[23] The range of application of undercover agents can serve various purposes and need not be restricted to investigating and disclosing the *modus operandi* within the organisation. For instance, should occasions arise, undercover agents could also attempt to actively prevent members of the organisation from infiltrating legal businesses or corrupting public officials. Hence, both investigative and preventive aims of State interventions could be considered.[24]

All of these investigative measures are tedious and costly. Therefore, law enforcement will only resort to them if the resources are available and there is a chance of a successful conclusion to the investigation. However, if the criminal organisation operates in a territory stretching far beyond local law enforcement's jurisdiction—as is usually the case—the prospects of the immediate

19 COM(2023) 641 final (n 11) 6.

20 See Boister, *An Introduction to Transnational Criminal Law* (n 3) 296–298 seq; Yvon Dandurand, 'Strategies and Practical Measures to Strengthen the Capacity of Prosecution Services in Dealing with Transnational Organized Crime, Terrorism and Corruption' (2007) 47 *Crime, Law and Social Change* 225, 237–238, on 'electronic surveillance, undercover operations and controlled deliveries'.

21 A description of the Italian approach as a double-track system differentiating between 'ordinary' crimes, on the one hand, and organised crime with enhanced investigative, prosecutorial, judicial powers, on the other hand, is discussed by Carnevale (n 4) 366–371.

22 Cf. von Lampe (n 4) 384–385.

23 Cf. Boister, *An Introduction to Transnational Criminal Law* (n 3) 294–296.

24 See also below: Section 2.4.4.

success of an investigation are very limited (see also below 2.4.3 on international cooperation).

Another problem stems from witnesses often being insiders of criminal organisations or victims of their crimes. Since such witnesses will often be intimidated by the threat of serious harm from members of the criminal networks, they must be motivated to overcome their (perfectly understandable) fears. In the case of former members or supporters of criminal organisations willing to testify against their previous accomplices, the prospect of a reduced sentence or even immunity from prosecution might be a powerful incentive for testimony. However, such testimony comes at a high price.[25] For one, the rule of law is affected if crimes committed by the witness go (partially) unpunished due to a negotiated testimony. Despite the waiver of punishment for mere 'underlings' being potentially justifiable through the greater interest in bringing more severe perpetrators to justice, there is a risk in playing this card. It presupposes that accomplices playing minor roles in the criminal organisation possess key information about the organisational context of the crimes committed. Closely related is the additional question of whether the information presented to law enforcement agencies is true. The more existential the involved interests of the witness/accomplice are, the less reliable the disclosed information is. There is no remedy for this problem other than to verify testimony by former accomplices with particular care, always bearing in mind the intricate situation of the witness.

Apart from this, intimidated witnesses must be protected against the risks they take by testifying.[26] Depending on how acute the danger is, different levels of witness protection programmes are provided in many countries. Countermeasures include keeping personal information of witnesses confidential, letting them testify anonymously, or even admitting them to institutionalised witness protection programmes providing them with a new identity, etc.[27]

2.4.2 *Access to illegally gained profits*

Organised crime seeks to generate illicit profits, whose criminal origin is subsequently concealed by channelling the profits back into legal financial and business cycles.[28] Criminal networks are therefore usually intertwined with legal business structures that are used to either commit or support serious crimes (for example, Value Added Tax fraud) or to disguise criminal acts and/or launder illegally gained profits.[29]

25 Cf. Heymann and Heymann (n 6) 41.

26 Von Lampe (n 4) 383, 388.

27 Carnevale (n 4) 369; Dandurand (n 20) 239–240; von Lampe (n 4) 387–388.

28 According to Europol (n 6) 10, 86% of the most powerful criminal networks active within the European Union infiltrate the legal business world; see also COM(2023) 641 final (n 11) 17.

29 Europol (n 6) 39–40.

A study released by Europol in April 2024 concludes that, next to their main field of activity, almost all of the most threatening criminal networks active in the territory of the European Union are at least also involved in money laundering to 'clean' the proceeds of their illegal activities.[30] The study names the following sectors as the most misused by these organisations: construction (used to invest illegally gained profits), hospitality (for example, nightclubs are run to traffic drugs), and logistics (businesses are run as instruments for drug or waste trafficking or for trafficking in human beings).[31] The fact that criminal organisations are active in multiple fields of crime, as well as using legal businesses, makes it hard(er) for law enforcement to 'isolate' and identify criminal conduct among their activities. Again, undercover investigations are an important tool to bring ties between legal and illegal 'business' structures to light (see above 2.4.1).

Moreover, since the motivation driving organised crime is the pursuit of illegal economic interests, the main goal of criminal policy must be that 'crime does not pay'. Therefore, the confiscation of assets—not necessarily based on a prior conviction but also non-conviction based and before the successful finalisation of a criminal investigation—is of utmost importance.[32] Since organised crimes are very often committed transnationally, profits need not be gathered in the same country as the one where the criminal acts are committed. In cases of online fraud, the recovery of illicit assets will be even more complex. Accordingly, international cooperation plays an important role in seizing illicit profits.[33]

In the territory of the European Union, the so-called 'follow the money approach'[34] has been established to hit the most important interest of criminal organisations. By uncovering money laundering flows, criminal organisations are to be kept from effectively securing their illegally obtained profits by laundering them through legal business structures. The 'follow the money approach' is strengthened by a new *EU Directive on Asset Recovery and Confiscation* that was introduced in April 2024.[35] It sets out specific requirements for the EU

30 According to Europol (ibid.) 14, 96% of the most threatening organised crime networks launder their illicit profits themselves.

31 Ibid., 41.

32 Dandurand (n 20) 234–237. For a detailed assessment of non-conviction-based confiscation of assets, see Jonathan Macziola, 'Non-Conviction-Based Confiscation as a Means to Combat Organised Crime', Chapter 4 of this volume.

33 See also COM(2023) 641 final (n 11) 6.

34 Ibid., 12; see also Council of the European Union, *Council Conclusions on Enhancing Financial Investigations to Fight Serious and Organised Crime*, Doc 8927/20 of 17 June 2020. For a comprehensive overview of the EU Strategy to fight organised crime, see Cyrille Fijnaut, 'The Strategy of the European Union Against Serious Transnational Crime (2020–2025)' in Felia Allum and Stan Gilmour (eds), *Routledge Handbook of Transnational Organized Crime* (Routledge, 2nd ed 2021) 522.

35 Directive (EU) 2024/1260 of the European Parliament and of the Council of 24 April 2024 on Asset Recovery and Confiscation [2024] OJ L 2024/1260.

Member States' legal systems to effectively recover and confiscate illicit profits not only on a national, but also on an EU level.[36]

2.4.3 *Strengthening law enforcement authorities and cooperative structures on the national and international level*

In many countries, specialised law enforcement units have been established within the police, prosecution, and judiciary to concentrate specialised expertise on criminal networks. This has strengthened the investigative, prosecutorial, and judicial strategies in countering organised crime on a national level.[37]

However, criminal networks are crossing borders that no longer form a serious barrier to their activities. This is all the more so as organised crime is increasingly carried out using modern technologies and telecommunication.[38] Consequently, organised crime cannot efficiently be addressed only on a national level; instead, effective law enforcement needs transnational cooperation in policing and prosecuting organised crime.[39] Therefore, national measures must be complemented by similar developments on a supranational level.[40]

A good example of such efforts can be found in the area of freedom, security, and justice of the European Union. Various EU institutions have been built to join forces and to support national proceedings on the European Union level.[41] Europol, the European Union's 'Police' Office, was already established in 1995 to serve as an intelligence centre for European police work investigating organised crime, terrorism, and other forms of serious crime.

36 See Directive 2024/1260 (n 35) Article 4, 19, 30.

37 See for the European Union: COM(2021) 170 final (n 9) 11; for the United States, see Heymann and Heymann (n 6) 44–45; for institutional changes in the Italian law enforcement system, see Carnevale (n 4) 368 on specialised regional bodies and the so-called Direzione Nazionale Antimafia, bringing together experts in this field of crime.

38 Heymann and Heymann (n 6) 115: 'TOC groups that take advantage of the Internet can be the most difficult of all to investigate'.

39 Cf. Boister, *An Introduction to Transnational Criminal Law* (n 3) 281–283; Dandurand (n 20) 240–244. For a critical stance on the current state of global cooperation in the fight against transnational organised crime, see Tuesday Reitano and Mark Shaw, 'The Global Fight against TOC: The Evolution of Approaches and Their Effectiveness' in Felia Allum and Stan Gilmour (eds), *Routledge Handbook of Transnational Organized Crime* (Routledge, 2nd ed 2021) 570, 580.

40 Cf. also Marilu Porchia, 'Joint Investigation Teams', Chapter 8 of this volume.

41 See, for an outline of several international instruments regarding the global fight on organised crime, Genevieve Rule and Andreas Schloenhardt, 'International Frameworks for Cooperation in Organised Crime Cases', Chapter 6 of this volume; cf. Valsamis Mitsilegas, 'Legal Responses to Transnational Crime: A Global Perspective' in Valsamis Mitsilegas, Saskia Hufnagel, and Anton Moiseienko (eds), *Research Handbook on Transnational Crime* (Edward Elgar, 2019) 5–16.

Europol's main competence lies in collecting data and supporting national law enforcement by providing information.[42]

Eurojust was founded in 2002 and serves as a similar institution in the judiciary.[43] The judicial level is further strengthened by the European Judicial Network, consisting of national liaison offices in the criminal justice systems to support transnational investigations.

The youngest institution in this ensemble is the European Public Prosecutor's Office (EPPO)[44] that was founded in 2017 and took up its operational work in June 2021. The EPPO can initiate proceedings against organised criminal groups harming the Union's financial interests, for example, by subsidy fraud. The EPPO has the authority to initiate criminal proceedings against persons participating in the activities of criminal organisations if the crimes committed affect the EU's financial interests. Additionally, the EU strives to establish an EU-wide network of specialised prosecutors and judges to lead complex cross-border investigations into organised crime.[45] The members of the network will also be supported by Eurojust at the EU level.

The list of more recent European Union efforts specifically dedicated to the fight against organised crime further entails a European Multidisciplinary Platform Against Crime Threats, an Operational Network Against Mafia-Style Organised Criminal Groups supporting complex investigations against high-risk criminal networks.[46] Moreover, six EU Member States[47] have founded a 'Coalition against Serious and Organised Crime' that is also supported by the Commission, Europol, and Eurojust and develops strategies to enhance the efficiency of the EU's fight against organised crime.[48]

Furthermore, particularly in the field of cybercrime, the EU is enhancing its capacity to efficiently answer organised crime by establishing several expert bodies. For example, the Commission established the EU High-Level Group on access to data for effective law enforcement in June 2023, bringing together law enforcement, judicial authorities, data protection, privacy and cybersecurity experts, the private sector, non-governmental organisations, and academia.[49] In 2021, the EU released recommendations on operational police cooperation, including the exchange of information between law enforcement

42 Cf. André Klip, *European Criminal Law. An Integrative Approach* (Intersentia, 4th ed 2021) 587–593, with further references.

43 Cf. ibid., 595–601, with further references.

44 The new institution was founded by Council Regulation (EU) 2017/1939 of 12 October 2017 Implementing Enhanced Cooperation on the Establishment of the European Public Prosecutor's Office [2017] OJ L 283/1.

45 COM(2023) 641 final (n 11) 12.

46 Ibid., 3–4; see for a brief summary of the roadmap eucrim 3/2023, 257.

47 Belgium, France, Germany, Italy, the Netherlands, and Spain.

48 See COM(2023) 641 final (n 11) 5.

49 Ibid., 14.

authorities to effectively fight organised crime.[50] Finally, the newly introduced *EU Regulation (EU) 2023/1543 of the European Parliament and of the Council of 12 July 2023 on European Production Orders and European Preservation Orders for Electronic Evidence in Criminal Proceedings and for the Execution of Custodial Sentences Following Criminal Proceedings*[51] provides for cross-border access to electronic evidence, a crucial element in the transnational investigation of organised crime(s) committed via the internet.

Naturally, all of these EU institutions only stand to strengthen national law enforcement's efforts if they are mirrored by a concentration of organised crime experts on the national level to coordinate the cooperation between the national and the supranational level.[52]

2.4.4 *Complementing criminal proceedings with an administrative approach to countering organised crime*

In recent years, the view has increasingly emerged that a criminal justice approach alone does not suffice to effectively fight the detrimental activities of criminal organisations. To strengthen legal retorts to organised crime, an additional administrative approach is advocated for.[53] In the European Union, the implementation of such an administrative approach is promoted by the European Commission and was already outlined in the EU Council Conclusions on an administrative approach to preventing and fighting serious organised crime in the year 2016.[54]

The EU administrative approach to fighting serious (and) organised crime[55] strives to meet numerous objectives. Persons involved in criminal activities shall be prevented from using the legal administrative infrastructure for criminal purposes. For example, they shall be denied public funds or administrative

50 EU Recommendations on Operational Police Cooperation (COM/2021/780 final); see also Directive (EU) 2023/977 of the European Parliament and of the Council of 10 May 2023 on the Exchange of Information Between the Law Enforcement Authorities of Member States and Repealing Council Framework Decision 2006/960/JHA [2023] OJ L 134/1.

51 OJ L 191/118.

52 Cf. COM(2023) 641 final (n 11) 16. From an international perspective, cf. Dandurand (n 21) 228.

53 See also COM(2023) 641 final (n 11) 17.

54 Doc 9935/16 of 9 June 2016 ('Doc 9935/16'); also referred to in the Council of the European Union, *Council Conclusions on a Way Forward for Crime Prevention in Europe*, Doc 16327/23 of 4 December 2023, 3; and in the EU Strategy to tackle organised crime, cf. COM(2021) 170 final (n 8) 21. For an analysis, see Yari Dennhardt, 'Der administrative Ansatz. Der Weg zu einem ganzheitlichen Konzept in der Bewältigung organisierter Kriminalität?' (2022) 1 (7–8) *Zeitschrift für Internationale Strafrechtswissenschaft* 507.

55 The European Network on the Administrative Approach, which tackles serious and organised crime, defines this administrative approach as '*a complementary way to prevent and tackle the misuse of the legal infrastructure through multi-agency cooperation by sharing information and taking actions in order to set up barriers*', see for more details <https://administrativeapproach.eu>.

permits, which are necessary for conducting legal business activities that could be used to support criminal activities (e.g. by laundering illicit proceeds). Preventive administrative measures, including the preventive screening and monitoring of applicants for administrative permits or funds, shall also be used in the prevention of organised crime.[56] Furthermore, national authorities are explicitly encouraged to consider utilising administrative measures to hamper business activities that are connected to organised crime.[57] As an example, the closing or expropriation of premises in case of occurring public nuisance is mentioned in the Council document of 2016.[58] Recently, it is also suggested that public–private partnerships, especially between law enforcement and the banking sector, should form part of the administrative approach as a helpful tool in detecting and recovering illegally obtained assets.[59]

To ensure a comparable level of administrative hurdles for organised criminal activities across the EU Member States, the European Network on the Administrative Approach tackling serious and organised crime has been founded. Within this network, research on an effective administrative approach is conducted and expertise shared with the national authorities.[60]

2.5 Conclusion

It has been demonstrated that the cooperative character of organised crime is the source of the procedural challenges faced when combating it. The remedy to these challenges lies in mirroring this cooperative character on the side of law enforcement. Cooperation is needed between local police authorities and specialised units, as well as between criminal law enforcement and administrative authorities on the national level. Furthermore, cooperation is also key on a transnational level, again not only between criminal law enforcement agencies but also in collaboration with administrative authorities. Numerous measures in different fields of the law must be brought together in a strategy to fight organised crime.

However, as helpful as this holistic concert of strategies and measures is to counter organised crime effectively, it is not to lose sight of the State's most eminent competence: ensuring that individual freedoms are not unduly impaired by State interventions. For example, it is very likely that the surveillance of a suspect's telecommunication will extend to private conversations and thus uninvolved persons unconnected to criminal activities. Furthermore,

56 Cf. COM(2023) 641 final (n 11) 6.
57 Ibid., 17.
58 Doc 9935/16 (n 54) 6.
59 COM(2023) 641 final (n 11) 13.
60 See, for example, ENAA (European Network on the Administrative Approach), *Third EU Handbook on the Administrative Approach in the European Union* (2020) <https://administrativeapproach.eu/sites/default/files/publication/files/2005_Third%20Handbook%20EU_ENG_LR_1.pdf>

if the administrative approach involves denying necessary business permits based on the suspicion of an intent to launder illicit profits, this may conflict with the presumption of innocence. These are only two examples of risks associated with forceful responses to organised crime. There is no doubt that all the measures described in this chapter are necessary to fight organised crime and ensure security in a democratic society, but it must be borne in mind that every measure comes at a price. Carefully striking the balance between effectively countering organised crime on the one hand and preserving a free society on the other is ultimately the biggest challenge in this field of the law.

3 Obstruction of justice in the context of organised crime

Benedikt Grünert

3.1 Introduction

In 1992, a meticulously planned assassination shook the Italian State to its core. On 23 May, the three-car motorcade of Giovanni Falcone, a judge, prosecuting magistrate, and the country's most prolific 'mafia hunter', was blown up using 500 kilogrammes of TNT hidden in a drainage pipe underneath the road the cars were travelling on. Just several weeks later, Falcone's friend and fellow magistrate, Paolo Borsellino, was assassinated with a car bomb. Both men were members of a group of magistrates nicknamed the 'Antimafia Pool'.[1] Falcone's work made him a primary target for the mafia. He made several mafiosi break their code of silence, the *omertà*, and was responsible for the indictment of 475 members of the mafia in the first *maxiprocesso*. The assassination of Falcone and Borsellino was ordered from the highest ranks of the Sicilian Cosa Nostra,[2] one of the mafia organisations the two men fought for years.[3]

This chapter explores obstruction of justice in the context of organised crime. Obstruction of justice describes any interference with the proper workings of the criminal justice system, by means of force, threats, intimidation, or the corruption of witnesses and other non-State actors participating in the criminal justice process.[4] Obstruction of justice not only compromises the integrity of legal systems but also threatens the safety, lives, and freedom of those involved in the fight against organised crime. The protection of these rights is particularly important in trials against members of organised criminal

1 Vincenzo Delle Donne, *Falcone; Die Biographie; Leben und Tod im Kampf gegen die Mafia* (Ullstein, 1993) 210.

2 Maurizio Cantino, *Mafia Organizations: The Visible Hand of Criminal Enterprises* (Cambridge University Press, 2019) 256.

3 For detailed reports on the lives and assassinations of Giovanni Falcone and Paolo Borsellino, see, among many, Delle Donne (n 1); Alexander Stille, *Excellent Cadavers: The Mafia and the Death of the First Italian Republic* (Vintage, 1996).

4 This definition is based on the *United Nations Convention against Transnational Organized Crime*, opened for signature 15 November 2000, 2225 UNTS 209 (entered into force 29 September 2003) Article 23.

DOI: 10.4324/9781003519317-4

groups, as these organisations have human and financial resources that enable them to outgun prosecutors and courts. Although closely related, obstruction of justice is different from the corruption of public officials (the latter is not covered further here). Bribery—the offering, promising, or giving of an unfair advantage—only constitutes obstruction of justice when employed 'specifically to interfere in the presentation of testimony or evidence'.[5]

Section 3.2 of this chapter provides an overview of the methods and targets of obstruction of justice in the organised crime context. In Sections 3.3 and 3.4, the most important international framework concerning the criminalisation of obstruction of justice, the *United Nations Convention against Transnational Organised Crime* (UNTOC), as well as different national models of implementing obstruction of justice as a criminal offence, are outlined and analysed for strengths and weaknesses. Section 3.5 includes several suggestions to address known problems and weaknesses and marks the conclusion of this chapter.

3.2 Purpose, methods, and targets

Obstruction of justice manifests in many forms and is as diverse and varied as organised crime itself.[6] What ties the different manifestations of obstruction of justice together is the special intention of interfering with the proper workings of the criminal justice system. Obstruction of justice aims to prevent investigations, hinder arrests, and influence testimony in court proceedings.

3.2.1 Methods of obstruction of justice

3.2.1.1 Physical Violence

Acts of extreme violence and brutality are often associated with organised crime.[7] Violence is frequently regarded as inherent to some illicit activities, such as drug trafficking,[8] and can constitute an effective measure to avoid interference by law enforcement officials[9] and to scare witnesses into silence.

5 United Nations Conference of the Parties to the United Nations Convention against Transnational Organized Crime, Working Group of Government Experts on Technical Assistance, *Identification of technical assistance needs and good practices relating to the criminalization of obstruction of justice* (Article 23), UN Doc CTOC/COP/WG.2/2016/3 (4 August 2016) [50] ('CTOC/COP/WG.2/2016/3').

6 Cf. Cyrille J Fijnaut, *The Containment of Organised Crime and Terrorism* (Brill, 2016) 176–187.

7 See Frank Vincent, 'Review of the Witness Protection Act 1991' (Government of Victoria, 2016) 56.

8 Angelica Duran-Martinez, 'To Kill and Tell? State Power, Criminal Competition, and Drug Violence' (2015) 59(8) *Journal of Conflict Resolution* 1377, 1378.

9 David Shirk and Joel Wallman, 'Understanding Mexico's Drug Violence' (2015) 59(8) *Journal of Conflict Resolution* 1348, 1361; Peter Reuter, 'Systemic violence in drug markets' (2009) 52 *Crime, Law and Social Change* 275, 279.

The assassinations of Falcone and Borsellino serve as prominent examples of the most extreme form obstruction of justice can take.

Indeed, some organisations distinguish themselves by their propensity for extreme violence and brutality.[10] Some Mexican drug trafficking organisations, for instance, show little reluctance in employing violence and extreme brutality against witnesses, judges, and police officers.[11] Margaret Beare refers to this as 'terrorist-style' violence used to constrain law enforcement altogether.[12] Roadblocks and ensuing gunfights with security personnel are utilised to extort the release of captured leaders.[13] The reasons for this extreme brutality are not conclusively determined in academic literature,[14] though the communicative aspects of violence are regarded as a considerable factor.[15]

Whilst in some cases symbolism[16] or mutilation[17] are used to expose the victim as a police informant or highlight an organised criminal group's responsibility for a killing, the link to organised crime is less obvious in many cases.[18] For example, some groups may attempt to cover up murders by making them look like narcotics overdoses or robberies.[19] It should, however, also be noted that although deliberate killings of police, prosecutors, and judicial officials

10 George W Grayson, *Mexico: Narco Violence and a Failed State?* (Routledge, 2010) 179, 271, 273; Pamela L Bunker, Lisa J Campbell, and Robert J Bunker, 'Torture, Beheadings, and Narcocultos' (2010) 21(2) *Small Wars & Insurgencies* 145, 150.

11 June S Beittel, 'Mexico; Organized Crime and Drug Trafficking Organizations' (2019) 21(2) *Current Politics and Economics* 181, 183.

12 Margaret E Beare, 'Narco-Terrorism', in Margaret E Beare (ed), *Encyclopedia of Transnational Crime and Justice* (Sage, 2012) 273, 274. See also Bunker, Campbell, and Bunker (n 10) 150; Duran-Martinez (n 8) 1396.

13 See Georgina Zerega, 'Arrest of Ovidio Guzmán, Sinaloa Cartel kingpin and son of "El Chapo" turns Culiacán into a war zone', *El Pais* (5 January 2023) <english.elpais.com/international/2023-01-05/ovidio-guzman-son-of-el-chapo-and-leader-of-sinaloa-cartel-recaptured-in-mexico.html>; 'Ovidio Guzmán-López: Twenty-nine killed during arrest of El Chapo's son', *BBC News* (January 2023) <bbc.com/news/world-latin-america-64179356>.

14 Laura Y Calderón, 'An Analysis of Mayoral Assassinations in Mexico, 2000–17' (2018) 15(1) *Justice in Mexico Working Paper Series* 10–22; Guillermo Trejo and Sandra Ley, *Votes, Drugs, and Violence: The Political Logic of Criminal Wars in Mexico* (Cambridge University Press, 2020).

15 Andrew Lantz, 'The Performativity of Violence: Abducting Agency in Mexico's Drug War' (2016) 25(2) *Journal of Latin American Cultural Studies* 253, 254.

16 Bunker, Campbell, and Bunker (n 10) 146; Laura H Atuesta, 'Narcomessages as a Way to Analyse the Evolution of Organised Crime in Mexico' (2017) 18(2) *Global Crime* 100, 107; Monica Massari, 'Mafia Violence: Strategies, Representations and Performances', in Monica Massari and Vittorio Martone (eds), *Mafia Violence: Political, Symbolic and Economic Forms of Violence in Camorra Clans* (Routledge, 2019) 21, 22.

17 Lantz (n 15) 261.

18 Massari (n 16) 32.

19 See Stephen Monterosso, 'Shortcomings in the Operation and Coordination of Witness Protection in Australia. Where to from Here?' (2022) 33 *Criminal Law Forum* 255, 275.

are not uncommon in the context of organised crime,[20] physical violence as a method of obstruction of justice more often involves less severe forms. In fact, some scholars note that some organised criminal groups tend to avoid violence for the possible negative effects on their illicit operations.[21]

3.2.1.2 Intimidation

Intimidation is a common and powerful tool used to obstruct the course of justice. In this context, intimidation refers to any behaviour that is intended to evoke fear in the target and prevent or manipulate participation in the criminal proceedings.[22] Viewed as a 'defining feature'[23] or 'inherent'[24] to organised crime, the lower visibility and traceability of intimidation compared to other methods make it particularly attractive to organised criminal groups.[25]

One of the most common forms of intimidation is the use of verbal threats.[26] Threats may be directed at a witness and relate to that person's safety, well-being, or economic livelihood,[27] or to that of people associated with the witness.[28] Additionally, organised criminal groups might threaten to reveal the criminal activities of the target or disclose their cooperation with law enforcement.[29] Disciplinary complaints and the threat of a possible lawsuit are sometimes used against law enforcement officers and can have a lasting effect

20 Cantino (n 2) 202; Margherita Stancati and Francesca Volpa, 'Italian Prosecutor Fights the Mafia—and Fears for His Life', *Wall Street Journal* (25 January 2022) <https://www.wsj.com/articles/italian-prosecutor-fights-the-mafiaand-fears-for-his-life-11579948200>.

21 Reuter (n 9) 289; Benjamin Lessing, 'Logics of Violence in Criminal War' (2015) 59(8) *Journal of Conflict Resolution* 1486, 1488–1489; Klaus von Lampe, *Organized Crime: Analyzing Illegal Activities, Criminal Structures, and Extra-Legal Governance* (Sage, 2016) 121–123.

22 Michael H Graham, 'Witness Intimidation' (1984) 2 *Florida State University Law Review* 239, 240; Vincent (n 7) 53.

23 Graham (n 22) 242; Lorenzo Picchi, *The State Mafia Deal. An Analysis of the Strategies and Patterns of the Sicilian Mafia. 1986–2006* (PhD thesis, Freie Universität Berlin, 2021) 243–244.

24 Liz Campbell, 'Organised Crime, Anonymous Witnesses and Fair Trials in Ireland: Responding to *R v Davis*' (2008) 6(1) *International Commentary on Evidence* 1, 1.

25 Cf. Yvonne Dandurand and Kristin Farr, *A Review of Selected Witness Protection Programs*, Report No 001 (Research and National Coordination Organized Crime Division Law Enforcement and Policy Branch Public Safety Canada, 2010) 9–10.

26 According to the British Crime Survey 1996, about 41% of intimidatory incidents involved threats; see UK Home Office, *Speaking up for Justice: Report of the Interdepartmental Working Group on the Treatment of Vulnerable or Intimidated Witnesses in the Criminal Justice System* (UK Home Office, June 1998) 114.

27 See Teresa M Garvey, *Witness Intimidation: Meeting the Challenge* (Aequitas, 2013) 8–9.

28 Julie M Bunck and Michael R Fowler, *Bullets, Bribes and Intimidation* (Pennsylvania State University Press, 2012) 58; Jana Arsovska, *Decoding Albanian Organized Crime: Culture, Politics and Globalization* (University of California Press, 2015) 186; Ruth Crocker et al., *The Impact of Organised Crime in* Local Communities, Report (The Police Foundation, June 2017) 44; Picchi (n 23) 243–244.

29 Garvey (n 27) 8–9.

on how police officers engage with members of organised criminal groups.[30] Social media plays an emerging role in intimidation efforts by enabling criminals to track and trace witnesses and issue threats in relative anonymity.[31]

Organised criminal groups may also use non-verbal threats to intimidate. At the extreme end, this includes arson by setting buildings, cars, or other property on fire.[32] Anecdotal reports include methods such as posting a dead rodent to a witness or using unambiguous gestures (e.g. hand signs or slashing motions).[33] Subtle and seemingly harmless acts may also be employed to threaten witnesses or criminal justice officials, which are less traceable and may thus be more difficult for the authorities to detect and prosecute. Such methods are characterised by creating a feeling of unease and constant surveillance in the target and include, for instance, stalking or observing private residences as well as harassment.[34]

Intimidation may not only result in silencing witnesses for imminent criminal proceedings,[35] but can also cause long-lasting damage to the functioning of the criminal justice system. The activities of organised criminal groups are often accompanied by an 'atmosphere of fear and menace'[36] seriously damaging trust in and cooperation with law enforcement.[37] Prior and repeated acts of violence or intimidation can create a 'reputation of intimidation',[38] with the effect that crimes related to organised criminal groups go unreported even if committed publicly.[39]

This effect can be a by-product of some obstruction methods, though some intimidation methods are used primarily to achieve this effect and are

30 Grégory Gomez del Prado, 'Outlaw Motorcycle Gangs' Attempted Intimidation of Quebec's Police Force' (2011) 12(2) *Police Practice and Research* 66, 71–72.

31 Linda A Seabrook and Jelahn Stewart, 'Snitches Get Stitches: Combating Witness Intimidation in Gang-Related Prosecutions' (2014) 62(3) *United States Attorneys' Bulletin* 83, 84; Anita Lavorgna, 'Organised crime goes online: realities and challenges' (2015) 18(2) *Journal of Money Laundering Control* 153, 157; Justin Nix et al., 'The Use of Social Media by Alleged Members of Mexican Cartels and Affiliated Drug Trafficking Organizations' (2016) 13(3) *Journal of Homeland Security and Emergency Management* 395, 410; cf. the graphs in Nilda M Garcia, *Mexico's Drug War and Criminal Networks: The Dark Side of Social Media*, (Routledge, 2020) 92–93, 117.

32 Kerry M Healy, *Victim and Witness Intimidation: New Developments and Emerging Responses*, Research Report (National Institute of Justice, October 1995) 4; Crocker et al. (n 28) 89.

33 Garvey (n 27) 10; Seabrook and Stewart (n 31) 83.

34 Healy (n 32) 4; Seabrook and Stewart (n 31) 85; Gomez del Prado (n 30) 71.

35 Dandurand and Farr (n 25) 9–10; Steven W Kayuni and Edister Jamu, 'Failing witnesses in serious and organised crimes: policy perspectives for witness protective measures in Malawi' (2015) 41(3) *Commonwealth Law Bulletin* 422, 442; Vincent (n 7) 56–58.

36 Crocker et al. (n 28) 29.

37 Garvey (n 27) 14–15; Monterosso (n 19) 257.

38 Gomez del Prado (n 30) 79.

39 Cf. Arsovska (n 28) 185; Stephen Monterosso, 'From bikers to savvy criminals, Outlaw motorcycle gangs in Australia: implications for legislators and law enforcement' (2018) 69 *Crime, Law and Social Change* 681, 684.

not aimed at a specific target but at the wider public and, from the perspective of the group, serve preventative purposes.[40] So-called 'narcomessages' are widely used by drug trafficking organisations in Mexico and are one example of this type of intimidation.[41] This practice involves a body or body part and a medium (e.g. sign or cloth wrapped around a body, a cut-off finger) to communicate that the victim is someone who has interfered with the group's interests and to warn others not to cooperate with police or State authorities to leave the organisation alone.[42]

In a similar manner, members of outlaw motorcycle gangs usually use their patched leather jackets and vests (commonly referred to as 'colours') to intimidate others.[43] The display of patches is believed to indicate a willingness to use violence against police officers.[44] This effect of 'wearing colours' is widely recognised, and for this reason some jurisdictions have banned the public display of such insignia.[45]

3.2.1.3 Evidence tampering

Besides trying to limit or eliminate any interference that may arise from witnesses, police officers, or prosecutors, organised criminal groups also conceal, destroy, or tamper with physical evidence as a way of obstructing the course

40 Howard Campbell, 'Narco-Propaganda in the Mexican "Drug War": An Anthropological Perspective' (2014) 41(2) *Latin American Perspectives* 60, 66–67; William Finnegan, 'Silver or Lead', *The New Yorker* (24 May 2011) <https://www.newyorker.com/magazine/2010/05/31/silver-or-lead>; Brian J Phillips and Viridiana Rios, 'Narco-Messages: Competition and Public Communication by Criminal Groups' (2020) 62(1) *Latin American Politics and Society* 1, 2.

41 Although the number of such messages has been declining, they still are a relevant issue. Laura Y Calderón et al. (eds), *Organized Crime and Violence in Mexico: 2021 Special Report* (Department of Political Science & International Relations, University of San Diego, October 2021) 11.

42 Blog del Narco, *Dying for the Truth: Undercover Inside the Mexican Drug War by the Fugitive Reporters of Blog del Narco* (Feral House, 2012) 247; Paul K Eiss, 'The Narcomedia: A Reader's Guide' (2014) 41(2) *Latin American Perspectives* 78, 78; Lantz (n 15) 259; Atuesta (n 16) 107.

43 Thomas Barker, *The Outlaw Biker Legacy of Violence* (Routledge, 2019) 15.

44 Michael Behrendt and Axel Lier, 'Ein Wunder, dass es in Berlin noch keine Toten gab', *Welt* (25 November 2008) <welt.de/welt_print/article2776837/Ein-Wunder-dass-es-in-Berlin-noch-keine-Toten-gab.html>.

45 See Germany, Bundesverfassungsgericht, 1. Kammer des Zweiten Senats (14 March 2012) 2 BvR 2405/11; Alexandra Humphries, 'Tasmanian Parliament Passes Law to Ban Bikies Wearing Club Colours', *ABC News* (30 August 2018) <https://www.abc.net.au/news/2018-08-30/tas-parliament-passes-law-to-ban-bikies-wearing-club-colours/10182046>; Joshua Robertson, 'Wearing Bikie Club Colours in Public Banned under Queensland Organised Crime Laws', *The Guardian* (30 November 2016) <theguardian.com/australia-news/2016/nov/30/wearing-bikie-club-colours-in-public-banned-under-queensland-organised-laws>.

of justice.[46] Although this problem is well-known and recognised,[47] it is difficult to point to specific cases and examples documented in the academic literature. Reported cases are often limited to failed attempts at destroying evidence or instigating others to do so.[48] Whilst evidence tampering by corrupt law enforcement officers is, by comparison, quite well documented and researched,[49] this should be classified as a subtype of corruption rather than obstruction of justice. Evidence tampering also needs to be distinguished from acts aimed at enabling the commission of a crime,[50] as the goal of evidence tampering is hindering the enforcement of justice.

3.2.1.4 Undue advantage

Although obstruction of justice and corruption may complement one another in the efforts of organised criminal groups to achieve impunity, the two involve different approaches.[51] In the case of corruption (or active bribery to be precise), the complicity of public officials is solicited or 'bought', whilst obstruction of justice focuses on the direct interference with the work of officials involved in the criminal justice process. Unlike corruption, obstruction of justice only captures the use of undue advantages to interfere with the cooperation of civilians in the criminal justice process, not with public officials.

Compared to witness intimidation, the extent of this problem is not extensively researched; evidence of 'buying' witnesses is mostly anecdotal.[52] Some sources refer to the 'informal settlement of disputes' as a way of silencing a witness or victim of a crime;[53] this can include an undue advantage.[54]

Organised criminal groups sometimes 'reinvest' their profits from illicit operations into local communities. Because the focus is on improving the public image of a criminal organisation and establishing loyalty and social control,

46 Yvon Dandurand, 'Strategies and Practical Measures to Strengthen the Capacity of Prosecution Services in Dealing with Transnational Organized Crime, Terrorism and Corruption' (2007) 47 *Crime, Law and Social Change* 225, 232.

47 David McClean, *Transnational Organized Crime: A Commentary on the UN Convention and its Protocols* (Oxford University Press, 2007) 256.

48 *United States of America v Coiro*, 922 F 2d, 1008 (2nd Cir, 1991).

49 See, for example, Cyrille J Fijnaut and Leo Huberts, *Corruption, Integrity and Law Enforcement* (Brill, 2002) 113; Luz E Nagle, 'Corruption of Politicians, Law Enforcement, and the Judiciary in Mexico and Complicity across the Border' (2011) 21(1) *Small Wars and Insurgencies* 95, 95.

50 *United States of America v Khan*, 729 Fed. Appx. 236 (4th Cir, 2018).

51 See Lessing (n 21) 1497 for the combination of violence and corruption.

52 Cf. Deutsche Presse Agenture (DPA), 'Kampf gegen Clan-Kriminalität: Justiz stellt Forderungen', *Die Zeit* (24 October 2019) <https://www.zeit.de/news/2019-10/24/clan-kriminalitaet-experten-kommen-zu-konferenz-zusammen?utm_referrer=https%3A%2F%2Fwww.google.com%2F>; Picchi (n 23) 243–244.

53 Anthony Harriot, *Police and Crime Control in Jamaica. Problems of Reforming Ex-Colonial Constabularies* (University of the West Indies Press, 2000) 109; Crocker et al. (n 28) 29.

54 Garvey (n 27) 9.

rather than interfering with the justice system, these acts should not be considered obstruction of justice in the context of this chapter.[55]

3.2.2 Targets of obstruction of justice

Obstruction of justice is aimed at the people participating in the criminal justice process. Although, generally, any such participant can be the target of any of the methods used to obstruct the course of justice, some methods are employed more often against particular targets.

With regard to public officials, police officers, judges, and prosecutors are primary targets when violence and intimidation[56] are used to obstruct, delay, or disable investigations or criminal proceedings or to prevent further interference with illicit operations.[57] Violence and intimidation may also be directed at elected representatives, such as local politicians. Such circumstances are better described as 'violent lobbying' if they are aimed at changing regulations or policies in favour of organised criminal groups, rather than obstructing criminal justice proceedings.[58]

Civilians typically participate in the criminal justice process by reporting crimes as well as testifying or producing evidence in front of a court. Witnesses play a crucial role in combating organised crime because the 'closed nature of … criminal … groups makes it very difficult to use traditional investigative methods successfully'.[59] In most cases it is difficult, if not impossible, to prosecute and convict members of organised criminal groups without witness testimony.[60] The vital role of witness testimony makes witnesses a primary target for obstruction of justice.[61] The situation is especially dangerous for former members of organised criminal groups who choose to 'turn' and cooperate

55 Cf. Alexander Gale, 'Narco-Philanthropy: How Mexico's Cartels are Using COVID-19 to Win Hearts and Minds', *SDAFA* (26 February 2022) <https://www.sdafa.co.uk/narco-philanthropy-how-mexicos-cartels-are-using-covid-19-to-win-hearts-and-minds>.

56 See, for example, [s.n.] 'Peru drugs trial judge shot dead', *BBC News* (20 July 2006) <news.bbc.co.uk/1/hi/world/americas/5201716.stm>; Grayson (n 10) 271; Bunck and Fowler (n 28) 262; Picchi (n 23) 198; Ernesto Dal Bo, Pedro Dal Bo, and Rafael Di Tella, '"Plata o Plomo?": Bribe and Punishment in a Theory of Political Influence' (2006) 100(1) *American Political Science Review* 41, 41.

57 Reuter (n 9) 279.

58 Lessing (n 21) 1497; Guillermo Trejo and Sandra Ley, 'High-Profile Criminal Violence: Why Drug Cartels Murder Government Officials and Party Candidates in Mexico' (2021) 51(1) *British Journal of Political Science* 203, 211.

59 Felföldi Enikö, 'The Rising Importance on the Protection of Witnesses in the European Union' (2006) 77 *Revue internationale de droit penal* 313, 314.

60 Liz Campbell, 'The Prosecution of Organised Crime: Removing the Jury' (2014) 18 *International Journal of Evidence and Proof* 83, 84; Vincent (n 7) 57.

61 Nicholas R Fyfe and Heather McKay, 'Desperately Seeking Safety: Witnesses' Experiences of Intimidation, Protection and Relocation' (2000) 40 *British Journal of Criminology* 675, 677; Nicholas R Fyfe and James Sheptycki, 'International Trends in the Facilitation of Witness Cooperation in Organized Crime Cases' (2006) 3(3) *European Journal of Criminology* 319, 333.

with law enforcement,[62] as well as for victim-witnesses who face the risk of re-victimisation.[63] Violence or intimidation is not only employed against witnesses but also against people associated with them, such as their family or lawyers, who may be harmed or threatened in order to interfere with the witnesses' testimony or production of evidence.[64]

3.3 Obstruction of justice and the United Nations Convention against Transnational Organized Crime

At the end of the 20th century, organised crime, especially operating across international borders, gained recognition as a serious international problem.[65] The efforts to combat organised crime on an international level led to the development of the United Nations Convention against Transnational Organized Crime, which entered into force on 29 September 2003. Among other things, UNTOC establishes four offences which States Parties must criminalise in their domestic laws: participation in an organised criminal group (Article 5), laundering of proceeds of crime (Article 6), corruption (Article 8), and obstruction of justice (Article 23). The inclusion of obstruction of justice underscores the significance of this problem in the organised crime context.[66] Article 25 of the United Nations Convention against Corruption ('UNCAC') includes an identical provision.[67]

Article 23 has two subparagraphs, dealing with both the protection of civilians (subparagraph a) and certain officials (subparagraph b) involved in the criminal justice process.

3.3.1 Offending against civilians, Article 23(a)

3.3.1.1 Conduct element

Article 23(a) firstly requires the use of coercive conduct. This includes 'physical force', such as deliberate killings as well as the lesser forms of violence discussed earlier.

'Threats or intimidation' can be interpreted broadly to capture 'any direct, indirect or potential threat to a witness, which may lead to interference with

62 Monterosso (n 19) 259–260.

63 UK Home Office (n 26) 26; Dandurand and Farr (n 25) 10; Vincent (n 7) 58.

64 Cantino (n 2) 307; Bunker, Campbell, and Bunker (n 10) 149; Bunck and Fowler (n 28) 244; [s.n.] 'Men Convicted in Shocking Murder of Attorney Derk Wiersum get 30 Years on Appeal', *NL Times* (23 February 2023) <nltimes.nl/2023/02/23/men-convicted-shocking-murder-attorney-derk-wiersum-get-30-years-appeal>.

65 Fijnaut (n 6) 862.

66 UNODC, *Legislative Guide for the Implementation of the United Nations Convention against Transnational Organized Crime* (UNODC, 2nd edn 2017) [223] ('*Legislative Guide*').

67 Opened for signature 31 October 2003, 2349 UNTS 41 (entered into force 14 December 2005).

his/her duty to give testimony free from influence of any kind whatsoever'.[68] There is no requirement that the target is placed in fear or otherwise perceives the threat or intimidation. Most of the intimidation tactics mentioned above would be captured by Article 23(a), but not so the 'violent lobbying', 'reputation of intimidation', and other threats that are made preemptively and without a connection to specific criminal justice procedures.

Article 23(a) further calls for the criminalisation of 'the promise, offering or giving of an undue advantage'. The *Legislative Guide for the Implementation of the United Nations Convention against Transnational Organized Crime* notes that 'an undue advantage may be something tangible or intangible, whether pecuniary or non-pecuniary' and adds that it should not matter if the advantage is given directly to the target or someone associated with it and that it is irrelevant whether the person promising, etc., the advantage is involved in the proceeding him- or herself.[69]

Evidence tampering in the manner described above is not expressly covered by Article 23(a). It would only be captured if coercive or manipulative means are used to instigate another to tamper with evidence.[70] Some jurisdictions may, however, interpret or implement Article 23(a) more broadly or criminalise tampering with evidence as a separate offence.[71]

3.3.1.2 Circumstance element

The conduct under Article 23(a) outlined before needs to occur in the context of 'a proceeding in relation to the commission of offences covered by this Convention'. The term 'proceeding' is to be interpreted widely and 'intend[s] to cover all official governmental proceedings, which may include the pre-trial stage of a case'.[72] The Working Group on Technical Assistance established by the Conference of the Parties to the UNTOC further suggests that it should be of no importance 'whether formal proceedings are in progress or not'.[73] The scope of Article 23(a) thus encompasses not only the obstruction of trials and investigations but also acts intended to prevent future proceedings.

68 Council of Europe Committee of Ministers, 'Recommendation NO R(97)13 Concerning the Intimidation of Witnesses and the Rights of the Defence' (adopted by the Committee of Ministers on 10 September 1997 at the 600th meeting of the Ministers' Deputies) 81.

69 *Legislative Guide* (n 66) [196]–[197].

70 Andreas Schloenhardt and Matthew R Taylor, 'Article 23: Criminalization of Obstruction of Justice', in Andreas Schloenhardt et al. (eds), *UN Convention Against Transnational Organized Crime: A Commentary* (Oxford University Press, 2023) 254, 257.

71 UNODC, *Model Legislative Provisions against Organized Crime* (United Nations, 2nd edn 2021) 43 ('*Model Legislative Provisions*').

72 UNODC, *Travaux Préparatoires of the negotiations for the elaboration of the United Nations Convention against Transnational Organized Crime and the Protocols thereto* (United Nations, 2006) 216 ('*Travaux Préparatoires*').

73 CTOC/COP/WG.2/2016/3 (n 5) [19].

3.3.1.3 Targets/objects of obstruction of justice

Article 23(a) does not limit the object of the offence to any type of group of persons. The Working Group further explains that the 'conduct in offences that fall under paragraph (a) may be employed against any person, private individuals and public officials'.[74] The inclusion of public officials may create some overlap with Article 23(b) if coercive conduct is used against justice and law enforcement officials and also with Article 8 on the criminalisation of corruption.[75] This is of no particular significance, though it appears to be preferable to view the use of corrupt means only as obstruction of justice if they are aimed at civilians participating in the criminal justice process.

The conduct element of Article 23(a) does not need to be 'directed against the victim or other specific individuals or interests'.[76] The requirements of a connection to a proceeding and the intention to interfere with it limit the scope of protected targets to civilians giving testimony or evidence in proceedings as well as people associated with them since harming, threatening, or otherwise manipulating any of them could obstruct the course of justice.

3.3.1.4 Mental element

Article 23(a) requires the special intention to 'induce false testimony or to interfere in the giving of testimony or the production of evidence'. This adds a mental element to ensure that the violent, threatening, or other conduct is employed deliberately to interfere with criminal justice proceedings. It also captures attempts at obstruction of justice;[77] it is not required that the interference of the proceedings actually occurs.

3.3.2 Offending against officials, Article 23(b)

3.3.2.1 Conduct element

The conduct element of Article 23(b), 'use of physical force, threats or intimidation', is much the same as that of paragraph (a), though the use of undue advantages is left out here. Promising, offering, or giving an undue advantage would amount to corruption (active bribery), which is covered separately by Article 8 of the UNTOC.[78] Article 23(b) thus only includes 'more direct attempts to pervert the course of justice'.[79]

74 Ibid., [15].
75 Ibid., [50].
76 Schloenhardt and Taylor (n 70) 258.
77 CTOC/COP/WG.2/2016/3 (n 5) [32].
78 Schloenhardt and Taylor (n 70) 260.
79 McClean (n 47) 258.

3.3.2.2 *Targets/objects*

Article 23(b) covers conduct aimed at 'justice or law enforcement officials'. In principle, this only includes 'police and other law enforcement personnel, as well as judges, magistrates, judicial officers, and other members of the judiciary'.[80] States Parties are free to extend the offence to other types of public officials, including elected representatives and municipal officials. Although not expressly mentioned, and not further discussed in the literature, consistent with and analogous to the interpretation of Article 23(a), it seems prudent to argue that the conduct under paragraph (b) may also be aimed at relatives and associates of justice and law enforcement officials.

3.3.2.3 *Circumstance and mental element*

Where Article 23(a) requires a connection to a 'proceeding', paragraph (b) only refers to the special intent of 'interfer[ing] with the exercise of official duties'. This allows for the inclusion of any acts preventing criminal proceedings from commencing in the first place as well as frustrating ongoing proceedings, such as investigations and trials.

If physical violence, threats, or intimidation are used to interfere with the testimony or production of evidence given by a criminal justice official, this would also amount to 'interference with the exercise of official duties' and would equally be covered by Article 23(a).

3.3.3 *Right to silence*

One issue frequently debated in the context of Article 23 is the principle *nemo tenetur prodere seipsum* ('no person is compelled to accuse themself'), which amounts to an absolute right to silence in some jurisdictions. To address this issue, an interpretative note has been issued to Article 23 explaining that '[i]t was understood that some countries may not cover cases where a person has the right not to give evidence and an undue advantage is provided for the exercise of that right'.[81]

> This note seems to add rather than remove confusion, considering that Article 23 sets out a separate offence so that the person … interfering in the giving of testimony … of another person can be held criminally responsible even if no case against the other person can be made out or if the other person is found to be not criminally responsible.[82]

80 CTOC/COP/WG.2/2016/3 (n 5) [27].
81 *Travaux Préparatoires* (n 72) 216.
82 CTOC/COP/WG.2/2016/3 (n 5) [48]–[49].

Article 23 does not aim to criminalise the person refraining from giving evidence, but the person who, in the stated circumstance, instigates another to do so. Nevertheless, the tension regarding the rights of the accused on the one hand, and the desire to prevent and suppress obstruction of justice needs to be recognised.

3.4 Models of implementation

The UNTOC is not a self-executing treaty and thus relies on implementation by its Parties whilst respecting their sovereignty as well as their administrative and constitutional traditions. One of the advantages of the Convention is the great flexibility it provides to States Parties in implementing its provisions, including the offence under Article 23.[83] Whilst transnational organised crime is the main target of the Convention, Article 34(2) stipulates that when implementing the Convention offences into domestic law, this may be done without the transnational and organised criminal group elements. Furthermore, States Parties are free to establish 'more strict or severe measures … for preventing and combatting transnational organised crime' (Article 34(3)). The freedom afforded to States Parties is also granted in relation to sanctions for Convention offences, as Article 11(1) only asks States to consider the grave nature of the offence when deciding on statutory penalties.

On this background, it is unsurprising that the domestic implementation of Article 23 varies greatly. The following sections attempt to categorise the main approaches and highlight some differences, strengths, and weaknesses.

3.4.1 Omnibus offences

Provisions under domestic law that capture the content of Article 23 in a single offence are, for the most part, an anomaly. Instead, some jurisdictions differentiate or limit the scope of these offences to particular conduct, such as witness intimidation. Rather than trying to legislate the full spectrum of obstruction of justice methods outlined earlier, some States Parties focus on the intention of interfering with the criminal justice system. By extension, these intent-based approaches also include the attempt and conspiracy to obstruct the course of justice.[84]

The use of broad 'catch-all' provisions relating to obstruction of justice can be problematic. Vague and general clauses on obstruction of justice face the

83 Ian Tennant, 'Fulfilling the Promise of Palermo? A Political History of the UN Convention Against Transnational Organized Crime' (2021) 2(1) *Journal of Illicit Economies and Development* 53, 62.

84 UNODC, *State of implementation of the United Nations Convention against Corruption: Criminalization, Law Enforcement and International Cooperation* (United Nations, 2nd edn 2017) 79, 94 ('*UNCAC State of Implementation*').

risk of exceeding the scope of Article 23 or falling short of it. The former runs the risk of jeopardising the right to silence, as discussed earlier.

3.4.2 *Covered conduct*

The various forms of coercive and corrupt conduct prescribed in Article 23 of the UNTOC are criminalised by the States Parties in different ways.

Some States rely on offences such as homicide, assault, threats, coercion, extortion, and the like to capture violent and intimidating behaviour regardless of the victim or target of the offences. Whether such conduct is employed to intimidate witnesses, prosecutors, judges, or to otherwise obstruct the course of justice is irrelevant for these offences.[85] These offences serve to protect persons and their physical integrity and freedom of choice, not to protect the integrity of the criminal justice system. Although these offences do not explicitly refer to proceedings or the criminal justice system, they generally fulfil the requirements of Article 23.[86] However, more subtle forms of obstruction of justice, such as harassing or stalking another to discourage that person from testifying, etc., may not be covered by these general offences.[87]

On the other hand, more problem-tailored offences that focus on specific aspects of Article 23 exist. These provisions offer protection to a certain group of targets or cover specific aspects of the criminal justice process. As the following section shows, not all of the offences meet the objective of 'creat[ing] primary liability for the person inducing or interfering'.[88] In some jurisdictions, this can also lead to problems regarding the criminalisation of attempts to interfere with the giving of testimony or evidence.[89] Although dividing the different aspects of obstruction of justice into separate offences can be useful, the 'excessive fragmentation of the applicable legislation' may present a limitation to the effective implementation of Article 23.[90]

3.4.3 *Protected targets*

3.4.3.1 *Participants in criminal justice proceedings*

The important role that witnesses play in criminal proceedings—not only but in particular in cases involving transnational organised crime—is recognised in the criminal laws of most States. This includes, first, offences seeking to protect the safety of witnesses. Harming or intimidating a witness may be

85 Ibid., 80.
86 Ibid., 81.
87 United Nations Conference of the States Parties to the United Nations Convention against Corruption, *Executive Summary: Addendum*, UN Doc CAC/COSP/IRG/I/3/1/Add.11 (4 April 2014) 4.
88 CTOC/COP/WG.2/2016/3 (n 5) [48].
89 See *UNCAC State of Implementation* (n 84) 80.
90 Ibid., 84.

criminalised in standalone offences or as aggravations to other offences involving assaults, threats, and the like. Such provisions often extend, expressly or impliedly, to persons closely associated with the witness. Some jurisdictions extend their offences beyond the conclusion of criminal proceedings by criminalising retaliation against a witness for testifying.[91] Second, most States have criminal offences protecting the integrity of the criminal justice system by criminalising the use of coercive and corrupt measures to interfere with the giving of testimony or evidence.[92] Some States also separately criminalise interferences with witness testimony, such as 'tampering' with or 'influencing' witnesses. In some jurisdictions, offences like perjury or false oath are used to criminalise interference with the criminal justice system. However, the *Legislative Guide* notes that

> Article 23 creates primary liability for the person inducing or interfering independent of the criminal liability of the other person giving false testimony or the like. Offences based on article 23 are complementary to provisions creating liability as a participant in or accessory to the perjury, false statements, false oaths, fabrication of false evidence or similar offences committed by another person. For these reasons, it is important that States parties criminalize obstruction of justice in the way envisaged by article 23 independently from offences relating to perjury.[93]

The UNTOC 'contains no provisions … on the criminalization of the person who … has been induced to give false testimony' but focuses on the instigator and considers the person giving a false statement the victim of a crime.[94] Furthermore, this approach might not cover instances where an undue advantage is given to encourage a witness to refrain from testifying.

Most jurisdictions have specific offences criminalising the use of coercive or corrupt measures against members of the judiciary (which sometimes extends to their relatives and other people associated with them). Additionally, there may be offences protecting the judiciary as an institution (rather than its members as individuals). Offences such as false reporting on judicial proceedings, publishing written statements intended to damage the reputation of the court or a judge, and contempt of court fall into this category.[95]

91 Charles Doyle, *Obstruction of Justice: An Overview of Some of the Federal Statutes That Prohibit Interference with Judicial, Executive, or Legislative Activities*, CRS Report RL34303 (United States, Congressional Research Service, 17 April 2014) 26.

92 CTOC/COP/WG.2/2016/3 (n 5) [37].

93 *Legislative Guide* (n 66) [238].

94 Ibid., [239].

95 UNODC, 'Israel', *SHERLOC* (Web Page, accessed 20 March 2023) <https://sherloc.unodc.org/cld//legislation/isr/penal_law/chapter_nine/236_-_255/article_236_-_255.html?lng=en&tmpl=sherloc>.

Obstruction of justice offences also include violence and intimidation used against law enforcement and other officials, which may be criminalised as standalone offences or aggravating circumstances.

3.4.3.2 *Journalists*

Much of the contemporary debate about obstruction of justice and the scope and interpretation of Article 23 of the UNTOC concerns the questions of whether and to what extent relevant offences and protections also cover journalists involved in investigating, uncovering, and reporting about criminal activities, elements, and justice.[96] There are ample reports about intimidation,[97] lawsuits,[98] and violence[99] faced by journalists for their work, especially in relation to reporting about organised crime.

Compared to the targets discussed previously, journalists typically only play a marginal, supplementary role, if any, in the judicial process. In situations where organised criminal groups have put in place an 'atmosphere of fear and noncooperation',[100] journalists may nevertheless become targets of violence, threats, and retaliation. Beyond uncovering, documenting, and analysing individual cases, groups, and criminal patterns, journalists can play an important role in raising public awareness about organised crime. This role is an important facet of criminal justice but also makes journalists targets.

For these reasons, some jurisdictions have introduced new offences or extended existing ones to criminalise acts of violence, intimidation, and harassment against journalists. The *Criminal Code* of Canada is often cited as

96 Cf. United Nations Conference of the Parties to the United Nations Convention against Transnational Organized Crime, Working Group of Government Experts on Technical Assistance, *Implementation of the provisions on technical assistance of the United Nations Convention against Transnational Organized Crime*, UN Doc CTOC/COP/2016/L.7 (19 October 2016) [10] ('CTOC/COP/2016/L.7'); *Model Legislative Provisions* (n 71) 42.

97 Dana Priest, 'Censor or Die: The Death of Mexican News in the Age of Drug Cartels', *The Washington Post* (11 December 2015) <https://www.washingtonpost.com/investigations/censor-or-die-the-death-of-mexican-news-in-the-age-of-drug-cartels/2015/12/09/23acf3ae-8a26-11e5-9a07-453018f9a0ec_story.html>; Cristina Marconi, 'Code of Silence: Why Italy's Press Treads Carefully between Threats from the Mafia and Defamation Laws from Fascist Times' (2016) 45(2) *Index on Censorship* 15, 15.

98 Picchi (n 23) 303–306.

99 Rubén Arnoldo González Macías and Victor Hugo Reyna García, '"They Don't Trust Us; They Don't Care If We're Attacked": Trust and Risk Perception in Mexican Journalism' (2019) 32(1) *Communication & Society* 147, 156; Clare R Seelke, 'Violence against Journalists in Mexico: In Brief' (2019) 21/2 *Current Politics and Economics* 225, 229–236; Garcia (n 31) 45. See also Maria B Marron, 'Shot Down in Her Car' (1996) 84(10) *The Quill* 15; Irva Mrvová and Martin Turček, 'In the Heart of Europe: The Murder of the Slovak Journalist Ján Kuciak' (2018) (4) *Südosteuropa Mitteilungen* 6; Edin Pašović, 'A Murdered Journalist's Last Investigation', *OCCPR* (26 February 2018). <occrp.org/en/amurderedjournalistslastinvestigation>.

100 Healy (n 32) 1.

a prominent example for comprehensive provisions and expressly criminalising the intention to impede journalists 'in the transmission to the public of information in relation to a criminal organisation'.[101] The debate about such offences, their advantages and disadvantages, their scope and application, goes beyond the purposes of the present chapter but should nevertheless be seen as a welcome development.[102] In the context of Article 23, however, it is clear that journalists are not covered unless they participate directly in the proceedings, for instance, by giving testimony or producing other evidence.

3.5 Observations, reflections, and conclusions

Given the great flexibility the UNTOC offers in relation to implementing its obligations, it is not surprising that a range of approaches can be found when looking at obstruction of justice-related offences under domestic law. Recognising this flexibility as a strength of the Convention (rather than an impediment), the following paragraphs set out some reflections about existing offences and future reforms relating to obstruction of justice.

Criminalising individuals who attempt to manipulate the proper functioning of criminal justice is the central objective of Article 23. This provision makes a person who (tries to) coerce, corrupt, or otherwise unduly influence participants in criminal proceedings the main offender. They are not merely accessories to offences such as perjury or evidence tampering committed by others.[103] Seen this way, a person giving false evidence, failing to testify, etc., is merely the object of the offence under Article 23; some may even view them as victims. One of the main messages of Article 23 is thus the call to establish separate offences focussing on the persons using violence, intimidation, or undue advantages to influence the criminal justice system.

Whilst the UNTOC permits criminalising obstruction of justice in the absence of the transnational and organised crime elements, it should nevertheless be recognised that the threat that criminal justice proceedings and actors are manipulated is all the greater in cases involving transnational organised criminal groups, as documented earlier in this chapter. For this reason, it may be advisable to consider using elements relating to organised criminal groups and cross-border offending as aggravating circumstances in domestic obstruction of justice offences. This could capture the increased risks associated with organised crime cases and reflect the spirit and purpose of the UNTOC, which is to prevent and combat transnational organised crime more effectively (Article 1).

Additionally, or alternatively, it is conceivable to use obstruction of justice as an aggravating circumstance for other offences. For example, if persons are

101 See *Criminal Code* (Canada), s 432.1.
102 CTOC/COP/2016/L.7 (n 96) [10].
103 See CTOC/COP/WG.2/2016/3 (n 5) [45]; *UNCAC State of Implementation* (n 84) 80.

harmed, threatened, coerced, extorted, stalked, harassed, or the like with the intention to hinder or manipulate their participation in criminal justice proceedings, that intention may serve as an aggravating mental element justifying higher statutory penalties in these circumstances. This may also be a simple way to include journalists within the scope of relevant offences.

At a minimum and regardless of any special intention, States should ensure that the persons most vulnerable to obstruction of justice, especially if violence and intimidation are involved, are properly protected. This involves, on the one hand, specific offences recognising the status of criminal justice participants and, on the other, practical measures to protect their physical safety such as victim and witness protection and security around courthouses, etc. Effective witness protection in particular is essential to gain the trust of witnesses and is inextricably linked to the fight against obstruction of justice.[104] Victim and witness protection are further discussed in other chapters of this volume.

Although this chapter primarily focuses on criminal offences relating to obstruction of justice, it is recognised 'that criminal law … [has] its limits and should be supplemented with administrative measures in order to achieve more long-lasting success against organised crime'.[105] Successful measures against organised crime and obstruction of justice need to tackle these problems from multiple directions. This also includes additional measures to better prevent and detect obstruction of justice. In keeping with the obligation under the UNTOC, this requires proper training of law enforcement and judicial officials,[106] the establishment of specialised law enforcement units in jurisdictions where obstruction of justice is widespread, and safe and anonymous channels for reporting crime.[107]

In conclusion, obstruction of justice remains a powerful tool for organised criminal groups to prevent their detection, arrest, investigation, prosecution, and conviction. As a result, many groups can operate with relative impunity, especially if they also engage in the corruption of criminal justice and other government officials. The UNTOC and chiefly its Article 23 go some way to address some of these issues and it is one of many novel features of the UNTOC that it expressly recognises the damage that can be done to criminal justice if witnesses, prosecutors, jurors, judges, and the like are harassed, intimidated, threatened, harmed, or even killed or otherwise manipulated. Article 25 of the UNCAC, which was opened for signature three years after the UNTOC, repeats the same obligations in relation to corruption.

104 Cf. Dandurand (n 46) 239; UNTOC, Article 24.
105 See Fijnaut (n 6) 860; cf. *UNCAC State of Implementation* (n 84) 84.
106 See Tennant (n 83) 63; cf. UNTOC, Article 29.
107 Cf. Carlos Martin, 'Categorization of Narcomessages in Mexico: An Appraisal of the Attempts to Influence Public Perception and Policy Actions' (2012) 35(1) *Studies in Conflict & Terrorism* 76, 85.

Article 23, however, is incapable of putting an end to the obstruction of justice. This responsibility rests with individual States and will depend on the quality of laws they implement pursuant to their obligation and the proper enforcement of these laws. Presently, these efforts remain rather patchy and luckless. It is important that all States pay proper attention to the threat posed by obstruction of justice, especially in the context of transnational organised crime. This also requires proper prevention measures, appropriate training and resources for law enforcement, prosecution services, and the judiciary, along with measures to protect the safety of victims and witnesses during investigations, prosecutions, trials, and beyond.

4 Non-conviction-based confiscation as a means to combat organised crime

Jonathan Macziola

4.1 Introduction

Organised crime is a phenomenon that States have been battling for some time. The confiscation of assets has been identified as one major cornerstone in these efforts. This recognition goes hand in hand with a multitude of ideas on how to further advance and broaden the confiscation of illicit assets. Whilst some proposals show the necessary respect for the rule of law, other proposals give the impression of originating from a populist competition between State actors to show who is the 'toughest' when it comes to combating organised crime. Unfortunately, sometimes such proposals then make it into the law.

In States governed by the rule of law, critically analysing existing provisions to ensure they are compatible with the principles of the rule of law is part of upholding the rule of law. To ensure that a critical analysis is part of the—often heated—debate about organised crime, it is necessary to approach the topic without prejudice and to subject it to the same level of scrutiny as all other issues within criminal law and legal policy.

Similar to many other jurisdictions, part of the German Government's strategy on tackling organised crime involves making extensive use of the possibilities criminal law provides for the confiscation of assets.[1] This includes confiscation under § 76a(4) *Strafgesetzbuch* [StGB, the *Criminal Code* of Germany], a provision which was introduced in 2017 to expand confiscation in the field of organised crime.[2] § 76a(4) allows for the confiscation of assets of unknown origin without a criminal conviction by a court of law (non-conviction-based confiscation).[3]

1 Sozialdemokratische Partei Deutschlands (SPD), Bündnis 90/Die Grünen, and Freie Demokraten (FDP), *Mehr Fortschritt Wagen: Bündnis für Freiheit, Gerechtigkeit und Nachhaltigkeit, Koalitionsvertrag 2021–2025* (2021) <https://www.spd.de/fileadmin/Dokumente/Koalitionsvertrag/Koalitionsvertrag_2021-2025.pdf> 107.

2 Bundesgesetzblatt ['BGBl'] I, 2017, 872.

3 Bundestagdrucksache ['BT-Drs'] 18/9525, 58. The scope of the provision extends to offences that fall under the umbrella term 'terrorism'. This chapter is limited to the provision as it pertains to organised crime.

DOI: 10.4324/9781003519317-5

Following this introduction, the role of asset confiscation (esp. non-conviction-based confiscation) in fighting organised crime is analysed in Section 4.2 of this chapter. Next, an examination of German law on non-conviction-based confiscation (Section 4.3) and notable amendments (Section 4.4) follows, along with a brief overview of the legal issues commonly raised in this context (Section 4.5). Last, Section 4.6 presents proposals for amendments of the current German provisions on non-conviction-based confiscation, focussing specifically on confiscation in cases of organised crime.

4.2 Fighting organised crime with confiscation

4.2.1 The idea

Confiscating assets derived from organised crime is often portrayed as one of the key instruments in the fight against organised crime and a manifestation of the 'crime must not pay' mantra.[4] Indeed, the origin of asset confiscation in criminal proceedings can be found in efforts to combat organised crime.[5] The confiscation of assets happens on the understanding that organised crime is largely a profit-driven endeavour: the motivation of individuals to engage in organised crime activities lies in the wealth to be gained.[6] This gives rise to the concept that by effectively confiscating these profits, organised crime will no longer be a worthwhile pursuit.[7] Deprived of their proceeds, the commission of crime by organised criminal groups will cease.[8]

Stemming from the principles of crime prevention, two rationales are commonly offered to explain how confiscation aids in the fight against organised crime. First, it is assumed that by confiscating the proceeds of crime it is

4 Arndt Sinn, 'Vermögenabschöpfung—ein wirksames Instrument bei der Verfolgung organisierter Kriminalität?' in Arndt Sinn, Mark A Zöller and Robert Esser (eds), *Reform der Vermögensabschöpfung* (Dr Kovač, 2019) 127, 127; Council of the European Union, *Analysis of non-conviction based confiscation measures in the European Union*, SWD(2019) 1050 final (12 April 2019) 1 ('SWD(2019) 1050 final'); European Commission, *Proposal for a Directive of the European Parliament and of the Council on asset recovery and confiscation*, COM(2022) 245 final (25 May 2022) 1 ('COM(2022) 245 final'); Milieu Consulting, *Study on freezing and asset recovery—what works, what does not work, Final report* (European Union, 2021) 131; cf. Albin Eser, 'Neue Wege der Gewinnabschöpfung', in Winfried Küper and Jürgen Welp (eds), *Festschrift für Walter Stree und Johannes Wessels zum 70. Geburtstag* (C F Müller, 1993) 833, 834.

5 Frank Meyer, '"Reformiert die Rückgewinnungshilfe!"—Denkanstöße für eine Generalüberholung der Vermögensabschöpfung' (2015) 127(2) *Zeitschrift für die gesamte Strafrechtswissenschaft* 241, 243.

6 COM(2022) 245 final (n 4) 1, recital (2); Directive 2014/42/EU of the European Parliament and of the Council of 3 April 2014 on the Freezing and Confiscation of Instrumentalities and Proceeds of Crime in the European Union [2014] OJ L 127/39, Recital (1) ('Directive 2014/42/EU'); SWD(2019) 1050 final (n 4) 2.

7 COM(2022) 245 final (n 4) 1–2.

8 Critical of this very concept is Eser (n 4) 851, who references the US, where similar measures have been able to significantly increase the amount of confiscated wealth, but this ultimately still represents an insignificant proportion of the profits resulting from organised crime.

possible to deter perpetrators from generating a regular income by repeatedly committing crimes in an organised fashion.[9] Second, confiscation is thought to deprive organised criminal groups of assets which they may use to commit further crimes.[10] Based on these assumptions, it is widely believed that asset confiscation plays a critical role in preventing and suppressing organised crime.[11]

4.2.2 *The reality*

The questions regarding how this theoretical idea of confiscation plays out in practice are twofold: First, there is the question of whether confiscation really has the intended effect, or, in other words, does asset confiscation in cases involving organised crime lead to a reduction of such crime? Second, if such an effect exists, does the confiscation of assets in organised crime cases occur to such an extent that it can justify even more extensive powers of intervention? Put differently, if highly intrusive confiscation measures have little actual impact, this raises serious concerns about proportionality and compatibility with rule of law principles.

Examining just how efficient confiscation is when it comes to organised crime is important because the justification of confiscation orders, which can deeply encroach on the rights and liberties of those affected by them,[12] is frequently based on the view that such measures are indispensable in fighting organised crime.[13]

4.2.2.1 *The concept*

The extent to which confiscation helps to prevent crime, both ordinary crime as well as organised crime, remains inconclusive among experts. Some research suggests that confiscation is perceived as a more severe sanction compared to other forms of criminal punishment (such as fines and imprisonment on

9 Meyer (n 5) 243; BT-Drs 12/989, 1, 20, 22; BT-Drs 12/731, 1, 4; BT-Drs 11/5461, 5.

10 Meyer (n 5) 243; BT-Drs 12/989, 1, 20, 22; BT-Drs 12/731, 1, 4; BT-Drs 11/5461, 5.

11 Europol, *Does crime still pay?, Criminal Asset Recovery in the EU, Survey of Statistical Information 2010–2014* (European Police Office, 2016) 5; see also Hellen Schilling, Johannes Corsten, and Yannic Hübner, 'Das Gesetz zur Reform der strafrechtlichen Vermögensabschöpfung' [2017] (3) *Strafverteidiger Forum* 305, 305.

12 On constitutional issues, see Albin Eser, *Die strafrechtlichen Sanktionen gegen das Eigentum* (Mohr Siebeck, 1969) 143–207. For the German implementation of non-conviction-based confiscation, see, for example, Bastian Heuer, *Einziehung ohne Verurteilung?* (Tectum, 2022) 187–238.

13 BT-Drs 18/9525, 48, 58, 73; BT-Drs 12/989, 1; Sinn (n 4) 127 speaks of a 'well-known pattern of argumentation'; for the European level see *Directive 2014/42/EU* (n 6) recitals (1), (3), (4), (6), (19).

probation).[14] Research in this field remains, however, limited.[15] Frank Meyer remarks that the assumption that asset confiscation contributes significantly to the fight against organised crime is 'more of an anecdotally enriched legal policy mantra than a scientifically substantiated fact'.[16]

4.2.2.2 The numbers

There have been attempts both on national and international levels to quantify the key financial aspects of the fight against organised crime. These encompass the estimated proceeds generated by organised crime, the amount of proceeds seized by investigation authorities (also referred to as 'frozen' proceeds), and the amount of proceeds confiscated by the courts. In this context, 'seizure' is an interim step on the way to confiscation. Pending a court decision on confiscation, objects are transferred to official custody by means of seizure. Ideally, statistics would allow for a direct comparison between, on the one hand, the estimated proceeds gained and, on the other, the confiscated proceeds. In the following, where figures for the confiscated proceeds are unavailable, a comparison between estimated proceeds and seized proceeds is drawn instead. The underlying assumption here is that, conservatively estimated, the confiscated assets will not exceed the seized assets as the usual course of events is that assets are seized prior to being confiscated.

By way of example, on a national level, for Germany, the proceeds of organised crime for the year 2022 are estimated to amount to EUR 1.1 billion.[17] The seized proceeds of organised crime for the year 2022 only amounted to EUR 228 million, approximately 21 per cent of the estimated proceeds.[18] Regrettably, figures for the confiscated proceeds are not available. German law enforcement authorities do not track the latter since such confiscation measures are within the responsibility of the courts. Whilst the courts do collect data on the number of confiscation orders, these are not classified by areas of crime.

At the level of the European Union (EU), a study conducted as part of the *Project Organised Crime Portfolio*, a project funded by the European Commission aiming to address the lack of data and information surrounding the economics of organised crime, looking at the years 2010 to 2014, puts the annual estimated profits generated by organised crime at roughly EUR 110

14 Denny Müller, 'Straftaten dürfen sich nicht lohnen', Vermögensabschöpfung als Mittel zur Korruptionsbekämpfung' (2010) 47 *Scheinwerfer, Transparency International Deutschland* 12.

15 Cf. Meyer (n 5) 244 n 15 for an assessment of the research with further references.

16 Ibid.

17 Germany, Bundeskriminalamt (BKA), *Organised Crime, National Situation Report 2022* (BKA, 2023) 2, 15.

18 Ibid., 2, 16.

billion.[19] Europol, the EU Agency for Law Enforcement Cooperation, estimates the annual seized proceeds for the same timeframe to amount to EUR 2.4 billion (approximately 2 per cent of the estimated proceeds)[20] and the confiscated proceeds are estimated at about EUR 1.2 billion (approximately 1 per cent of the estimated proceeds).[21]

At the global level, the United Nations Office on Drugs and Crime (UNODC) estimates that proceeds of organised crime amounted to USD 2.1 trillion for the year 2009.[22] The seized laundered proceeds are estimated to amount to USD 4.2 billion or just 0.2 per cent of the estimated proceeds.[23] Figures for confiscated proceeds were not part of the study.

It should be noted, however, that the figures are merely (conservative) estimates.[24] Further, the definitions of organised crime slightly differ between the organisations that produced the referenced research. Nevertheless, the picture emerging from the data is very clear: seized and confiscated proceeds are a fraction of the estimated generated proceeds.

4.2.2.3 *First observations*

The facts presented thus far demonstrate that the question of whether confiscation truly is an efficient tool to combat organised crime remains unanswered. For this reason, caution should be exercised before making bold claims about confiscation being essential for fighting organised crime.[25] Furthermore, particular caution should be exercised when asserting that extensive confiscation measures are indispensable for targeting organised crime. It should not remain unsaid, however, that even if confiscation were to be inefficient in fighting organised crime, it remains an essential part of bringing justice and indemnifying victims of crime for the financial losses they have suffered.

4.2.3 *The problem*

The question remains why seizure and confiscation of proceeds of organised crime fall so far behind the estimated proceeds generated by organised crime. A closer look at the requirements for issuing a confiscation order sheds some light on this problem.

19 Ernesto U Savona and Michele Riccardi (eds), *From Illegal Markets to Legitimate Businesses: The Portfolio of Organised Crime in Europe*, Final Report of the Project OCP—Organised Crime Portfolio (Transcrime, 2015) 7.

20 Europol (n 11) 4, 8–9.

21 Ibid., 4, 9–10.

22 UNODC, Estimating illicit financial flows resulting from drug trafficking and other transnational organised crime, research report (UNODC, 2011) 7, 38.

23 Ibid., 7.

24 See the disclaimers in BKA (n 17) 7; Europol (n 11) 6; UNODC (n 22) 5.

25 Cf. Eser (n 4) 851.

Traditionally, confiscation was conceived to require a conviction in a criminal trial by a court.[26] The confiscation of assets is ordered in the judgment as part of the sentencing. Due to the opaque structures of organised criminal groups and the efforts of many groups to conceal and shield their activities, assets, and members, it is often not possible to achieve a conviction in organised crime cases.[27] For the same reason, law enforcement often struggles to identify, seize, and confiscate the proceeds obtained by organised criminal groups.[28] Even when specific assets which are believed to derive from a specific crime are identified and seized, they cannot be confiscated without a conviction for the crime these assets are linked to. Linking specific assets to specific crimes is challenging at the best of times, but all the more complicated in organised crime cases.[29]

This is particularly the case with organised criminal groups that are layered or hierarchically structured, involving leaders and directors who orchestrate the crimes and ultimately receive the majority of the proceeds but who themselves are not involved in physically committing the crimes.[30] Such structures can make it especially difficult to establish a link between proceeds and the offence.[31]

Further, organised criminal groups often set up elaborate schemes to hide the true origin of their wealth.[32] Assets often pass through multiple businesses, accounts, or people before they end up with the group. Such layering makes it difficult to trace assets back to the crime they originate from.[33] In many cases, otherwise lawful entities, wittingly or unwittingly, become involved in the layering and are used deliberately by organised criminal groups to cover up the laundering of proceeds and other illicit trade.[34] These problems are all the

26 Jon Petter Rui, 'Introduction', in Jon Petter Rui and Ulrich Sieber (eds), *Non-Conviction-Based Confiscation in Europe* (Duncker & Humblot, 2015) 1, 2.

27 See COM(2022) 245 final (n 4) recital (28).

28 Eurojust, *Report on non-conviction-based confiscation*, General Case 751/NMSK-2012 (Eurojust, 2013) 5.

29 Alexander Retemeyer, 'Das Gesetz zur Neuregelung der strafrechtlichen Vermögensabschöpfung vom 13. April 2017', in Arndt Sinn, Mark A Zöller, and Robert Esser (eds), *Reform der Vermögensabschöpfung* (Dr Kovač, 2019) 1, 2.

30 Rui (n 26) 1.

31 Bright Line Law, The Use of Non-Conviction-Based Seizure and Confiscation (Council of Europe, 2020) 16.

32 See, for example, the complex transnational value-added tax fraud scheme uncovered by the European Public Prosecutor's Office (EPPO) during 'Operation Admiral' involving close to 9000 legal entities and more than 600 natural persons. EPPO, 'Operation Admiral: EPPO Uncovers Organised Crime Groups Responsible for VAT Fraud Estimated at €2.2 billion', EPPO News (29 November 2022) <https://www.eppo.europa.eu/en/news/operation-admiral-eppo-uncovers-organised-crime-groups-responsible-vat-fraud-estimated-eu22>.

33 SWD(2019) 1050 final (n 4) 2.

34 Savona and Riccardi (n 19) 7; SWD(2019) 1050 final (n 4) 2; BKA (n 17) 17–19.

greater if multiple crimes are committed over an extended period,[35] as is often the case with organised crime.

4.2.4 The solution?

After decades of struggling to enhance the confiscation of proceeds from organised crimincal groups,[36] many policymakers and legislators have resorted to a new approach they believe fixes the problem outlined above.[37] The solution seemingly is simple and obvious: confiscation without a conviction, so-called non-conviction-based confiscation. Different jurisdictions use different models of non-conviction-based confiscation, some in civil proceedings, others in criminal proceedings.

Non-conviction-based confiscation can occur in civil proceedings, where the court can order the confiscation of proceeds based on the conclusion that the assets have been acquired via unlawful conduct. This may lead to confiscation based on evidence below the threshold necessary to initiate criminal proceedings.[38] Whether confiscation takes place is determined on a balance of probability/preponderance of evidence test.[39] Once an indirect link between the assets and a crime has been established, for example, large amounts of cash are found on a person during a border control without the person being able to give a plausible explanation for the origin of the money, the burden of proof is reversed such that in order to prevent confiscation the party concerned has to prove that they lawfully acquired the asset.[40]

Non-conviction-based confiscation is also possible in civil courts without any (indirect) link between a specific crime and specific assets. In proceedings related to so-called 'unexplained wealth', assets can be confiscated if a comparison of a person's legal income with the assets found in their possession cannot explain the legal acquisition of said assets. It is then upon the person to prove the legal acquisition of said assets (effectively reversing the burden of proof).[41]

In criminal proceedings, so-called 'extended confiscation' allows for the confiscation of assets believed to stem not from the crime for which the defendant is convicted, but from other unlawful conduct occurring prior to the conviction, for which the court, however, cannot convict the defendant

35 Cf. COM(2022) 245 (n 4) 10.
36 Eurojust (n 8) 6; similar Sinn (n 4) 131.
37 Although the term 'new' is to be liberally understood within the EU, Italy introduced preventive confiscation as early as 1965 (Law 575/1975, Disposizioni contro le organizzazioni criminali di tipo mafioso, anche straniere).
38 Eurojust (n 28) 10.
39 Ibid., 7, 19.
40 Ibid., 10.
41 Ibid.

due to a lack of evidence.[42] Extended confiscation as part of a conviction can also be possible if the defendant's assets cannot be accounted for by their lawful income, and the court is therefore convinced that the assets stem from other unlawful conduct, which the defendant can, however, not be convicted for due to a lack of evidence.[43]

Finally, non-conviction-based confiscation is possible in criminal proceedings if proceedings have been launched against a defendant and cannot be brought to a conviction either due to a lack of evidence or because a conviction is not possible for legal reasons such as immunity, death, or illness of the defendant, statutes of limitations, etc.[44] In these circumstances, confiscation is possible if the court is convinced that the concerned assets stem from an unlawful activity.[45]

These examples are not an exhaustive list of possibilities for employing non-conviction-based confiscation, and combination as well as entirely different approaches are conceivable.[46] The specific criminal law approach used in Germany is outlined in the following part.

4.3 Non-conviction-based confiscation in Germany

The German *Criminal Code* sets out several avenues of non-conviction-based confiscation. The focus here is on non-conviction-based confiscation in cases of wealth of unexplained origin without the need to prove a specific crime.[47] Relevant provisions can be found in § 76a(4) StGB and § 437 of the *Code of Criminal Procedure* [*Strafprozessordnung* (StPO)]. Both provisions were introduced in July 2017 as part of a major reform of confiscation laws. Whilst

42 Ibid. Implementing extended confiscation for certain crimes is mandatory in the EU for its member states under Article 5(1) of *Directive 2014/42/EU* (n 6). See also Marie-Lena Marstaller, *Grenzüberschreitende Einziehung* (Nomos, 2022) 56.

43 Eurojust (n 28) 10.

44 Ibid., 9–10. Implementing such confiscation is also mandatory under Directive 2014/42/EU (n 6) for cases at least where such impossibility is the result of illness or absconding of the suspected or accused person; see also Marstaller (n 42) 56. The proposal in COM(2022) 245 final (n 4) goes even further: Under Article 15, member states would be required to provide for confiscation, e.g. in cases of death, immunity, or amnesties. Article 16 would require providing for confiscation in cases of unexplained wealth linked to organised crime.

45 Eurojust (n 28) 10; Schilling, Corsten, and Hübner (n 11) 310.

46 See Eurojust (n 28) 11–12. Some examples of international implementation can be found in Bright Line Law (n 31) 10–13.

47 In the remaining parts of this chapter, the term 'non-conviction-based confiscation' therefore refers to this modality of confiscation independent of a conviction. In the present context, the term 'unexplained origin' is not to be understood literally as origins that are completely unknown. The term is commonly used to refer to assets believed to be obtained illegally (in violation of criminal laws), Frank Saliger, 'Die Einziehung von Vermögen unklarer Herkunft aus deutscher Sicht', in Arndt Sinn, Mark A Zöller, and Robert Esser, *Reform der Vermögensabschöpfung* (Dr Kovač, 2019) 91, 92.

the German framework on confiscation had to be amended to comply with EU obligations,[48] the introduction of non-conviction-based confiscation for unexplained wealth was not mandated by EU law.[49] Rather, inspiration was drawn from Italian and US legislation on non-conviction-based confiscation.[50]

The reform further pursued the ambitious goal of reducing the notorious complexity of Germany's confiscation law, which had proven to be a significant barrier to a wider use of the existing provisions on confiscation.[51] The amendment sought to, at long last, grant confiscation the importance in practice that criminal policy assigns to it.[52] Criticism on whether the reform is suitable for this purpose was not only made by defence lawyers,[53] but also by the German Judges' Association (Deutscher Richterbund), who feared a considerable increase in their workload and pointed out that the implementation is not practical at all.[54]

Although no direct mention of organised crime is made in the new provisions, the introduction of non-conviction-based confiscation in

48 *Directive 2014/42/EU* (n 6).

49 A critical perspective on exceeding the EU requirements can be found in Hellen Schilling and Yannic Hübner, '"Non-conviction-based confiscation"—Ein Fremdkörper im neuen Recht der strafrechtlichen Vermögensabschöpfung?' (2018) 38(1) *Strafverteidiger* 49, 53; Markus Meißner, 'Die Reform der strafrechtlichen Vermögensabschöpfung—ein Ehrgeizprojekt oder: Höher, schneller, weiter ... das neue Abschöpfungsrecht aus Sicht des Strafverteidigers' (2017) 2(4) *Kriminalpolitsche Zeitschrift* 237, 240–241.

50 BT-Drs 18/9525, 73. For a closer look at the Italian model, see Till Bettels, *Gewinnabschöpfung zur Bekämpfung Organisierter Kriminalität am Beispiel Italiens* (Nomos, 2016) 176–270; Michele Panzavolta and Roberto Flor, 'A Necessary Evil? The Italian "Non-Criminal System" of Asset Forfeiture', in Jon Petter Rui and Ulrich Sieber (eds), *Non-Conviction-Based Confiscation in Europe* (Duncker & Humblot, 2015) 111. For the US model, see Stefan D Cassella, 'Civil Asset Recovery – The American Experience', in Jon Petter Rui and Ulrich Sieber (eds), *Non-Conviction-Based Confiscation in Europe* (Duncker & Humblot, 2015) 13.

51 BT-Drs 18/9525, 2; see further Patrick Hinderer and Lisa Blechschmitt, 'Die "erweiterte selbstständige Einziehung" nach § 76a Abs. 4 StGB i.V.m. § 437 StPO' (2018) 7(5) *Neue Zeitschrift für Wirtschafts- Steuer- und Unternehmensstrafrecht* 179, 179; Folker Bittmann, 'Commentary on Bundesgerichthof—3 StR 238/21' (2022) 11(10) *Neue Zeitschrift für Wirtschafts-, Steuer- und Unternehmensstrafrecht* 406, 406; Sinn (n 4) 145.

52 BT-Drs 18/9525, 1. Frank Meyer, 'Die selbstständige Einziehung nach § 76a StGB-E, oder: Don't Bring a Knife to a Gunfight' (2017) 37(5) *Strafverteidiger* 343, 343, expresses high hopes on § 76a(4) StGB in this respect.

53 Meißner (n 49) 241.

54 Deutscher Richterbund, 'Stellungnahme zum Referentenentwurf eines Gesetzes zur Reform der strafrechtlichen Vermögensbschöpfung', Nr. 9/16 (June 2016) <https://www.drb.de/fileadmin/DRB/pdf/Stellungnahmen/2016/DRB_160602_Stn_Nr_09_Vermoegensabschoepfung.pdf>; Deutscher Richterbund, 'Zweite Stellungnahme zum Gesetzesentwurf zur Reform der strafrechtlichen Vermögensbschöpfung', Nr. 19/16 (October 2016) <https://www.drb.de/fileadmin/DRB/pdf/Stellungnahmen/2016/DRB_161018_Stn_Nr_19_Zweite_Stellungnahme_Vermoegensabschoepfung.pdf>.

Germany—allegedly—sought to close existing gaps in the confiscation regime concerning assets of unknown origin in the field of organised crime.[55]

The legislative material contains some scenarios where the legislator envisions non-conviction-based confiscation to close existing gaps. One insightful example is a situation where customs and police authorities seize considerable amounts of cash, for instance, at airports or during traffic controls, which appear to stem from organised crime, but where it is not possible to trace the exact origin of the money.[56] Under the old law, if a specific offence could not be proven, such assets had to be returned to their previous holder, even if there was no reasonable doubt that the money originated from a criminal offence.[57] Confiscation was not possible. Non-conviction-based confiscation is designed to close such gaps by surrendering the requirement to prove a specific crime. Procedural safeguards, such as the principle of proving the guilt of an individual (i.e. a criminal conviction), do not apply,[58] because, at least according to the legislator, § 76a(4) StGB embodies an *in rem* procedure, that is, a proceeding against an object rather than a proceeding against a subject (*in personam*).[59]

The first sentence of § 76a(4) StGB sets out the requirements for non-conviction-based confiscation through the courts:

> An object and any benefits derived thereof, seized on suspicion of an offence referred to in sentence 3, shall also be confiscated independently if the object originates from an unlawful act and the person affected by the seizure cannot be prosecuted or convicted for the underlying offence.

The StGB refers to non-conviction-based confiscation as 'independent confiscation' ['selbständige Einziehung']. § 76a(4) StGB is commonly referred to as extended independent confiscation (erweiterte selbstständige Einziehung) to emphasise that confiscation is not only possible independent of a conviction

55 The legislative material only ever mentions non-conviction-based confiscation in the context of organised crime (and terrorism); see, for example, BT-Drs 18/9525, 3, 48, 58; and BT-Drs 18/11640, 77, 83.

56 BT-Drs 18/9525, 48; further (detailed) examples are provided by Marcus Köhler and Christiane Burkhard, 'Die Reform der strafrechtlichen Vermögensabschöpfung—Teil 2/2' (2017) 37(12) *Neue Zeitschrift für Strafrecht* 665, 671–672; Retemeyer (n 29) 13.

57 BT-Drs 18/9525, 48.

58 Ibid., 92.

59 BT-Drs 18/9525, 92; Wilhelm Schmidt and Patrick Scheuß, '§ 437 StPO', in Christoph Barthe and Jan Gericke (eds), *Karlsruher Kommentar zur Strafprozessordnung* (C H Beck, 9th ed 2023) [3]. Critical: Karsten Gaede, '§ 437 StPO', in Jörg-Peter Becker et al. (eds), *Löwe-Rosenberg. Die Strafprozessordnung und das Gerichtsverfassungsgesetz* (De Gruyter, 27th ed, 2022) [2]; Silke Hüls, 'Zur Reform des Rechts der Vermögensabschöfpung im Strafrecht' [2017] (9) *Zeitschrift für Wirtschaftsstrafrecht und Haftung im Unternehmen* 242, 251; Schilling and Hübner (n 49) 53, 54.

but also 'extended' in comparison to 'ordinary' confiscation, as the offence the confiscated object derives from does not have to be identical with the offence that triggered the seizure of the object. The following sections further explore the individual requirements.

4.3.1 Investigation into listed offence

The first requirement for non-conviction-based confiscation under § 76a(4) StGB is an investigation into one of the listed offences (also referred to as 'catalogue offences') found in the third sentence of § 76a(4). The list includes, *inter alia*, offences the legislator associates with organised crime,[60] such as trafficking in persons, forced prostitution, and forced labour committed commercially and/or by a gang (§§ 232–232b StGB); establishing a criminal organisation (§ 129(1) StGB); dissemination, procurement, and possession of child abuse material (§ 184b(2) StGB); money laundering (§ 261 StGB); as well as offences relating to illicit drugs and arms set out in statutes outside the *Criminal Code.*

When it comes to what constitutes an investigation 'into' such an offence, different scenarios are conceivable. For one, an investigation can be launched into one of the listed offences, resulting in the object being seized, and then non-conviction-based confiscation commences based on the belief that the object derives from said listed offence.

Controversial was the scenario in which an investigation was originally launched into a non-listed offence, and this suspicion was only later dismissed at some point during the investigation in favour of the suspicion of a listed offence. After the German Federal Court of Justice [Bundesgerichtshof (BGH)] ruled that confiscation under § 76a(4) StGB was not permissible in such a case,[61] the legislator in the following reworded the provision.[62] The accompanying legislative materials suggest that the provision shall now also capture the scenario where an investigation started into a non-listed offence and only later turned into an investigation for a listed offence.[63] With this interpretation it is thus only necessary that the suspicion of a listed offence existed at some point during the entire confiscation process.

60 BT-Drs 18/9525, 73, Thomas Fischer, '§ 76a StGB', in Thomas Fischer (ed), *Strafgesetzbuch mit Nebengesetzen* (C H Beck, 71st ed 2024) [11]. Possible explanations for the composition of the list are given by Meyer 'Die selbstständige Einziehung' (n 52) 345.

61 Bundesgerichtshof [German Federal Court of Justice], 1 StR 320/18, 18 September 2019, reported in (2019) 64 BGHSt 186.

62 BGBl I 2021, 327.

63 BT-Drs 19/26602, 8. Cf. Mohamad El-Ghazi, Marie-Lena Marstaller, and Till Zimmermann, 'Die erweiterte selbstständige Einziehung gem. § 76 a Abs. 4 StGB nach der Reform des Geldwäschestrafrechts' (2021) 10(8) *Neue Zeitschrift für Wirtschafts-, Steuer- und Unternehmensstrafrecht* 297, 303–304.

It is not required that there is a high degree of suspicion that a listed offence was committed; a mere initial suspicion ['Anfangsverdacht'] under §§ 152(2), 160(1) StPO suffices.[64] The initial suspicion is the lowest degree of suspicion provided for in the StPO, which is present if there are sufficient facts indicating that an offence that can be prosecuted has been committed.[65]

4.3.2 *Object seized on suspicion of listed offence*

As part of the investigation, the object in question needs to be seized by the authorities. The term 'object' includes any proceeds generated by the offence, including surrogates that have substituted (the value of) the original object.[66] It is contentious if the term also encompasses the products of the offence, meaning objects produced through the commission of the crime, for example, producing counterfeit currency.[67]

4.3.3. *Person cannot be persecuted/convicted for the underlying offence*

A third requirement is that the person concerned (i.e. the person the object was seized from) cannot be prosecuted or convicted for the offence, for example, because the suspicion cannot be confirmed or the suspicion turns out to be false.[68] Other scenarios envisioned by the legislator are cases where a conviction cannot be achieved because mental elements such as intention cannot be established, or where the person concerned is assumedly involved in some criminal activity but the involvement in a specific statutory offence cannot be proven.[69] If a conviction is obtained, conviction-based confiscation (under provisions outside § 76a StGB) takes precedence. Subsidiarity further applies to all other means of non-conviction-based confiscation under § 76a(1) to (3), such that extended independent confiscation under § 76a(4) is subsidiary to all other forms of confiscation.[70]

64 Steffen Barreto da Rosa, 'Die Reform der Vermögensabschöpfung: Offene Fragen des neuen Sicherstellungsrechts' (2018) 7(6) *Neue Zeitschrift für Wirtschafts- Steuer- und Unternehmensstrafrecht* 215, 218; Felix Kraushaar, 'Die Einziehung nach § 76 a Abs. 4 StGB—Zivilprozess im Strafprozess?' (2019) 8(8) *Neue Zeitschrift für Wirtschafts-, Steuer- und Unternehmensstrafrecht* 288, 289–290, on the other hand, refers to 'probable suspicion'.

65 Markus Mavany, '§ 152 StPO', in Jörg-Peter Becker et al. (eds), *Löwe-Rosenberg. Die Strafprozessordnung und das Gerichtsverfassungsgesetz* (De Gruyter, 27th ed, 2020) [27]–[32].

66 Hans Kornprobst, '§ 33 Betäubungsmittelgesetz', in Klaus Weber, Hans Kornprobst, and Stefan Maier (eds), *Betäubungsmittelgesetz* (C H Beck, 6th ed 2021) [456].

67 Cf. El-Ghazi, Marstaller, and Zimmermann (n 63) 301–302.

68 Lena-Marie Marstaller and Till Zimmermann, *Non-conviction-based Confiscation in Deutschland?* (Nomos, 2018) 38 including n 67.

69 BT-Drs 18/9525, 92–93.

70 BT-Drs 18/9525, 73; Susanne Beck and Thomas C Knierim, 'Kapitel 16: Vermögensabschöpfung', in Thomas C Knierim et al. (eds), *Gesamtes Strafrecht aktuell* (Nomos, 2018) [103]; cf. Kornprobst (n 66) § 33 Betäubungsmittelgesetz [460]–[464].

Meyer criticises the legislator for failing to specify the extent of the effort the authorities have to undergo to achieve confiscation under other provisions before resorting to non-conviction-based confiscation.[71] Hans Kornprobst suggests there has to be a need for a 'serious will' to prosecute.[72] It is unclear, however, how such a 'serious will' would be proven in court.

4.3.4. Court is convinced that object derives from an unlawful act

Even though no specific offence needs to be proven,[73] the court ordering non-conviction-based confiscation needs to be convinced that the object derives from an unlawful act.[74] § 437 StPO, entitled 'special provisions concerning independent confiscation proceedings' sets out the criteria to aid the court in its decision on whether the object in question derives from an unlawful act.[75]

> When deciding on independent confiscation pursuant to § 76a(4) StGB, the court may base its persuasion that the object derived from an unlawful act in particular on the gross discrepancy between the value of the object and the lawfull income of the person concerned. In addition, the court may in particular also take the following into account when reaching its decision:

1. the outcome of the investigations into the offence giving rise to the proceedings,
2. the circumstances under which the object was found and secured, and
3. the other personal and financial circumstances of the person concerned.

71 Meyer 'Die selbstständige Einziehung' (n 52) 345 criticises in particular the lack of provisions on the use of mutual legal assistance; see also Frank Meyer, 'Abschöpfung von Vermögen unklarer Herkunft' (2018) 7(6) *Neue Zeitschrift für Wirtschafts-, Steuer- und Unternehmensstrafrecht* 246, 247 (Meyer, 'Abschöpfung von Vermögen unklarer Herkunft').

72 Kornprobst (n 66) § 33 Betäubungsmittelgesetz [459].

73 Fischer (n 60) § 76a StGB [9a]; Tim Gebauer, 'Reform der strafrechtlichen Vermögensabschöpfung', *Zeitschrift für Rechtspolitik* (2016) 49(4) 101, 104; Kersten Höft, '§ 76a Abs. 4 StGB—Ein neues und verfassungswidriges Instrument im deutschen Vermögensabschöpfungsrecht' (2018) 19(5) *Höchstrichterliche Rechtsprechung zum Strafrecht* 196, 196.

74 Saliger (n 47) 96 points out that this requirement bears a fundamental contradiction within itself: How is the court supposed to come to a definitive conclusion that an object derives from an unlawful act if the specific unlawful act it derives from remains unknown?

75 BT-Drs 18/9525, 92–93. On the controversial question of what purpose the provision serves (a rule of evidence, a shift of the burden of proof, a prima facie standard of evidence, a legal presumption, or a factual presumption and others), see Katharina Beckemper, 'Die zweifelhafte Rechtsnatur des § 437 StPO' (2022) 134(2) *Zeitschrift für die gesamte Strafrechtswissenschaft* 456; Frank Saliger, 'Grundfragen der Vermögensabschöpfung' (2017) 129(4) *Zeitschrift für die gesamte Strafrechtswissenschaft* 995, 1027–1029 ('Saliger, "Grundfragen der Vermögensabschöpfung"'); Saliger (n 47) 107–108; Heuer (n 12) 61–67; Nils E Wilfert, *Die Beweissituation im Recht der selbstständigen Einziehung in Deutschland und England* (Nomos, 2022) 87–102.

The first sentence of § 437 StPO states that in making its decision, the court may rely, in particular, on a gross discrepancy between the value of the confiscated object vis-à-vis the lawful income of the person concerned. It is the intention of the legislator that this circumstance should be of 'particular importance' when determining the origin of an object in question, especially as this circumstance is given special importance in other jurisdictions in the context of non-conviction-based confiscation.[76]

Additional optional criteria are set out in a non-exhaustive list in the second sentence of § 437 StPO.[77] These criteria relate to the results of the investigation into the listed offence, the circumstances under which the object was secured, and other personal and economic circumstances of the person concerned. It is important to note that § 437 does not intend to affect the principle of free judicial assessment of evidence enshrined in § 261 StPO.[78] The criteria set out in § 437 are to be treated merely as specifics which the court may take into consideration when making its decision;[79] they need to be examined on a case-by-case basis.[80] It is the legislator's intention, however, 'that no excessive demands should be placed on the [judicial] conviction' that the object derives from an illegal origin,[81] which indicates that a general reasoning based on the criteria set out in § 437 should suffice for the court's conviction that the object derives from an unlawful act.[82]

In addition, some sources argue that the rules on presenting evidence and the corresponding burden of proof applicable to civil law cases should serve as guidance.[83] If the prosecution presents verifiable facts that lead to a conclusion that the object in question derives from an unlawful origin, the persons concerned shall, in general, not be able to defend themselves by exercising their right to silence or by claiming a lack of knowledge.[84] Rather it is then up to them to substantiate the legal origin of the object.[85]

76 BT-Drs 18/9525, 92.
77 BT-Drs 18/9525, 92; Schmitt and Scheuß (n 59) § 437 StPO [4].
78 Schmidt and Scheuß (n 59) § 437 StPO [2]. A clarification which the legislator first intended to codify in subsection (2) of the provision (see BT-Drs 18/9525, 58, 93) but then later deemed redundant (see BT-Drs 18/11640, 89).
79 Schmidtt and Scheuß (n 59) § 437 StPO [3].
80 Ibid.
81 BT-Drs 18/9525, 73. The legislative materials then reference several decisions by the German Federal Court of Justice (BGH 4 StR 516/94 (22 November 1994); BGH 5 StR 184/10 (4 August 2010)) concerning the standard of evidence as developed by the court in reference to extended confiscation.
82 Gaede (n 59) § 437 StPO [3].
83 BT-Drs 18/9525, 92; Amtsgericht Nürtingen [Local Court Nürtingen], 16 DS 211 Js 53509/17 (21 June 2017) reported in (2019) BeckRS 15406 [15]. Disapproving: Kraushaar (n 64) 291–293; El-Ghazi, Marstaller, and Zimmermann (n 63) 304.
84 BT-Drs 18/9525, 92; Amtsgericht Nürtingen, 16 DS 211 Js 53509/17 (21 June 2017) reported in (2019) BeckRS 15406 [15].
85 BT-Drs 18/9525, 92.

3.4.5 Confiscation in the court's discretion

Even if all other requirements are met, the court retains discretion to order (or not to order) the confiscation of the object. The phrase 'shall be confiscated' in the first sentence of § 76a(4) StGB means that confiscation should in principle take place, but that the court may refrain from ordering confiscation if this produces disproportionate results, especially as articulated in the case law of the European Court of Human Rights.[86] One example of such disproportionate results provided in the legislative material is the acquisition of the asset by a third-party beneficiary in good faith on the basis of a lawful transaction.[87]

4.4 Amendments since implementation

Substantial changes were made to the scope of § 76a(4) StGB in relation to money laundering (§ 261 StGB), a listed offence in the third sentence of § 76a(4) and itself an offence that was originally introduced to combat organised crime.[88] Up until 18 March 2021, the money laundering provision contained a list of suitable predicate offences.[89] This meant that the scope of § 76a(4), too, was limited in relation to money laundering by the restriction on predicate offences under § 261 as this resulted in non-conviction-based confiscation only being possible for the laundered proceeds of limited crimes included in the list of § 261.

Pursuing an 'all-crimes-approach'[90] regarding money laundering, the list of predicate offences in § 261 StGB was dropped altogether in March 2021 such that any offence is now a suitable predicate offence for money laundering.[91] Removing the limitation on predicate offences for money laundering also resulted in a significant expansion of the scope of § 76a(4) StGB as non-conviction-based confiscation is now possible for any criminal offence so long as an initial suspicion of money laundering arises at some stage of the proceedings.[92]

86 BT-Drs 18/9525, 73. On the exercise of this discretion, see also Kammergericht Berlin [Higher Regional Court Berlin], 4 Ws 46/20 (30 September 2020) [2021] *Zeitschrift für Wirtschafts- und Steuerstrafrecht* 121, 124.
87 BT-Drs 18/9525, 73.
88 BT-Drs 12/989, 21, 26.
89 See BGBl 2021 I, 327 and BR-Drs 620/20; BT-Drs 19/24180; BT-Drs 19/26602.
90 On this see Nikolaos Gazeas, 'Das neue Geldwäsche-Strafrecht: Weitreichende Folgen für die Praxis' (2021) 74(15) *Neue Juristische Wochenschrift* 1041; Frank Böhme and Markus Busch, 'Das Gesetz zur Verbesserung der strafrechtlichen Bekämpfung der Geldwäsche: Richtlinienumsetzung und Neuausrichtung von § 261 StGB' [2021] 5 *Zeitschrift für Wirtschafts- und Steuerstrafrecht* 169, 171.
91 El-Ghazi, Marstaller, and Zimmermann (n 63) 301.
92 Ibid; Fischer (n 60) § 76a StGB [10]; Anja Schiemann, '"Bekämpfungsstrafrecht" außer Rand und Band: Zur unverhältnismäßigen Reform des Geldwäschetatbestands' (2021) 6(3) *Kriminalpolitische Zeitschrift* 151, 156; see also BT-Drs 19/24180, 19, 27–28. It has to be noted that prior to the 2021 amendment, the list of predicate offences was already quite extensive,

4.5 Legal issues with non-conviction-based confiscation

A plethora of legal issues, controversies, and open questions continue to arise in the context of non-conviction-based confiscation in Germany. Controversies include whether and if so to what extent the constitutional right to property laid down in Article 14(1) of the *Grundgesetz* (Basic Law) applies.[93] The legal nature of non-conviction-based confiscation is a hotly debated issue, with some scholars arguing that it has a penal character, whilst others argue that confiscation merely restores the balance of assets back to the original situation and is thus not of a penal nature.[94] Closely tied to this debate is the question of the application of the principle of guilt and the presumption of innocence.[95] These only apply under German law if § 76a(4) StGB is considered to be of a penal nature.

Issues also arise concerning the principle that the accused cannot be compelled to self-incriminate in relation to the shift of the burden of proof triggered by non-conviction-based confiscation, whereby the persons concerned must potentially give evidence that could be later used against them. This is particularly relevant, for instance, in situations where not giving a statement is not feasible for economic reasons and, therefore, the principle of not being compelled to self-incriminate is effectevily circumvented.[96] As mentioned, it is additionally questionable if the criteria set out in § 437 StPO to 'aid' the court's decision are compatible with the principle of free judicial assessment under § 261 StPO.[97]

A further concern is the extensive scope of application of non-conviction-based confiscation given the broad requirement that the objects merely need to derive from an unlawful act. The term 'derive' is to be interpreted in line with § 261 StGB (money laundering) where 'derives from' is fulfilled if, from an economic point of view, there is a causal link between the object and the predicate offence, i.e. the object has its origin in the unlawful act.[98] As all causal factors are treated equally to determine whether an object derives from

covering all offences with a minimum penalty of one year imprisonment and a long list of further suitable offences.

93 See Höft (n 73) 202–204; Marstaller and Zimmermann (n 68) 91–98; cf. Robert Esser, 'A Civil Asset Recovery Model: The German Perspective and European Human Rights', in Jon Petter Rui and Ulrich Sieber (eds), *Non-Conviction-Based Confiscation in Europe* (Duncker & Humblot, 2015) 69, 83–91.

94 See Beck and Knierim (n 70) [9]–[16]; El-Ghazi, Marstaller, and Zimmermann (n 63) 298; Höft (n 73) 199–201; Marstaller and Zimmermann (n 68) 60–80; Frank Meyer, 'Verfassungsfragen der Einziehung' in Matthias Bäcker and Christoph Burchard (eds), *Strafverfassungsrecht* (Mohr Siebeck, 2022) 349, 353–366; Thomas Rönnau and Moritz Begemeier, 'Die Vermögensabschöpfung ist keine Strafe!?' (2021) 41(12) *Neue Zeitschrift für Strafrecht* 705.

95 See Hinderer and Blechschmitt (n 51) 183; Hüls (n 59) 251; Heuer (n 12) 189–192. Cf. Esser (n 93) 80–81, 102–103.

96 Meißner (n 49) 243. Cf. Esser (n 93) 82–83; Hinderer and Blechschmitt (n 51) 183.

97 Hüls (n 59) 251; Höft (n 73) 201–202; Kraushaar (n 64) 292; see also n 75.

98 BT-Drs 18/9525, 73.

an unlawful act, 'derives' also includes objects that do not stem exclusively from a criminal offence but rather were combined with incriminated objects.[99] An asset (for example, a house) that is suspected to have been financed to a not insignificant part by incriminated funds can therefore be confiscated in its entirety (and not only to the extent that incriminated funds are suspected). Some authors have raised concerns whether the limitations placed on § 76a(4)StGB and § 437 StPO are sufficient to comply with the principle of proportionality.[100]

Criticism has also been raised that the subsidiarity of § 76a(4) StGB to other confiscation provisions might not be taken all that seriously by the authorities. The fact that § 76a(4) does not require a conviction entails the risk that attempts to confiscate using regular means (i.e. by obtaining a conviction) will be abandoned all too quickly in order to confiscate via § 76a(4) without a conviction.[101] Whilst this might aid the political goal of clamping down on organised crime, such an approach is not compatible with the original justification of the provision, which is merely to close confiscation loopholes in this context.[102]

At the time of its introduction, some authors already questioned whether the list of offences in the third sentence of § 76a(4) StGB provided an adequate restriction to the scope of application of non-conviction-based confiscation.[103] In light of the amendments that have been made since, this concern is all the more relevant today.

These concerns and several other issues raised by other sources are beyond the scope of the present chapter and warrant further, separate research and analysis.

The German federal parliamentary Committee on Legal Affairs and Consumer Protection ['Ausschuss für Recht und Verbraucherschutz'] expressly noted that the provisions 'fully exhaust' the scope of what is constitutionally permissible.[104] This is a rare acknowledgement by the legislator and begs the question at what point the line of what is constitutionally permissible will be (or has been) crossed. This question is all the more important because, as discussed earlier, the provisions have seen further amendments since this worrying statement was made by the Committee. At the European level, the Council of the European Union has similarly identified the compatibility of non-conviction-based confiscation with fundamental rights, including the

99 Ibid; Höft (n 73) 196–197; Gebauer (n 73) 104; Meyer 'Die selbstständige Einziehung' (n 52) 345; Hüls (n 59) 251; Schilling and Hübner (n 49) 52; Heuer (n 12) 31–45.

100 See Hinderer and Blechschmitt (n 51) 184; Hüls (n 59) 251; Gebauer (n 73) 104. Cf. Esser (n 93) 104–105.

101 Meyer 'Die selbstständige Einziehung' (n 52) 345.

102 BT-Drs 18/9525, 58.

103 See Schilling, Corsten and Hübner (n 11) 310.

104 BT-Drs 18/11640, 83.

right to a fair trial, effective judicial remedy, the presumption of innocence, and the right to property, as a 'key challenge'.[105]

In sum, the many issues raised in relation to Germany's rules relating to non-conviction-based confiscation call for a restrictive interpretation. Where this is not possible, a restrictive implementation through further legislative amendments of the provisions is warranted.

4.6 Proposal for amendment

The following sections contain some suggestions for legislative amendments to non-conviction-based confiscation under § 76a(4) StGB. The underlying proposal seeks to restore proportionality by reverting the provision to its original purpose of confiscating the proceeds of organised crime (and only of organised crime).

4.6.1 Amending the list in the third sentence of § 76a(4) StGB

By removing the requirement of a predicate offence for money laundering (§ 261 StGB), the scope of § 76a(4) StGB experienced a major extension. The list of offences in the third sentence of § 76a(4) no longer serves its purpose of ensuring proportionality by limiting the scope of § 76a(4),[106] making a restriction to offences of organised crime all the more important. A reversal of the amendments to the money laundering provision to rein in the scope of § 76a(4) seems highly unlikely, if not impossible, as the incorporation of significant parts of the (existing and newly added) predicate offences is necessary to comply with EU law.[107] For this reason the focus here shall be on an amendment of the list in the third sentence of § 76a(4).

Several provisions included in the current list of offences have been identified as not necessarily being tied to organised crime but rather as 'ordinary' white-collar crimes.[108] These include money laundering [Geldwäsche], § 261 StGB,[109] tax evasion (as a member of a gang) [Steuerhinterziehung (als Mitglied einer Bande)], § 370(3) 5 *Fiscal Code* [*Abgabenordnung*],[110] tax fraud (commercially or as a member of a gang) [Steuerhehlerei (gewerbsmäßig

105 SWD(2019) 1050 final (n 4) 8.
106 El-Ghazi, Marstaller, and Zimmermann (n 63) 303.
107 See BT-Drs 19/24180, 15–16.; Directive (EU) 2018/1673 of the European Parliament and of the Council of 23 October 2018 on combatting money laundering by criminal law [2018] OJ L 284/22.
108 See Heuer (n 12) 214–215 who, however, sees the confiscation from non-listed offences as a tolerable by-product.
109 Gina Greeve, 'Das neue Recht der strafrechtlichen Vermögensabschöpfung' [2017] 10 *Zeitschrift für Wirtschaftsstrafrecht und Haftung im Unternehmen* 277, 279; Hüls (n 59) 251; Schilling, Corsten and Hübner (n 11) 310; Hinderer and Blechschmitt (n 51) 181.
110 Hinderer and Blechschmitt (n 51) 181.

oder als Mitglied einer Bande)], § 374(2) *Fiscal Code*,[111] as well as several offences under §§ 17 and 18 of the *Foreign Trade Act* [*Außenwirtschaftsgesetz*] concerning violations of trade embargoes and national and EU foreign trade law.[112] Susanne Beck and Thomas C Knierim further argue that, despite contrary assertions by the legislator, these offences cannot be classified as 'serious crimes' but are merely simple offences targeting individual offenders rather than groups, or offences involving a medium level of criminality.[113]

Of the offences mentioned in the previous paragraph, money laundering is of particular interest since almost all the published cases in which § 76a(4) StGB was applied, the required initial suspicion of a listed offence related to a suspicion of money laundering.[114] Given the very broad understanding of what constitutes money laundering under German criminal law, a suspicion of some form of money laundering can very easily arise.[115] As Alexander Retemeyer points out, anytime hard cash is found by the investigation authorities, there are reasonable grounds for the suspicion of money laundering under § 261 StGB.[116] Money laundering has been referred to as a 'door opener': it brings white-collar crimes far removed from the field of organised crime into the realm of Germany's non-conviction-based confiscation regime.[117]

A closer look at the reasons why some offences were included in the list in the third sentence of § 76a(4) StGB shows that the German parliamentary Committee on Legal Affairs and Consumer Protection argued that adding the offences of tax evasion (committed by a member of a gang that has joined forces to commit such offences on a continuing basis) and tax fraud (on a commercial basis or by a member of a gang that has joined forces to commit such offences on a continuing basis) as well as living off the earnings of another person's prostitution (i.e. pimping [*Zuhälterei*], § 181a(1), (3) StGB) to the list would not raise any concerns because the minimum penalty of six months imprisonment for these three offences is sufficiently similar to that of the other offences comprising the list.[118]

Based on this reasoning, one decisive factor for the inclusion of an offence into the list is a minimum penalty of a certain duration (six months

111 Ibid.

112 Greeve (n 109) 279; Schilling, Corsten and Hübner (n 11) 310.

113 Beck and Knierim (n 70) [106].

114 El-Ghazi, Marstaller, and Zimmermann (n 63) 297.

115 See Meißner (n 49) 243.

116 Retemeyer (n 29) 14; similar Amtsgericht Nürtingen, 16 DS 211 Js 53509/17 (21 June 2017) reported in (2019) BeckRS 15406 [16], arguing that cash payments as such in this day and age are highly suspicious in regard to money laundering.

117 Gerson Trüg, 'Die Reform der strafrechtlichen Vermögensabschöpfung' (2017) 80(27) *Neue Juristische Wochenschrift* 1913, 1916; cf. Christian Pelz, 'Abschöpfung von Vermögen unklarer Herkunft in Deutschland' (2018) 7(6) *Neue Zeitschrift für Wirtschafts-, Steuer- und Unternehmensstrafrecht* 251, 253. See also Meyer 'Die selbstständige Einziehung' (n 52) 352.

118 BT-Drs 18/11640, 83.

imprisonment) in order to include the offence in a category of crimes that are sufficiently severe to justify non-conviction-based confiscation. By this logic, however, money laundering does not make a good fit, since the penalty also includes monetary fines and thus a minimum penalty that is much less severe than six months imprisonment. The same goes for some of the offences under § 18 of the *Foreign Trade Act*, which have a minimum penalty of only three months imprisonment or merely a fine.

Adopting the Committee's reasoning of using the minimum penalty as an indicator for inclusion into the list, these offences do not fit the picture. As money laundering plays a critical role in organised crime,[119] removing § 261 StGB from the list would seriously diminish the efforts to 'drain the swamp of organised crime'. A sustainable amendment should therefore find a way to restrict the listed offences in § 76a(4) StGB in such a way that only cases of more serious crime, especially cases of organised crime, are captured.

In relation to money laundering, inspiration for an amendment may be drawn from other offences in the list. In some parts, the personal commission of the offence is not sufficient for non-conviction-based confiscation; rather, commission by a member of a gang set up to commit such offences on a continuing basis[120] or commission on a commercial basis[121] is required. The aforementioned offence of tax fraud under § 374(2) of the *Fiscal Code* is one such example.

These specific prerequisites (commission by a member of a gang set up to commit such offences on a continuing basis or comission on a commercial basis) already surface in the context of aggravated money laundering. § 261(5) StGB makes particularly serious cases of money laundering punishable by imprisonment for six months to ten years. The subsection then sets out two examples: commission by a member of a gang set up to commit such offences on a continuing basis or comission on a commercial basis. The list of offences in the third sentence of § 76a(4) StGB could thus be amended in a way that a suspicion of money laundering in an aggravated case under § 261(5) is required.

With regards to the offences under the *Foreign Trade Act* that have a low minimum statutory penalty, the scope of § 76a(4) StGB could be restricted to § 17(3) and § 18(7) and (8) of the *Foreign Trade Act*, which similarly refer

119 BT-Drs 12/989, 1; critical of whether the current concept of the offence does justice to this goal, Schiemann (n 92) 151.

120 The concept of a gang requires the association of at least three persons who have joined together with the intention of committing several independent offences of the type of offence specified by the law for a certain period: BGH GSSt 1/00 (22 March 2001) reported in (2001) 46 BGHSt 321, 321.

121 A person acts commercially if he or she intends to obtain not only temporary and not entirely insignificant source of income by repeatedly committing an offence: BGH 4 StR 563/51 (8 November 1951) reported in (1951) 1 BGHSt 383, 383.

to commission by a member of a gang set up to commit such offences on a continuing basis or commission on a commercial basis.

A somewhat similar proposal to the one suggested here was put forward by the Federal Government of Germany. In light of the amendments to the money laundering offence which greatly expanded the scope for non-conviction-based confiscation, the Government suggested, for reasons of proportionality, to limit non-conviction-based confiscation to cases of serious crime.[122] It feared that otherwise the list of offences in the third sentence of § 76a(4) StGB, which is intended to limit the scope for non-conviction-based confiscation to serious offences in the fields of organised crime, would be rendered meaningless.[123] It proposed to limit § 76a(4) to cases of money laundering where the predicate offence either carries a minimum penalty of one year of imprisonment (i.e. is a felony, § 12(1) StGB) or if the predicate offence was committed by a member of a gang set up to commit such offences on a continuing basis or was committed on a commercial basis.[124] As the Federal Parliament never adopted this proposal by the Government, the underlying issue, i.e. the drastic expansion of the scope of non-conviction-based confiscation, remains unaddressed. For this reason, the Government's proposal is still a suggestion worthy of further consideration.

One option would be to combine the two proposals discussed above, such that money laundering is included under the third sentence of § 76a(4) StGB if it was committed by a member of a gang set up to commit such offence on a continuing basis or committed on a commercial basis and if the predicate offence, too, was committed in one of these circumstances.

Alternatively, the list could be refocused on serious organised crime by limiting the application of money laundering as a suitable listed offence. As detailed above, money laundering requires a predicate offence from which the money to be laundered is derived. Under the current law, any criminal offence can be a predicate offence to money laundering. A possible amendment, within the spirit of the provision, to § 76a(4) StGB would be to limit money laundering as a suitable listed offence to such cases of money laundering where the predicate offence is any one of the offences currently already listed in the third sentence of § 76a(4). This amendment would be very much within the spirit of the provision, as these are the offences the legislator considers to be serious organised crime offences for which non-conviction-based confiscation was specifically intended.

122 BT-Drs 19/24180, 19, 27–28.
123 Ibid., 27–28.
124 Ibid., 7, 27–28. Differently already then BR-Drs 620/20 (B), 3.

4.6.2 *Confiscation of proceeds only from listed offences*

A further option to revive the link to organised crime would be to ensure that confiscation under § 76a(4) StGB is only possible in cases where the court's view that the assets derive from an unlawful act is specified to the effect that the court is also convinced that the asset is derived from a listed offence.

As laid out above, § 76a(4) StGB initially requires the suspicion of a listed offence at some point during the investigation. The link to the list gets lost, however, if the suspicion of a listed offence is dropped in favour of the object now deriving from a non-listed offence. In such cases confiscation nevertheless remains possible because all that is required is that the suspicion of a listed offence is present at some point during the investigation. This opens the door to extensive confiscation measures which are not in line with the legislator's intentions as stated when non-conviction-based confiscation was introduced into German law. Not requiring a nexus between the initial suspicion on the one hand and the offence the asset is believed to derive from on the other is rightly viewed critically.[125]

The requirement of such a nexus has been called for by authors in reference to the position of § 76a(4) StGB within Germany's confiscation regime and its low threshold that a mere suspicion is sufficient to order confiscation.[126] Others argue, however, that such a restrictive reading of the provision is not mandated, neither by the wording of § 76a(4) nor by the reasons provided in the government draft.[127] Even if there is no definite answer to the requirement of such a nexus when looking at the aforementioned interpretation of the provision, a strong case for a restrictive interpretation can be made when taking the above-mentioned concerns into account.

4.6.3 *Origin from organised crime in each individual case*

Whilst the list of offences in the third sentence of § 76a(4) StGB is a compilation of offences the legislator associates with organised crime, there is no certainty that the actual cases in which the court suspects the assets to derive from organised crime turn out to be such cases, even if there is the suspicion of a listed offence.

A reasonable fix in line with the legislator's intentions would be to add a further element to § 76a(4) StGB, requiring the court to be convinced that the object to be confiscated derives from an unlawful act which the court is convinced was committed within the context of organised crime. In the literature and case law there is some consensus that, for reasons of proportionality, a measure as intrusive as non-conviction-based confiscation under § 76a(4)

125 See Meyer 'Die selbstständige Einziehung' (n 52) 345.
126 Ibid.; but then contrary Meyer 'Abschöpfung von Vermögen unklarer Herkunft' (n 71) 247.
127 Pelz (n 117) 253; Saliger 'Grundfragen der Vermögensabschöpfung' (n 75) 1024–1025.

should only be employed in cases where a suspicion of organised crime is present.[128]

Such a restriction is not unheard of for non-conviction-based confiscation aimed at organised crime. At the EU level, Article 16(1)(c) of the *Proposal for a Directive of the European Parliament and of the Council on Asset Recovery and Confiscation* (COM(2022) 245 final), a proposal for a directive to further asset confiscation in cases of organised crime across the EU, would require Member States to

> take the necessary measures to enable the confiscation of property, where … the property is frozen in the context of an investigation into criminal offences committed in the framework of a criminal organisation … and the national court is satisfied that the frozen property is derived from criminal offences committed in the framework of a criminal organisation.[129]

The national legislator is, of course, free to go beyond the EU proposal (within the limits of the constitution) as these only set out minimum standards and omit the additional requirement of the court being convinced that the object in question derives from organised crime. Once more referencing the aforementioned concerns, there are, however, convincing grounds for a narrow handling of the provision. Such a restriction would pose further challenges, as the German *Criminal Code* does not recognise the term 'organised crime' as an established concept and it is therefore unclear how exactly the courts should determine if an unlawful act was committed within the context of organised crime.

4.7 Conclusion

In conclusion, it has to be noted that legal arguments about the effectiveness of confiscation as a tool to fight organised crime need to be supported by relevant data demonstrating this effect. Until such data is presented, calls for more far-reaching confiscation measures should be met with caution. It is a welcome development that EU law now requires Member States to collect such data.[130] Remarkably, the motivation for the collection of data on non-conviction-based confiscation in Germany seems to be rather low.[131]

On a national level, it seems that an erosion of non-conviction-based confiscation is already underway. Surprisingly, little has remained of the instrument

128 El-Ghazi, Marstaller, and Zimmermann (n 63) 299 with further references in n 29.

129 COM(2022) 245 final (n 4).

130 See Articles 11, 27 *Directive 2014/42/EU* (n 6); COM(2022) 245.

131 See the inquiry of several members of the Bundestag and the group of the *Freie Demokratische Partei* (BT-Drs 19/20858 and 19/21156).

introduced some years ago to confiscate assets deriving specifically from serious offences in the field of organised crime. In combination with the limitless expansion of the money laundering provision, the list in § 76a(4) StGB has degenerated into nothing more than a fig leaf. Several easy possibilities for amendment are readily available; the main question is whether the required political motivation to implement one of them can be mustered.

It remains to be seen whether § 76a(4) StGB will ultimately succumb to the same 'all crimes' approach the offence of money laundering has already witnessed. The first steps in that direction appear to have already been taken; with the rule of law in mind, one would have wished otherwise.

5 Protection of victim-witnesses of trafficking in persons

Problems, principles, and practice

Joseph Lelliott

5.1 Introduction

Trafficking in persons is a serious crime and an issue of significant global concern. While accurate statistics on the scale of the phenomenon are difficult to come by, it is clear that millions of people around the world are trafficked each year.[1] Trafficking is associated with a range of exploitative practices that entail severe violations of the human rights of those affected, such as slavery and servitude, debt bondage, forced labour, sexual exploitation, and forced marriage.

Action against trafficking in persons has rapidly increased over the past three decades, with States employing a range of measures designed to address its root causes, criminalise perpetrators, protect victims, and facilitate cross-border cooperation and action. At the international level, trafficking is subject to a comprehensive international legal framework. This includes, principally, the *Protocol to Prevent, Suppress and Punish Trafficking in Persons, Especially Women and Children* (*Trafficking in Persons Protocol*),[2] which supplements the *United Nations Convention against Transnational Organized Crime* (UNTOC).[3] Numerous regional instruments now also address trafficking.[4]

Despite the serious nature of trafficking in persons and the scale of global action to combat it, successful prosecutions of trafficking have remained low. There are many reasons for this, including difficulties in uncovering and investigating what is often a clandestine criminal activity, the complexity of trafficking offences, and a simple lack of awareness of what is (and what is not) trafficking. A further key issue is the lack of participation of victims in

1 Joan A Reid and Bryanna Fox, 'Reforming the Criminal Justice Response to Human Trafficking Victims and Offenders: An Introduction' (2023) 18(3) *Victims & Offenders* 393, 393.

2 Opened for signature 15 November 2000, 2237 UNTS 319 (entered into force 25 December 2003).

3 Opened for signature 15 December 2000, 2225 UNTS 209 (entered into force 29 September 2003).

4 For example, *Council of Europe Convention on Action against Trafficking in Human Beings*, opened for signature 16 May 2005, ETS 197 (entered into force 1 February 2008); *ASEAN Convention against Trafficking in Persons, Especially Women and Children*, adopted 20 November 2015 (entered into force 8 March 2017).

DOI: 10.4324/9781003519317-6

prosecutions.[5] Though there are a range of reasons why victims of trafficking may not wish to act as witnesses, a significant factor is the threat of intimidation or retaliation from traffickers or their associates. The common involvement of organised criminal groups in trafficking only accentuates this risk,[6] given that such groups are likely to have a greater capacity to intimidate victims and witnesses, interfere with prosecutions, and otherwise obstruct justice.

This chapter examines the protection of victim-witnesses of trafficking in persons, with a focus on measures that safeguard such persons from intimidation or retaliation by perpetrators and their associates. It explains that while traditional measures designed to protect witnesses, such as modifications to court and evidence-giving procedures, remain important, the unique circumstances of victim-witnesses of trafficking require consideration of other approaches. This includes mechanisms tied to the immigration status and removal of victims, their liability for unlawful acts committed as a consequence of their trafficking, and an awareness of the trauma they have likely experienced. This chapter highlights the importance of a human-rights-centred approach to victim-witnesses and explains that remedying deficiencies in protecting victims can have positive flow-on impacts on their likelihood to assist with prosecutions of traffickers.

This chapter begins with a brief overview of the definition of trafficking and identifies the meaning and scope of 'victim' and 'witness' in the context of the UNTOC and the *Trafficking in Persons Protocol.* Following this, the chapter turns to an explanation and analysis of the particular circumstances of victims of trafficking in criminal justice processes and the risks of intimidation and retaliation. Next, the chapter examines States' obligations under international law that must guide how they treat victim-witnesses of trafficking, as well as key best practices. It then examines these issues in the Australian context, before concluding with several observations on the protection of victim-witnesses.

5.2 Definitions

5.2.1 Trafficking in persons

The *Trafficking in Persons Protocol*, which, as of March 2024, has 181 States Parties, sets out an internationally agreed definition of trafficking. Article 3(a) of the Protocol states that 'trafficking in persons' means

> [t]he recruitment, transportation, transfer, harbouring or receipt of persons, by means of the threat or use of force or other forms of coercion, of abduction, of fraud, of deception, of the abuse of power or of a position

5 Anne Gallagher and Paul Holmes, 'Developing an Effective Criminal Justice Response to Human Trafficking Lessons from the Front Line' (2008) 18(3) *International Criminal Justice Review* 318, 332–333.

6 UNODC, *Global Report on Trafficking in Persons 2022* (United Nations, 2023) xiii.

> of vulnerability or of the giving or receiving of payments or benefits to achieve the consent of a person having control over another person, for the purpose of exploitation. Exploitation shall include, at a minimum, the exploitation of the prostitution of others or other forms of sexual exploitation, forced labour or services, slavery or practices similar to slavery, servitude or the removal of organs.

This definition combines act, means, and purpose elements. The only exception is for trafficking of children; in this case the means element is not required.[7]

In addition to this definition, the Protocol articulates a uniform approach to addressing trafficking in persons, including the criminalisation of perpetrators, protection of victims, and cooperation among States Parties to these ends. Of particular relevance to this chapter are the provisions of the Protocol addressing the forms of protection and assistance that States must afford to victims of trafficking, as well as articles concerning their legal status in the host country and potential return to their countries of origin.

It should be stressed that trafficking in persons is a fundamentally different phenomenon from smuggling of migrants, a crime that it is nonetheless often confused with.[8] Smuggling of migrants is addressed and defined in the *Trafficking in Persons Protocol's* sister instrument, the *Protocol against the Smuggling of Migrants by Land, Sea and Air*.[9] Trafficking centres on the purpose of perpetrators to exploit victims of trafficking, whereas the purpose of migrant smugglers is to obtain a financial or material benefit through the 'illegal entry of a person into a state party of which the person is not a national or a permanent resident'.[10] Smuggling also requires a cross-border element, while trafficking can occur completely within one State.[11]

It is also worth noting that trafficking in persons is not one and the same as 'modern slavery', a term that has emerged in recent years and increasingly found its way into State's domestic legislation.[12] Unlike trafficking, modern slavery is not defined in international law and lacks the precision of trafficking's carefully crafted three-pronged definition. It is generally used as an umbrella

7 *Trafficking in Persons Protocol*, Article 3.

8 See, for example, Marika McAdam, 'Victim Naming and Blaming in Rights-Based Distinctions between Human Trafficking and Migrant Smuggling' (2015) 4(1) *International Human Rights Law Review* 1.

9 Opened for signature 15 December 2003, 2241 UNTS 507 (entered into force 28 January 2004).

10 *Smuggling of Migrants Protocol*, Article 3(a).

11 Andreas Schloenhardt and Joseph Lelliott, 'Migrant Children and the United Nations Protocols against Smuggling of Migrants and Trafficking in Persons' in Mary Crock and Lenni B Benson (eds), *Protecting Migrant Children: In Search of Best Practice* (Edward Elgar, 2018) 119–120.

12 For example, the Australian *Modern Slavery Act 2018* (Cth) and *Modern Slavery Act 2015* (UK).

term for various (legally defined) practices including trafficking in persons, forced labour, and slavery.[13]

5.2.2 Victim

The scope of the term 'victim' affects various obligations States attract with regard to victim-witnesses of trafficking in criminal proceedings. Protection and assistance measures apply to persons who are victims of trafficking in persons under the *Trafficking in Persons Protocol*, while victims of all offences covered by the UNTOC are given protection under Article 25 of the Convention. Victims of trafficking are also victims of crime and human rights violations,[14] which are additional categories of persons to which certain obligations are owed under international law more broadly.

Despite common use of the term 'victim', it is not often defined. The UNTOC, for instance, does not include a definition, despite the fact that determination of who is, and who is not, a victim is necessarily key to the application of States' obligations under Article 25. The *Model Legislative Provisions against Organized Crime*, published by the United Nations Office on Drugs and Crime (UNODC), explains that States may look to the definition of victim in the *Declaration of Basic Principles of Justice for Victims of Crime and Abuse of Power*.[15] The Declaration states that:

> 'Victims' means persons who, individually or collectively, have suffered harm, including physical or mental injury, emotional suffering, economic loss or substantial impairment of their fundamental rights, through acts or omissions that are in violation of criminal laws operative within Member States, including those laws proscribing criminal abuse of power.[16]

The Declaration further notes that it is immaterial whether or not a perpetrator is 'identified, apprehended, prosecuted or convicted' for consideration of victim status, as is any familial relationship between the victim and perpetrator.[17] A similar definition is provided by the *Basic Principles and Guidelines on the Right to a Remedy and Reparation for Victims of Gross Violations of*

13 See Janie Chuang, 'The Challenges and Perils of Reframing Trafficking as "Modern-Day Slavery"' (2015) 5 *Anti-Trafficking Review* 146.

14 OHCHR, *Recommended Principles and Guidelines on Human Rights and Human Trafficking: Commentary* (United Nations, 2010) 130.

15 UNODC, *Model Legislative Provisions against Organized Crime* (United Nations, 2nd ed 2021) 120; UN General Assembly, *Declaration of Basic Principles of Justice for Victims of Crime and Abuse of Power*, UN Doc A/RES/40/34 (29 November 1985) (hereafter 'UN Doc A/RES/40/34').

16 UN Doc A/RES/40/34 (n 15) [1].

17 Ibid., [2].

International Human Rights Law and Serious Violations of International Humanitarian Law.[18]

5.2.3 Witness

Like 'victim', the term 'witness' is not defined in the UNTOC. Article 24 of the Convention, which sets out obligations in relation to the protection of witnesses, covers those who 'give testimony concerning offences covered by [the UNTOC]' in criminal proceedings. The act of 'giving testimony' could be given a restrictive interpretation and limited to persons who actually provide testimony (or who will do so). It could also be interpreted more broadly and be 'extended to persons merely willing to testify, or even persons who have only identified key evidence'.[19] The *Legislative Guide* to the Convention notes that this is likely preferable, given the practical need to grant protection to anyone willing to cooperate in criminal proceedings.[20] Frank Zimmerman, commenting on an equivalent use of the term in the *United Nations Convention against Corruption*,[21] is also of the view that the

> broad understanding is probably the most convincing one: when citizens share information with the police, for instance, it will often be impossible to predict whether their testimony will be needed in court. Nevertheless they may risk intimidation and retaliation already at that early stage.[22]

5.3 Threats against victim-witnesses of trafficking

Many types of crime that fall under the umbrella of organised crime do not have a victim in the narrow sense, such as drug offences, firearms trafficking, smuggling of migrants, wildlife trafficking, and other forms of organised environmental crime. For these offences, evidence supporting a successful prosecution may well not involve any person impacted by the offending. This is

18 United Nations General Assembly, *Basic Principles and Guidelines on the Right to a Remedy and Reparation for Victims of Gross Violations of International Human Rights Law and Serious Violations of International Humanitarian Law*, UN Doc A/RES/60/147 (21 March 2006) [8]–[9].

19 Joseph Lelliott, 'Article 24: Protection of Witnesses' in Andreas Schloenhardt et al. (eds), *UN Convention Against Transnational Organized Crime: A Commentary* (Oxford University Press, 2023) 267.

20 UNODC, *Legislative Guide for the Implementation of the United Nations Convention against Transnational Organized Crime* (UNODC, 2nd ed 2017) [409].

21 Opened for signature 31 October 2003, 2349 UNTS 41 (entry into force 14 December 2005).

22 Frank Zimmerman, 'Article 32: Protection of Witnesses, Experts, and Victims' in Cecily Rose, Michael Kubiciel, and Oliver Landwehr (eds), *The United Nations Convention Against Corruption* (Oxford University Press, 2019) 331.

not the case for trafficking in persons, which, by definition, involves acts committed against human victims.

For cases of trafficking, victim testimony is commonly central to a prosecution case.[23] Often it is only victims who can provide insight into the means of trafficking, particularly where these means are subtle and involve threats, deception, coercion, or the abuse of power and vulnerability.[24] The importance of victim-witnesses to trafficking prosecution means that cases can frequently turn on the credibility of a victim. While this is generally undesirable, given the burden and stress placed on already traumatised and vulnerable persons, other forms of physical and corroborating evidence are often hard to come by in trafficking cases.[25]

Despite the importance of victim evidence, it has frequently been observed that victims of trafficking are often reluctant to involve themselves in criminal proceedings against their traffickers. Studies in Australia, Europe, India, and the United States, for example, have all observed low rates of prosecution and attributed this, at least in part, to the difficulty of obtaining victim testimony.[26] The reasons for this are multiple and complex.

At the outset, persons who have been trafficked may not identify as victims at all. They may not see themselves as victims of crime, particularly where they had some appreciation of the situation they entered into and do not see themselves as 'saved' by authorities.[27] If their trafficker was a family member, emotional ties may also make them unwilling to be labelled a victim or assist in any action against the perpetrator.[28]

Even if they do accept the victim label, like many victims of crime, victims of trafficking commonly want to move past their experiences and 'go on with their lives', a desire that is stymied by their participation in the criminal process. Recalling experiences of trafficking is likely to be re-traumatising, a process sometimes referred to as 'secondary victimisation'.[29] As Biljana Meshkovska et al.

23 Fiona David, 'Prosecuting Trafficking in Persons: Known Issues, Emerging Responses' in *Trends and Issues in Crime and Criminal Justice* (No 358, Australian Institute of Criminology, 2008) 2–3.

24 See *Trafficking in Persons Protocol*, Article 3(a).

25 Amy Farrell et al., 'The Prosecution of State-Level Human Trafficking Cases in the United States' (2016) 6 *Anti-Trafficking Review* 48, 66.

26 David (n 23); Jo Goodey, 'Sex Trafficking in Women from Central and East European Countries: Promoting a "Victim-Centred" and "Woman-Centred" Approach to Criminal Justice Intervention' (2004) 76 *Feminist Review* 26–45; Vibhuti Ramachandran, '"These Girls Never Give Statements": Anti-Trafficking Interventions and "Victim-Witness Testimony" in India' (2022) 11(9) *Social Sciences* 1–25; Farrell et al. (n 25) 48.

27 Ramachandran (n 26) 5.

28 Biljana Meshkovska et al., 'Trafficking of Women for Sexual Exploitation in Europe: Prosecution, trials and their impact' (2016) 6 *Anti-Trafficking Review* 71, 86.

29 Deana Davy, 'Justice for Victims of Human Trafficking in Australia? Issues Associated with Australia's Criminal Justice Response to Trafficking in Persons' (2017) 20(1) *Contemporary Justice Review* 115, 123.

observe, '[v]ictim testimonies during trials, in often intimidating and sometimes hostile court environments, can hinder the recovery and reintegration process of victims'.[30] Victims may also fear the potential stigma from others in their family or communities discovering the details of their exploitation and avoid giving evidence for this reason.

Added to these dynamics is the fact that victims of trafficking may fear reprisals from their traffickers if they choose to give evidence against them. As experts have long observed, a key obstacle to 'securing convictions is the fear of victims of trafficking that they, or their families, will face some kind of retribution from the traffickers or their associates should they give evidence against them'.[31] For example, a study of trafficked women in Germany found that the threat of violence was a major factor in the willingness of victims to make a statement to the police, as was the ability of authorities to offer effective protection from offenders.[32] The International Organization for Migration (IOM) has also observed that

> [i]t is a fact that traffickers have taken reprisals against their victims who were rescued and who subsequently testified against them in legal proceedings, and they can be expected to continue to do so as their business comes under increasing threat from a concerted international effort to stop it.[33]

While any witness in a trafficking prosecution may be threatened, victim-witnesses are particularly vulnerable to intimidation. As already noted, as victims of crime, and having likely experienced severe exploitation at the hands of those they are asked to testify against, their fear will be heightened. It is also not uncommon for traffickers to have ties to, or otherwise be active in, the communities that victims come from. This can enhance their ability to make threats against victims' families, particularly when they are able to act with impunity due to corruption.[34]

Two further issues are also worth highlighting. The first is the potential removal of victims of trafficking from the country in which the prosecution is to take place. As noted above, though persons may be trafficked within their countries of residence, it is common for trafficking to occur across international borders. In such cases, victims may have no legal migration status in

30 Meshkovska et al. (n 28) 77.

31 Ryszard Piotrowicz, 'European Initiatives in the Protection of Victims of Trafficking who Give Evidence Against Their Traffickers' (2002) 14(2–3) *International Journal of Refugee Law* 263, 264.

32 Cornelia Helfferich, Barbara Kavemann, and Heike Rabe, 'Determinants of the Willingness to Make a Statement of Victims of Human Trafficking for the Purpose of Sexual Exploitation in the Triangle Offender–Police–Victim' (2011) 14 *Trends in Organized Crime* 125, 132, 146.

33 IOM, *The IOM Handbook on Direct Assistance for Victims of Trafficking* (IOM, 2007) 277.

34 Meshkovska et al. (n 28) 83.

the country to which they have been trafficked and, as a result, are liable to removal. As well as making victims more fearful of authorities and potentially depriving them of social supports, lack of legal status may make them fearful of removal to places where their traffickers (or their associates) are more able to carry out their threats.[35] In this context, it has been observed that the ability of authorities to offer victims protection from removal can make them more willing to testify against their traffickers.[36]

The second factor is the potential liability of victims of trafficking for unlawful acts committed as a consequence of their trafficking. For example, their exploitation may have involved criminal offending (such as drug production or illegal sex work), while the process of trafficking may have entailed breaches of immigration laws. It is not uncommon for traffickers to use this fact to instil further fear into victims, threatening that if they contact or cooperate with authorities, they will be punished themselves.[37] Manifestly, punishment of victims may mean they are treated as perpetrators, rather than protected as victims, and can make them less disposed to participate in criminal processes against their traffickers.[38]

All of these issues make it imperative that national criminal justice systems develop ways to ensure that victims of trafficking can, insofar as possible, participate safely in court processes. This goal requires a protection-centred approach to the treatment of victims that addresses their fears and hesitations over involvement in prosecutions, as well as providing effective protection from potential intimidation and retaliation. This is, of course, subject to the caveat that authorities will rarely be able to offer a victim-witness complete protection. As Anne Gallagher and Paul Holmes note:

> In many cases, law enforcement officials cannot provide victims with the level of protection they may need or want, either through lack of mandate, resources, or both. It is essential that victims are made to understand the limits of protection and are not lured into cooperating with false or unrealistic promises regarding their safety and that of their families.[39]

35 UNODC, *Toolkit to Combat Trafficking in Persons* (United Nations, 2008) 344. Though not further addressed here, victims may apply for international protection on this basis: Vladislava Stoyanova, 'Complementary Protection for Victims of Human Trafficking under the European Convention on Human Rights' (2011) 3(2) *Göttingen Journal of International Law* 777–817.

36 Helfferich, Kavemann, and Rabe (n 32) 135–136.

37 UN General Assembly, Human Rights Council, *Trafficking in Persons, Especially Women and Children: Report of the Special Rapporteur on Trafficking in Persons, Especially Women and Children*, UN Doc A/HRC/44/45 (6 April 2020) 8 [29].

38 Inter-Agency Coordination Group against Trafficking in Persons, 'Issue Brief 8: Non-Punishment of Victims of Trafficking' (2020) 2.

39 Gallagher and Holmes (n 5) 333.

In view of the risks faced by victim-witnesses of trafficking, it is crucial that States comply with their international obligations to protect these persons. The following section identifies relevant provisions of the UNTOC and the *Trafficking in Persons Protocol*, before briefly turning to other instruments and best practice guidance.

5.4 UNTOC and the Trafficking in Persons Protocol

5.4.1 UNTOC

The UNTOC contains several articles broadly relevant to the protection of victim-witnesses of trafficking. Article 24 mandates that States Parties take effective measures to protect witnesses, their families, and others close to them from potential retaliation or intimidation when they testify in criminal proceedings concerning offences covered by the Convention. Closely related to Article 24 is Article 25, which places an obligation on States Parties to protect victims of offences covered by the Convention. These articles also intersect with Article 23, which deals with the criminalisation of obstruction of justice, including the production of evidence and witness testimony.

5.4.1.1 Protection of witnesses

While Article 24(1) requires States Parties to provide witnesses with 'effective protection', it is subject to the qualification that States only need to do so 'within their means'. Some forms of protection that can be provided to witnesses may require significant technological or organisational capabilities or may be costly, and States are at liberty to employ more economical and less complex measures as necessary. In addition, what protection is 'effective' and appropriate in any case will depend on the identity and individual needs of the witness, the scale of the threat they face, and the degree to which particular measures' benefits outweigh their negative impacts, including on the rights of the defendant.[40] Only extreme risks to victim-witnesses will justify certain measures, such as changes in identity or victim relocation.[41]

Article 24(2) gives a non-exhaustive list of examples of measures that States may employ in seeking to give witnesses effective protection. These include non-disclosure and limits on information about a witness' whereabouts or identity, relocation, and evidentiary rules that ensure witness safety, such as mechanisms that permit testimony to be given remotely. Article 24(3) encourages States Parties to enter into agreements or arrangements for international relocation, while Article 24(4) simply notes that the provisions of Article 24 apply to victims.

40 Lelliott (n 19) 268.

41 UNODC, *Good Practices for the Protection of Witnesses in Criminal Proceedings Involving Organized Crime* (United Nations, 2008) 1.

Article 24 stresses that the rights of the defendant should not be prejudiced by any measures taken. Of course, procedural rights are generally not absolute and may be limited where reasonable, necessary, and proportionate to the goals of prosecuting serious crime and protecting witnesses and/or victims.[42] Where such limitations are justified, however, measures should be taken to ensure fairness to the defendant.[43]

5.4.1.2 Protection of victims

Article 25 addresses the protection of victims of trafficking and other offences covered by the Convention from retaliation and intimidation, the presentation of their views and concerns in criminal proceedings, and access to compensation and restitution. Article 25(1), which is of principal relevance to the present chapter, requires States Parties 'to take appropriate measures within its means to provide assistance and protection to victims of offences covered by this Convention, in particular in cases of threat of retaliation or intimidation'.

While mandatory, it is qualified with the words 'within its means', indicating that—like the obligations under Article 24—States Parties only need to act within their economic and practical constraints. As to what measures are 'appropriate' will depend on the needs of individual victims (taking into account status such as gender, age, and disability) as well as their consent to any proposed measures.[44] In cases of threatened retaliation or intimidation, the gravity of the risk will necessarily guide the measures required.

An *Interpretative Note* to this article states that '[w]hile the purpose of this article is to concentrate on the physical protection of victims, the Ad Hoc Committee was cognizant of the need for protection of the rights of individuals as accorded under applicable international law'.[45] As further discussed below, States have obligations under international human rights law to protect persons from violations of their rights to the standard of due diligence, and provide victims of violations with an effective remedy.

Article 25(2) obliges States Parties to provide victims with avenues to access compensation and restitution, while Article 25(3) mandates that the views and concerns of victims must be able to be presented and considered during criminal proceedings. This paragraph is of principal relevance to victims who are not witnesses, though there may be cases where a victim appears both as a witness and also wishes to make additional statements on the offending, such

42 Laura Salvadego, 'Witness Protection and Inter-State Cooperation: Current and Emerging Challenges in the Fight against Transnational Organised Crime' (2015) 58 *German Yearbook of International Law* 379, 391–392.

43 Lelliott (n 19) 269.

44 UNODC (n 15) 120.

45 UNODC, *Travaux Préparatoires of the Negotiations of the United Nations Convention against Transnational Organized Crime and the Protocols thereto* (United Nations, 2006) 224.

as through a post-conviction victim impact statement.[46] The obligation here is subject also to the rights of the defence, as well as States' domestic law.

5.4.1.3 *Obstruction of justice*

Where force, threats, or intimidation are used against victim-witnesses to interfere with their testimony, including pressuring them to give false evidence, States Parties to the Convention should ensure that this conduct is criminalised. Article 23 makes such an offence mandatory. Importantly, the offence should extend to unsuccessful attempts and should be criminalised independently of offences relating to the giving of false evidence.[47]

5.4.1.4 *Summary*

Though Articles 23, 24, and 25 of the UNTOC do not specifically address victim-witnesses of trafficking, the provisions of these articles set out a range of measures key to their protection. The general obligations in Articles 24 and 25 to provide protection to witnesses and victims are manifestly relevant, while Article 23 effectively adds an extra layer of deterrence to those intending to threaten or intimidate victim-witnesses.

It may be noted, however, that Article 25 is fairly cursory and leaves out many key rights for victims of crime, including information, legal assistance, and privacy. The particular needs of women, children, and other groups are also not addressed. Tom Obokata characterises the Article as 'very general' and its 'lack of due regard to the victims of organised crime' as problematic.[48] Similar comments are made by Jan Van Dijk, who observes that Article 25 is a 'missed opportunity for the advocates of victim rights'.[49]

46 Joseph Lelliott, 'Article 25: Assistance to and Protection of Victims' in Schloenhardt et al. (eds), *UN Convention Against Transnational Organized Crime: A Commentary* (Oxford University Press, 2023) 278.

47 UN Conference of the Parties to the United Nations Convention against Transnational Organized Crime, *Working Group of Government Experts on Technical Assistance, Identification of Technical Assistance Needs and Good Practices Relating to the Criminalization of Obstruction of Justice* (Article 23), UN Doc CTOC/COP/WG.2/2016/3 (4 August 2016) 9, 12–13.

48 Tom Obokata, *Transnational Organised Crime in International Law* (Hart 2010) 90.

49 Jan J M Van Dijk, 'Empowering Victims of Organized Crime: On the Concurrence of the Palermo Convention with the UN Declaration on Basic Principles of Justice for Victims' (2002) 9 *International Review of Victimology* 15, 18.

5.4.2 *Trafficking in Persons Protocol*

Though the *Trafficking in Persons Protocol* is principally a criminal justice instrument, one of its purposes is the protection of victims of trafficking.[50] Provisions in several articles of the Protocol are directly relevant to victim-witnesses.

5.4.2.1 *Assistance and protection*

Article 6 of the Protocol sets out various measures for the assistance and protection of victims of trafficking in persons. While these measures are all of general relevance to victim-witnesses, including those providing for physical, psychological, and social recovery of victims,[51] and access to compensation,[52] several are of particular significance to victim-witnesses. It should be stressed that each must be applied in a way that takes into account the 'age, gender and special needs of victims of trafficking in persons, in particular the special needs of children'.[53]

The first is the obligation in Article 6(1) to protect the privacy and identity of victims in appropriate cases and to the extent possible. These qualifiers acknowledge that States have different laws around privacy in court proceedings, as well as the fact that it is not always possible to fully protect victims' privacy. Critically, Article 6(1) is not restricted to legal proceedings. Privacy should be ensured at all stages and settings in which the State deals with victims, noting that this is key to preventing intimidation or harm from traffickers, in addition to secondary victimisation through media reporting or other forms of information dissemination.[54]

Second, Article 6(2)(a) requires States Parties to make sure that, in appropriate cases, victims are provided with information on 'relevant court and administrative proceedings'. This is a straightforward obligation, but essential to the safety of victim-witnesses. For example, they must be kept informed as to the progress of proceedings, which perpetrators have been apprehended and whether they are at large or on bail, and the outcome of trials and sentencing. Such information can help victims make informed decisions about their own safety, which protection measures they consent to, and whether and to what degree they wish to participate in proceedings.

Third, Article 6(5) mandates that States 'endeavour to provide for the physical safety of victims of trafficking in persons'. Though the use of 'endeavour' somewhat weakens the obligation in this paragraph, it should 'entail, at

50 *Trafficking in Persons Protocol*, Article 2(b).
51 Ibid., Article 6(3).
52 Ibid., Article 6(6).
53 Ibid., Article 6(4).
54 OHCHR, *Recommended Principles and Guidelines on Human Rights and Human Trafficking, Report of the United Nations High Commissioner for Human Rights*, UN Doc E/2002/68/Add.1 (20 May 2002) guideline 6.6.

a minimum, efforts to … and protect them from any reprisals or intimidation from traffickers or their associates'.[55]

5.4.2.2 Legal status and removal

Protection from removal from the country in which criminal proceedings are taking place, together with legal immigration status, is commonly central to the protection of victim-witnesses of trafficking. The Protocol does not grant any particular rights in either respect, but it does ask States Parties to (1) consider permitting victims to remain in 'territory, temporarily or permanently, in appropriate cases' and (2) to give due regard to 'the safety of that person and for the status of any legal proceedings related to the fact that the person is a victim of trafficking', under Articles 7(1) and 8(2) respectively.

With regard to permission to remain, Article 7 does not clarify what 'appropriate cases' entails, save for an ambiguous reference to 'humanitarian' and 'compassionate' factors in Article 7(2). The *Legislative Guide* does, however, observe that victims are less likely to 'assist law enforcement in investigations, participate in proceedings against an accused, access compensation, and, in some cases, recover sufficiently from their experiences and trauma' without some form of legal status.[56] UNODC's *Model Legislative Provisions* go further and suggest allowing all victims to remain on temporary permits for at least six months, irrespective of any cooperation with authorities,[57] a recommendation that reflects calls from both the Special Rapporteur on Trafficking in Persons, Especially Women and Children, and the Conference of the Parties.[58]

In relation to removal (the term 'repatriation' is used in Article 8), specific reference is made to legal proceedings in recognition of the potential involvement of victims in prosecutions of traffickers. Reference is also made to safety, and the obligations under Articles 6(5) and 9(1)(b) of the Protocol, which address physical safety and revictimisation, should be noted here. Whilst 'safety' is not further explained in the Protocol, the context of victim-witnesses'

55 Joseph Lelliott, 'Article 6: Assistance and Protection of Victims of Trafficking in Persons' in Andreas Schloenhardt et al. (eds), *UN Convention Against Transnational Organized Crime: A Commentary* (Oxford University Press, 2023) 450.

56 UNODC, *Legislative Guide for the Protocol to Prevent, Suppress and Punish Trafficking in Persons, Especially Women and Children, Supplementing the United Nations Convention against Transnational Organized Crime* (United Nations, 2nd ed 2020) 56 [197].

57 UNODC, *Model Legislative Provisions against Trafficking in Persons* (United Nations, 2nd ed 2020) 79.

58 UN General Assembly, *Report of the Special Rapporteur on Trafficking in Persons, Especially Women and Children*, UN Doc A/75/169 (17 July 2020) 7 [18]; UN, Conference of the Parties to the United Nations Convention against Transnational Organized Crime, Working Group on Trafficking in Persons, *Effective Criminal Justice Responses to Trafficking in Persons Centred on Addressing the Protection and Assistance Needs of Different Groups and Types of Victims, with Particular Reference to Victims of Trafficking within Mixed Migration Movements*, UN Doc CTOC/COP/WG.4/2017/2 (3 July 2017) 5 [14].

involvement in criminal proceedings may put them at greater risk upon their return; interpretative materials to the Protocol recognise that safety should be pursued generally and must include protection of victims' 'privacy, dignity, and health', as well as their human rights.[59]

5.4.2.3 Summary

The provisions identified here articulate several key elements of effective protection of victim-witnesses, including ensuring their privacy and providing them with information and physical protection (an obligation that intersects with that in Article 25 of the UNTOC to protect victims from retaliation and intimidation). The measures dealing with legal status and removal, meanwhile, are important for victim-witnesses who would benefit from secure legal status to participate effectively in criminal proceedings and who may fear for their safety if returned to their countries of origin.

The shortcomings of these provisions are, however, evident. As noted above, the text of Articles 6, 7, and 8 is often framed in non-mandatory or qualified language and has been subject to frequent critique. Nonetheless, the 'ungenerous and equivocal' content of the protection provisions has been increasingly fleshed out by a wide variety of interpretative and other soft law materials.[60] Among other things, these have lent clarity to issues such as where permission to remain should be granted and how 'safety' should be interpreted in return decisions.

Furthermore, notwithstanding any deficiencies in the Protocol itself, its saving clause in Article 14 clarifies that the Protocol does not affect any other rights of victim-witnesses of trafficking under international law. Particular attention is called to rights against refoulement and discrimination, as well as States' obligations under international human rights and humanitarian law.

5.5 Other principles

International law relevant to the protection of victim-witnesses of trafficking is not limited to the UNTOC and the *Trafficking in Persons Protocol*. Their treatment is also informed by States' obligations under international human rights law, as well as key sets of principles and guidelines that, while not strictly binding on States, influence the level and form of protection to which they are entitled. Important materials in this regard include the OHCHR's (Office of the High Commissioner for Human Rights) *Recommended Principles and Guidelines on Human Rights and Human Trafficking* and the *Declaration of Basic Principles of Justice for Victims of Crime and Abuse of Power*. The latter

59 UNODC (n 56) 83.
60 Anne T Gallagher, *The International Law of Human Trafficking* (Cambridge University Press, 2010) 336.

Principles call on States to '[take] measures to minimize inconvenience to victims, protect their privacy, when necessary, and ensure their safety, as well as that of their families and witnesses on their behalf, from intimidation and retaliation'.[61] OHCHR's *Recommended Principles*, meanwhile, emphasise that the safety of trafficked persons is the primary responsibility of law enforcement. Among other things, these Principles note that appropriate protection of victim-witnesses should include ensuring their privacy, giving them access to legal counsel, and 'identification of options for continued stay, resettlement or repatriation'.[62]

Whilst it is beyond the scope of this chapter to review international law and best practices in depth, it is worth noting that there is now broad acceptance of a non-punishment principle, despite the fact it is not included in the *Trafficking in Persons Protocol*. The punishment of victims for unlawful acts committed as a consequence of their trafficking is deleterious to their protection, inconsistent with a human-rights approach to trafficking, and, as noted above, a potential barrier to their participation in criminal proceedings against perpetrators.[63] As the Special Rapporteur on Trafficking in Persons stated in 2021:

> The principle of non-punishment of victims of trafficking is critical to the recognition of trafficking in persons as a serious human rights violation. Punishment of a victim marks a rupture with the commitments made by States to recognize the priority of victims' rights to assistance, protection and effective remedies.[64]

While the exact scope and preferable mode of implementation of the principle is contested, its support by the UN Security Council, OHCHR, the Conference of the Parties to the UNTOC, and the European Court of Human Rights, among others, undergirds its significance.[65]

61 UN Doc A/RES/40/34 (n 15) principle 6.

62 OHCHR (n 54) guideline 5.

63 See generally Ryszard Piotrowicz and Liliana Sorrentino, 'Human Trafficking and the Emergence of the Non-Punishment Principle' (2016) 16 *Human Rights Law Review* 669.

64 UN General Assembly, Human Rights Council, *Implementation of the Non-Punishment Principle: Report of the Special Rapporteur on Trafficking in Persons, Especially Women and Children, Siobhán Mullally*, UN Doc A/HRC/47/4 (17 May 2021) 3 [18].

65 UN Security Council, *Resolution 2331*, UN Doc S/RES/2331 (20 December 2016) [2(b)]; OHCHR (n 54); UN, Conference of the Parties to the United Nations Convention against Transnational Organized Crime, *Report of the Conference of the Parties to the United Nations Convention against Transnational Organized Crime on its Tenth Session, held in Vienna from 12 to 16 October 2020*, UN Doc CTOC/COP/2020/10 (3 November 2020) Resolution 10/3 [13(g)]; *VCL and AN v the United Kingdom*, App nos 77587/12, 74603/12 (ECHR, 16 February 2021).

5.6 National example: victim-witness protection in Australia

Many of the problems concerning victim-witnesses of trafficking explained in Section 5.3 above have been observed in Australia. As in many countries around the world, the number of prosecutions of trafficking have remained low, despite estimates that there are many hundreds of victims of trafficking in Australia each year.[66] For example, between 2004 and 2019, only 24 people were convicted of trafficking and slavery offences.[67] Again, as in other countries, this is attributable to a range of issues, including difficulties identifying victims. The reluctance of victims to appear as witnesses has, however, been cited as a key contributing factor.[68] Samantha Lyneham observes that even where victims are initially eager to participate, 'complex trauma, lack of English language skills, and cultural and institutional issues related to mistrust in police or misunderstanding of the police's role' can still lead to disengagement during the investigation and prosecution process.[69]

The Australian Government has responded to this issue with a range of legal and policy frameworks intended to encourage victims to give evidence against their traffickers and protect them from potential retaliation or intimidation. These included a range of amendments in 2013 to the country's *Crimes Act 1914* (Cth) and *Criminal Code* (Cth). Among other things, these amendments legislated protections including:

- Limitations on the ability of defendants to cross-examine victims;
- Allowing the use of closed-circuit television, video-link or video-recording to give evidence;
- Allowing witnesses to have an accompanying support person;
- Enabling court proceedings to be closed to the public;
- Prohibiting the publication of material identifying a vulnerable person and making it an offence to do so.[70]

This legal framework is supplemented by the Commonwealth Director of Public Prosecutions' (CDPP) *Victims of Crime Policy*, which specifies the information that should be provided to all victims of federal offences, including victims of trafficking. This includes information on decisions to prosecute, the dates and places of any court proceedings, plea negotiations, bail

66 Samantha Lyneham, Christopher Dowling, and Samantha Bricknell, *Estimating the Dark Figure of Human Trafficking and Slavery Victimisation in Australia*, Statistical Bulletin 16 (Australian Institute of Criminology, February 2019) 2.

67 Samantha Lyneham, 'Attrition of Human Trafficking and Slavery Cases Through the Australian Criminal Justice System' in *Trends and Issues in Crime and Criminal Justice* (No 640, Australian Institute of Criminology, 2021) 1.

68 David (n 23).

69 Lyneham (n 69) 12.

70 *Crimes Legislation Amendment (Law Enforcement Integrity, Vulnerable Witness Protection and Other Measures) Act 2013* (Cth).

outcomes, and the outcome of any proceedings including appeals. Victims should also generally be advised on the progress and stages of a matter.[71] In certain cases, including those involving slavery, servitude, and forced marriage offences, victims have further rights to be given reasons for a decision not to prosecute and to request a review of this decision.[72] The Policy also states that '[a] victim's privacy and personal information will be protected as appropriate and as far as possible', and that their views on their safety will be sought when applications for bail are made.

Where there is an especially high risk to a victim-witness, the Commonwealth National Witness Protection Program may be used. Established and regulated by the *Witness Protection Act 1994* (Cth) and coordinated by the Australian Federal Police, the Program authorises, inter alia, the creation of new identities for witnesses and their placement and removal in/from certain locations.[73]

In addition to legal and policy protections during court proceedings, a 'Support for Trafficked People Program' provides assistance to victims of trafficking. This can be put in place before, during, and after court proceedings. The Program has five 'streams' including, as of July 2023 when the Program was last updated, the Intensive Support Stream, Forced Marriage Support Stream, Justice Support Stream, Temporary Trial Support Stream, and the Transition Stream. The Intensive Support Stream applies to all victims of trafficking referred to the Program and provides intensive social and welfare supports for 90 days, irrespective of participation in the investigation or prosecution of trafficking offences. The Justice Support Stream is of particular relevance to victim-witnesses and provides additional support until a matter is finalised. It gives victims safe accommodation and access to legal services, as well as health, social, educational, and employment supports. The Temporary Trial Support Stream, meanwhile, applies to victims who return to Australia to give evidence. It entitles them to safe accommodation and living expenses.[74]

Victim-witnesses of trafficking also have access to visas that enable them to stay in Australia during criminal proceedings as well as permanently in some cases. In particular, the Referred Stay Visa (Subclass 852, previously known as the Witness Protection (Trafficking) (Permanent) visa) may be granted to victims who have made a contribution to an investigation or prosecution and

71 CDPP, 'Victims of Crime Policy' (2021) <https://www.cdpp.gov.au/victims-and-witnesses/victims-crime-policy>.

72 CDPP, 'NLD—Right of Review—Prosecutions Involving Child and Certain Other Complainants' (2021) <https://www.cdpp.gov.au/publications/nld-right-review-prosecutions-involving-child-and-certain-other-complainants>.

73 See further Stephen Monterosso, 'Shortcomings in the Operation and Coordination of Witness Protection in Australia. Where to from Here?' (2022) 33 *Criminal Law Forum* 255–282.

74 See Australian Government, Department of Social Services, 'Support for Trafficked People Program' <https://www.dss.gov.au/women/programs-services/reducing-violence/anti-people-trafficking-strategy/support-for-trafficked-people-program>.

would be in danger if returned to their home country. Immediate family members of the victim may also receive the visa.[75]

A key gap remaining in Australia's treatment of victims is the fact that it is yet to incorporate the principle of non-punishment into its legal framework for trafficking. It receives no mention in the country's current *National Action Plan to Combat Modern Slavery (2020–2025)*, nor is it included in any form in the *Criminal Code* (Cth) or *Modern Slavery Act* (Cth), unlike, for example, the UK's equivalent legislation.[76]

5.7 Conclusion

Best practice guidance and scholarship on trafficking in persons has increasingly emphasised the importance of protecting victims' human rights to ensure effective criminal justice responses. Given that the evidence of victims is often integral to successful prosecutions of perpetrators and organised criminal groups, measures that allay fears over involvement in court proceedings and allow them to participate safely in legal processes are critically important. As this chapter has shown, victims of trafficking may face intimidation and threats of retaliation if they agree to give evidence. This fear is especially acute for victim-witnesses due to their frequently traumatic experiences, the ties their traffickers may have to their communities, and the potential risk of removal to places where reprisals are more likely.

For these reasons, States must provide mechanisms to protect victim-witnesses. As outlined in Sections 5.4 and 5.5, the form and extent of these mechanisms must be guided by States' international obligations, including, principally, under the UNTOC and the *Trafficking in Persons Protocol*. A significant body of other materials, such as the principles on human rights and trafficking and those on the rights of victims, should also be drawn upon. Together, this international legal framework identifies the key components and considerations necessary to create effective measures for the protection of victim-witnesses of trafficking. Many of these components are incorporated into Australian law, as shown in Section 5.6.

75 *Migration Regulations 1994* (Cth) sch 2, subclass 852.511.
76 *Modern Slavery Act 2015* (UK) s 45.

Part 2

International cooperation

6 International frameworks for cooperation in organised crime cases

Andreas Schloenhardt and Genevieve Rule

6.1 Introduction

Organised criminal groups are highly mobile, and their activities frequently transcend international borders. They often seek to evade detection, arrest, and punishment by moving to other jurisdictions or by laundering the proceeds of crime through offshore companies or financial institutions. Organised criminal groups avoid interference by taking advantage of the discrepancies between criminal justice systems and the inability or reluctance of law enforcement authorities to engage in complicated and expensive international investigations and prosecutions. Because State sovereignty and the principle of non-intervention prohibit 'all kinds of territorial encroachment', States must rely on international instruments to investigate and prosecute organised crime cases across borders.[1]

Deficiencies in any one State's capacity to address these threats effectively translate into an overall weakness of the international regime of criminal justice cooperation. This is why comprehensive cross-border cooperation is essential to ensure the appropriate investigation and prosecution of transnational organised crime. International cooperation is therefore a central feature of global and regional frameworks which aim to prevent and combat organised crime.

This chapter explores the main mechanisms in international law which enable and enhance cross-border prosecutorial and judicial cooperation in organised crime cases. The main focus is on the provisions of the *United Nations Convention against Transnational Organized Crime* (UNTOC),[2] though relevant frameworks established by regional organisations are also considered. An outline of extradition, mutual legal assistance, transfer of criminal proceedings, and transfer of sentenced persons under the UNTOC and regional frameworks is provided. Not further discussed here are confiscation (discussed in

1 UN, *Commentary on the United Nations Convention Against Illicit Traffic in Narcotic Drugs and Psychotropic Substances 1988* (United Nations, 1988) 45 [2.17].
2 Opened for signature 15 November 2000, 2225 UNTS 209 (entered into force 29 September 2003).

DOI: 10.4324/9781003519317-8

Chapter 4 of this volume), joint investigations (discussed in Chapter 8 of this volume) and other forms of law enforcement cooperation.

6.2 International frameworks

International criminal justice cooperation occurs when States share information, resources, investigators, and prosecutors to achieve the common goal of combating criminal activities, such as organised crime.[3] The basis of such cooperation may be formal or informal. Formal cooperation can be based on international, regional, or bilateral treaties; informal cooperation generally involves direct officer-to-officer or agency-to-agency contact across borders. Generally, informal cooperation is not dealt with by legislation but may be based on a memorandum of understanding (MoU) between the cooperating States or their agencies.

6.2.1 United Nations Convention against Transnational Organized Crime

The need for comprehensive international criminal justice cooperation was one of the main motivators behind the development of the UNTOC, and this is captured in the statement of purpose in its Article 1.[4] International cooperation under the UNTOC comprises a range of mechanisms that facilitate exchange and collaboration between States and their law enforcement, prosecution, and judicial authorities. Among other things, this Convention creates avenues for obtaining evidence, accessing information, confiscating assets, transferring persons, transferring proceedings, and arresting and returning fugitives across borders, thus 'closing the gap that existed in international cooperation in an area generally regarded as one of the top priorities of the international community in the 21st century'.[5] The main provisions relating to international cooperation under the Convention include extradition (Article 16), mutual legal assistance (Article 18), transfer of criminal proceedings (Article 21), and the transfer of sentenced persons (Article 17). Many of these provisions are based on provisions under the *Convention against Illicit Traffic*

3 UNODC, *In-depth Training Manual on Investigating and Prosecuting Smuggling of Migrants* (United Nations, 2011) 91; UNODC, *International Framework for Action to Implement the Smuggling of Migrants Protocol* (United Nations, 2011) 11.

4 Alexandra V Orlova and James W Moore, '"Umbrellas" or "Building Blocks": Defining International Terrorism and Transnational Organised Crime in International Law' (2005) 27 *Houston Journal of International Law* 267, 285; also cited in Neil Boister, 'The Cooperation Provisions of the UN Convention against Transnational Organised Crime: A "Toolbox" Rarely Used?' (2016) 16 *International Criminal Law Review* 39, 45.

5 Dimitri Vlassis, 'The United Nations Convention against Transnational Organized Crime and its Protocols: A New Era in International Cooperation' in Daniel Préfontaine (ed), *The Changing Face of International Criminal Law* (International Centre for Criminal Law Reform and Criminal Justice Policy, 2002), 75.

in Narcotic Drugs and Psychotropic Substances of 1988.[6] Most of the UNTOC articles on international cooperation have also been adopted by the *United Nations Convention against Corruption* (UNCAC).[7]

6.2.2 Regional conventions

Regional organisations in Africa, the Americas, Asia, and Europe have developed a range of agreements and conventions on crime and criminal justice matters. Some of these were concluded specifically to facilitate international cooperation, such as extradition and mutual legal assistance, across a range of criminal offences. Other treaties focus on specific crime types, such as cybercrime, corruption, or trafficking in persons, and provide mechanisms for international cooperation in cases concerning these types of offences. Treaties in the latter category are not further discussed in this chapter.

Among American States, several agreements to facilitate international cooperation have been developed with the assistance of, or are deposited with or administered by, the Organization of American States (OAS). In Europe, the Council of Europe has a long history of promoting criminal justice cooperation and has developed a plethora of conventions to facilitate international cooperation in criminal matters. Several of these conventions have also been signed by non-Member States. In addition, the European Union has issued a range of directives and framework decisions concerning international criminal justice cooperation, organised crime, or both. Several regional agreements pertaining to criminal justice cooperation have also been concluded in Africa and, to a much lesser extent, in Asia and the Pacific.

Purpose, design, and depth vary greatly between these instruments, and it is not possible to make generalisations about their scope and application. It is worth noting, though, that these instruments are widely used among the parties to these regional agreements and among Member States of the relevant regional organisations. Because these regional agreements bring together a smaller number of States, they sometimes contain mechanisms that exceed those set out in global conventions such as the UNTOC or the UNCAC. If the agreements are tied to, or developed under the auspices of, a regional organisation, they usually bring together countries in geographical proximity, with shared histories and values, and with greater levels of trust and more experience of cooperation. As a result, States sometimes favour international cooperation in criminal matters based on regional agreements with which they are more familiar, and which may provide administrative and other mechanisms

6 Opened for signature on 20 December 1988, 1582 UNTS 95 (entered into force 11 November 1990).

7 Opened for signature 31 October 2003, 2349 UNTS 41 (entered into force 14 December 2005).

to effect cooperation that are not available under global treaties. Official statements made by parties to the UNTOC seem to confirm this.[8]

6.3 Extradition

Extradition is a formal process to return or deliver fugitives from the jurisdiction where they are present (the requested State) to the jurisdiction where they are wanted in relation to criminal activities (the requesting State).[9] Extradition 'allows States lawfully to acquire custody of alleged criminals located in other States in order to exercise an already established criminal jurisdiction'.[10]

Extradition is the oldest form of international cooperation in criminal matters. Since the late 19th century, States have signed bilateral extradition treaties in their efforts to eliminate safe shelters for serious offenders.[11] The earliest multilateral extradition treaties date back to the 1930s and 1950s.[12] Multilateral conventions containing extradition provisions, such as the UNTOC, provide the legal basis and set basic minimum standards for extradition for offences within the scope of the convention. They also encourage the adoption of a variety of mechanisms designed to streamline the extradition process.[13]

In the past, extradition treaties commonly set out a list of offences for which extradition could be sought or granted. These set lists create difficulties when a new crime type emerges for which no corresponding extraditable offence can be found, and require the legislator to constantly review and amend the list of extraditable offences.[14] For this reason, more recent extradition treaties define extraditable offences by reference to a minimum penalty or other criteria for the purpose of establishing dual criminality, rather than requiring

8 UN Conference of the Parties to the United Nations Convention against Transnational Organized Crime, *Catalogue of examples of cases of extradition, mutual legal assistance and other forms of international legal cooperation on the basis of the United Nations Convention against Transnational Organized Crime*, 5th sess, UN Doc CTOC/COP/2010/CRP.5 (22 September 2010) 2 [5], 17 [86]–[89], 18 [95].

9 UNODC, *Legislative Guide for the Implementation of the United Nations Convention against Transnational Organized Crime* (UNODC, 2nd edn 2017) [470] ('UNODC, *Legislative Guide*').

10 Neil Boister, *An Introduction to Transnational Criminal Law* (Oxford University Press, 2nd edn 2018) 353.

11 Christopher Blakesley, 'The Practice of Extradition from Antiquity to Modern France and the United States: a Brief History' (1981) 4(1) *Boston College International and Comparative Law Review* 39, 39; Joanna Harrington, 'Extradition of transnational criminals' in Neil Boister and Robert Currie (eds), *Routledge Handbook of Transnational Criminal Law* (Taylor & Francis, 2014) 153, 153.

12 See further, Matti Joutsen, 'International Cooperation against Transnational Organized Crime: Extradition and Mutual Legal Assistance in Criminal Matters' (2003) 59 *UNAFEI Resource Material Series* 364, 366.

13 UNODC, *Criminal Justice Assessment Toolkit* (United Nations, 2006) International Cooperation, 8 ('UNODC, *Criminal Justice Toolkit*').

14 UNODC, *Legislative Guide* (n 9) 482.

strict observance of a prescribed list of offences.[15] The relevant thresholds may be different depending on the different stages of the prosecution and trial. Defining extraditable offences in this manner obviates the need to list individual offences and renegotiate or supplement a treaty if States pass laws dealing with a new type of criminal activity, or if the list inadvertently fails to cover a type of criminal activity punishable by both States.[16]

6.3.1 *Article 16 UNTOC: Scope and application*

Article 16 of the UNTOC provides the legal basis and sets minimum standards for extradition for offences covered by the Convention. Article 16 comprises 17 subsections that can be broadly grouped as follows:

- (1) and (2) set out the offences to which the extradition provisions apply;
- (3) to (6) concern the relationship between this extradition provision and other extradition treaties;
- (7), (8), and (17) relate to the conditions of extradition;
- (9) concerns custody or other measures against the person whose extradition is sought in the requested State Party;
- (10) to (12) set out special provisions concerning the extradition of nationals;
- (13) concerns the treatment and rights of persons whose extradition is sought; and
- (14) to (16) deal with situations in which extradition may be refused.

The obligation to extradite applies 'to the offences covered by this Convention' (Article 16(1)). By reference to Article 3(1), this includes:

- offences established in accordance with Articles 5 (participation in an organised criminal group), 6 (money laundering), 8 (corruption), and 23 (obstruction of justice);
- serious crimes (defined in Article 2(b)); and
- offences established in accordance with the three Protocols supplementing the UNTOC.[17]

15 Gavan Griffith and Claire Higgins, 'Recent Developments in the Law of Extradition' (2005) 6 *Melbourne Journal of International Law* 33, 37–38.

16 UNODC, *Legislative Guide* (n 9) [471].

17 *Protocol to Prevent, Suppress, and Punish Trafficking in Persons, especially Women and Children*, opened for signature 15 November 2000, 2237 UNTS 319 (entered into force 25 December 2003), Article 1(3); *Protocol against the Smuggling of Migrants by Land, Sea and Air*, opened for signature 15 November 2000, 2241 UNTS 507 (entered into force 28 January 2004), Article 1(3); and *Protocol against the Illicit Manufacturing of and Trafficking in Firearms, their Parts and Components, and Ammunition*, opened for signature 31 May 2001, 2326 UNTS 208 (entered into force 3 July 2005) Article 1(3).

Article 3(1) requires that the offences to which the UNTOC applies must meet two criteria: they must involve an organised criminal group, and they must be transnational in nature. According to Article 3(2), an offence under the Convention is transnational in nature if it is committed:

a) in more than one State;
b) in one State but a substantial part of its preparation, planning, direction, or control takes place in another State;
c) in one State but involves an organised criminal group that engages in criminal activities in more than one State; or
d) in one State but has substantial effects in another State.

The obligation under Article 16(1) further applies 'in cases where an offence referred to in Article 3(1)(a) or (b) involves an organised criminal group and the person who is the subject of the request for extradition is located in the territory of the requested State party'. Under this alternative, transnationality of the offence is not strictly necessary as extradition is possible where the subject of the request is merely located in the requested State.[18] Extradition under the first alternative of Article 16(1) further extends to 'serious crime' as defined in Article 2(b), namely 'conduct constituting an offence punishable by a maximum deprivation of liberty of at least four years or a more serious penalty'.

Article 16(1) further requires 'that the offence for which extradition is sought is punishable under the domestic law of both the requesting State party and the requested State party'. This dual criminality requirement reflects the *nullum crimen sine lege* maxim.[19]

Article 16(2) permits States to use Article 16 as a legal basis to extradite so long as one of the offences for which extradition is sought is covered by the Convention. The provision may therefore also be used if the request includes other offences outside the scope of the UNTOC. In such circumstances, the requested State is encouraged, but not required, to extradite.[20]

18 UN Conference of the Parties to the United Nations Convention against Transnational Organized Crime, *Use of the United Nations Conventions against Transnational Organized Crime as a Legal Basis for International Cooperation against All Forms of Transnational Organized Crime*, UN Doc CTOC/COP/WG.3/2015/3 (18 August 2015) 6 [29] ('CTOC/COP/WG.3/2015/3'); UNODC, *Manual on Mutual Legal Assistance and Extradition* (United Nations, 2012), 26 [59], 46 [98] ('UNODC, *Manual*').

19 Boister (n 10) 359; see further, Robert Currie and Joseph Rikhof, *International and Transnational Criminal Law* (Irwin Law, 2nd edn 2014) 481.

20 CTOC/COP/WG.3/2015/3 (n 18) 6 [27]; see further, Andreas Schloenhardt, 'Article 16: Extradition', in Andreas Schloenhardt et al. (eds), *UN Convention against Transnational Organized Crime, A Commentary* (Oxford University Press, 2023) 155, 164–165.

6.3.2 *Relationship between UNTOC other extradition treaties*

Article 16(3) obliges States Parties to treat the offences described in Article 16(1) as automatically included in existing extradition treaties between them.[21] States Parties are further obliged to include them in all future extradition treaties between them.[22]

The UNTOC can provide a basis for extradition in addition to other bilateral or multilateral agreements into which the States have entered. Article 16(4) allows, but does not require, States Parties to use the Convention as a treaty basis for extradition if such a treaty basis is a prerequisite.[23] In these circumstances, the UNTOC may serve as a 'surrogate extradition convention'.[24] The law of some States prevents the use of the UNTOC as a legal basis for extradition in the absence of other relevant treaties between the requesting and requested States. Under Article 16(5)(a), States Parties that require a treaty basis for extradition must notify the Secretary-General as to whether or not they will permit the UNTOC to be used for extradition.

States Parties that can extradite pursuant to a domestic statute (i.e. those that do not require a treaty basis for extradition) are required under Article 16(6) to include the offences described in Article 16(1) as extraditable offences under their applicable statute governing international extradition.

6.3.3 *Conditions and execution of extradition under Article 16 UNTOC*

Differences between prosecutorial practices can make effective international cooperation difficult. In the field of extradition, such differences are even more acute in relation to the documents to be presented to the requested State and the evidentiary requirements for granting an extradition request.[25] Modern extradition practice tends to simplify requirements with respect to the form of extradition requests and the channels of transmission, as well as the evidentiary standards. For this reason, Article 16(8) encourages States Parties to expedite extradition procedures and simplify evidentiary requirements.[26]

Provisions on provisional arrest and detention pending extradition are standard features of extradition treaties.[27] Accordingly, Article 16(9) provides that the requested State Party may take a fugitive into custody or take other appropriate measures to ensure his or her presence for the purposes of extradition.[28] For States that consider the UNTOC as a treaty basis for extradition

21 Ibid., 155, 166.
22 UNODC, *Legislative Guide* [494]–[495].
23 See also CTOC/COP/WG.3/2015/3 (n 18) 6 [26].
24 Boister (n 10) 358.
25 UNODC, *Manual* (n 19) 15 [39]; Schloenhardt (n 20) 155, 169–170; Currie and Rikhof (n 19) 484–485.
26 UNODC, *Legislative Guide* [517].
27 Ibid., [520].
28 See further, UNODC, *Manual* (n 19) 57–58 [136].

(Article 16(4)), Article 16(9) provides the treaty basis needed for the provisional arrest of a person pending the outcome of extradition proceedings.[29]

Many States are reluctant to extradite their own nationals, and some have incorporated a prohibition from doing so in their domestic law; some are even constitutionally prohibited from extraditing their nationals.[30] 'The rationale for such a view', notes Joutsen,

> is a mixture of the obligation of a State to protect its citizens, a lack of confidence in the fairness of foreign legal proceedings, the many disadvantages that defendants face when defending themselves in a foreign legal system, and the many disadvantages of being in custody in a foreign country.[31]

Article 16(10) provides that where a requested State Party does not extradite a person found in its territory for an offence set forth in Article 16(1) on grounds that the person is its national, that State shall, at the request of the State Party seeking extradition, be obliged to submit the case without undue delay to its competent authorities for the purpose of prosecution. This reflects the *aut dedere aut judicare* principle, which is the obligation to either extradite or prosecute. Article 16(10) does not go so far as to compel a State to prosecute. Instead, the authorities of the requested State that refuses extradition are to determine whether to proceed with a prosecution and conduct their proceedings in the same manner as in the case of any other offence of a grave nature under domestic law. This means that 'the State in question should make an earnest effort to bring the suspect to justice'.[32]

The difficulty of successfully mounting a prosecution in these types of cases is, of course, compounded by the fact that the crime was not perpetrated in the State Party where the suspect now resides. Differences in legal traditions and systems between where the investigation was conducted and where the case is to be tried can further increase the problem. This is particularly the case if there is a question as to whether the requested State has jurisdiction to prosecute the case domestically. Mutual legal assistance should be utilised in cases of this type to aid in the proposed prosecution in the requested State. Evidence gathered to date by the requesting State can be provided, and any additional evidence can be acquired through further mutual legal assistance requests.[33]

Article 16(11) refers to the possibility of temporary surrender of the person on condition that he or she will be returned to the requested State Party for the purpose of serving the sentence imposed. This option can serve as a tool

29 Schloenhardt (n 20) 155, 170; Joutsen (n 12) 364, 375–376.
30 See further Currie and Rikhof (n 19) 480.
31 Joutsen (n 12) 364, 369.
32 Ibid., 364, 370; see also Boister (n 10) 371.
33 UNODC, *Manual* (n 19) 50 [109].

to overcome the reluctance of some States to extradite their own nationals. It is a further illustration of the *aut dedere aut judicare* principle and requires the establishment of an appropriate jurisdictional basis.[34] Where extradition is requested for the purpose of enforcing a sentence, the requested State, rather than extraditing the national, may choose to enforce the sentence itself. Article 16(12) calls upon a State Party that has denied, on the ground of nationality, a request by another State Party to extradite a fugitive to serve a sentence, to consider enforcing the sentence itself.

Article 16(14) provides that nothing in the UNTOC is to be interpreted as imposing an obligation to extradite if the requested State has substantial grounds for believing that the request has been made for the purpose of prosecuting or punishing a person on account of that person's sex, race, religion, nationality, ethnic origin, or political opinions, or that compliance with the request would cause prejudice to that person's position for any one of those reasons.[35] Article 16(15) provides that States Parties may not refuse a request for extradition on the sole ground that the offence is also considered to involve fiscal matters. This is particularly important since many cases of transnational organised crime have fiscal implications.[36] States Parties must therefore ensure that no such ground for refusal may be invoked under their extradition laws or treaties.[37] Article 16(16) provides that, where appropriate, the requested State Party shall consult with the requesting State Party before refusing extradition. This process could enable the requesting State Party to present additional information or explanations that may result in a different outcome.[38]

6.3.4 *European Convention on Extradition*

One of the earliest criminal justice treaties developed by the Council of Europe was the *European Convention on Extradition* of 1957.[39] Article 1 of this Convention creates an obligation 'to surrender to each other ... all persons against whom the competent authorities of the requesting party are proceeding for an offence or who are wanted by said authorities for the carrying out of a sentence or detention order'. Any offence with a minimum statutory penalty of one year imprisonment is an extraditable offence for the purpose of this treaty (Article 2(1)).

By defining the offences to which the Convention applies in terms of the statutory penalty rather than a list of specific offences, the Convention increases the scope of offences to which it can apply and allows for new offences to be

34 See further, ibid., 50 [110].
35 Ibid., 52–53 [115]–[119].
36 Boister (n 10) 375.
37 UNODC, *Legislative Guide* (n 9) [509].
38 Ibid., [511]; UNODC, *Manual* (n 19) 55 [129].
39 Opened for signature 13 December 1957, ETS No 024 (entered into force 18 April 1960).

included more easily;[40] unlike the UNTOC, the scope of application is not limited to organised and serious crime. It is also noteworthy that the European Convention contains no requirement that the offence be committed within the borders of the requesting State and thereby acknowledges that parties can exercise criminal jurisdiction over crimes committed abroad.[41] Just like the UNTOC, the European Convention stipulates several limitations on the obligation to extradite, including where the offence is political or military in nature and the right of parties to refuse to extradite their nationals.[42]

6.3.5 *Inter-American Convention on Extradition*

The *Convention on Extradition*,[43] adopted in Montevideo in 1933, was the first multilateral extradition treaty in the world. It creates an obligation for States Parties 'to surrender to any one of the States which may make the requisition, the persons who may be in their territory and who are accused or under sentence' (Article 1 châpeau). Pursuant to Article 1(b), the Convention applies to any offence that is punishable in the requesting and the requested States by a minimum of one year imprisonment.

The *Inter-American Convention on Extradition* of 1981 substituted the 1933 Convention for those States that became a party to the 1981 Convention.[44] Under Article 1 of the latter Convention, States Parties are obliged to extradite 'persons who are judicially required for prosecution, are being tried, have been convicted, or have been sentenced to a penalty involving deprivation of liberty'. Article 2 provides that an extradition request may be granted where the relevant offence was committed in the territory of the requesting State or where the requesting State had jurisdiction to try the offence. The Convention only applies to offences punishable by 'a penalty of not less than two years of deprivation of liberty under the laws of both the requesting State and the requested State' (applying the condition of dual criminality).[45] Article 4 lists six grounds for denying extradition, which include where the offence is a political offence or where 'it can be inferred that persecution for reasons of race, religion or nationality is involved'.[46] Additionally, nationality can be invoked as a ground for denying an extradition request where the law of the requested State provides.[47]

40 Harrington (n 11) 156.
41 Ibid.
42 *European Convention on Extradition*, arts 3, 4, 6.
43 Opened for signature 26 December 1933, OAS Treaty Series No 34 (entered into force 26 December 1934).
44 Opened for signature 25 February 1981, OAS Treaty Series No 60 (entered into force 28 March 1982).
45 *Inter-American Convention on Extradition*, Article 3(1).
46 Ibid., Article 4(4), (5).
47 Ibid., Article 7(1).

6.4 Mutual legal assistance

Broadly, mutual legal assistance enables States to receive and provide assistance for gathering evidence for investigations and criminal prosecutions, including where coercive measures are required. In order to allow law enforcement, prosecution, and judicial authorities to collaborate internationally, States have enacted laws permitting them to provide such cooperation and have increasingly resorted to treaties enabling mutual legal assistance in criminal matters (often referred to as MLATs). Such treaties commonly list the kinds of assistance to be provided, the rights of the requesting and requested States relative to the scope and manner of cooperation, the rights of alleged offenders, and the procedures to be followed in making and executing requests. Information sharing and agency-to-agency communication are also important to facilitate mutual legal assistance and may make it possible to provide assistance without a formal request.

6.4.1 Application and scope of Article 18 UNTOC

Under Article 18(1) of the UNTOC, States Parties are required to provide the widest measure of mutual legal assistance in relation to the offences covered by the Convention. It further requires the provision of mutual legal assistance where the requesting State has reasonable grounds to suspect that the offence is transnational in nature and that the offence involves an organised criminal group.[48] In merely requiring 'reasonable grounds to suspect' that the offence is transnational in nature and involves an organised criminal group, a lower evidentiary standard than that applying to other provisions of the Convention applies to Article 18.[49] Simply showing that 'victims, witnesses, proceeds, instrumentalities or evidence ... are located in the requested State party' has been indicated to be sufficient for a State to reasonably suspect that an offence is transnational in nature.[50] This lower evidentiary burden provides an 'enlarged notion of transnationality' and allows for assistance in the early stages of investigations where evidence proving the commission of an offence within the scope of the Convention may be weak.[51] This is a significant advantage of the UNTOC as it is suggested that without this lower evidentiary standard, evidence that could show that an offence falls within the scope of the Convention may not be obtained and other mechanisms for cooperation (such as extradition) would not be available.

Article 18(6) and (7) address the interplay between the Convention and bilateral and multilateral mutual legal assistance treaties. The UNTOC does not override any existing treaty already in place between States Parties (Article

48 UNODC, *Legislative Guide* (n 9) [547].
49 UNODC, *Manual* (n 19) 38.
50 Ibid.
51 CTOC/COP/WG.3/2015/3 (n 18) 6–7 [31].

18(6)). Instead, the Convention gives States the option to use Article 18(9) to (29) if this would facilitate cooperation. These provisions have been referred to as 'a very detailed mini mutual legal assistance treaty in [their] own right', reflecting the UNTOC's goal of departing from long-winded rogatory processes where requests are sent through diplomatic channels and foreign courts facilitate the taking of evidence.[52]

Article 18(3) sets forth eight specific types of mutual legal assistance that a State Party must be able to provide. This list is not exhaustive and extends to 'any other type of assistance that is not contrary to the domestic law of the requested State Party' (Article 18(3)(i)). In cases involving transnational organised crime, witnesses and victims, along with other persons who have relevant information, are frequently located abroad. As a result, it is necessary to ask the State where those persons are located to take evidence or statements from them (Article 18(3)(a)). Under Article 18(3)(b), mutual legal assistance may be sought to affect the service of judicial documents in another State Party. The requesting State may specify the mode of service which the requested State should follow, if its laws permit. If the request does not specify a mode of service, the law of the requested State will apply. Under Article 18(3)(c), a State Party may request another to conduct searches, seize assets, or freeze bank accounts. Article 12 provides additional guidance on the freezing and seizure of proceeds of crime and of property, equipment, and other instrumentalities used in or destined for offences covered by the UNTOC.

Pursuant to Article 18(3)(d), States Parties to the UNTOC may request that another party examine objects or sites that may be of relevance for a case pending in the requesting State. This may include, for instance, the viewing or taking of photographs or the taking and supply of measurements or descriptions of the objects or sites concerned.[53] Article 18(3)(e) broadly refers to requests to obtain information, evidentiary items, and expert evaluation from another State Party. The supply of evidence under Article 18(3)(e) is only unproblematic if that evidence is in the possession of the requested State. Otherwise, the measure may either require permission from the owner or the person in possession of that item or may require seizure of the item (Article 18(3)(c)).[54]

Article 18(3)(f) makes specific mention of mutual legal assistance requests for the purpose of obtaining certain official documents and financial transaction records. This subsection needs to be read in conjunction with Article 18(8), which mandates that States Parties 'shall not decline to render mutual legal assistance pursuant to this article on the basis of banking secrecy'. It

52 Boister (n 4) 39, 52–53.

53 Andreas Schloenhardt, 'Article 18: Mutual Legal Assistance', in Andreas Schloenhardt et al. (eds), *UN Convention against Transnational Organized Crime, A Commentary* (Oxford University Press, 2023) 187, 199.

54 Ibid.

has been argued that this subsection applies regardless of whether there are other binding mutual legal assistance treaties between the requesting and requested States, and that banking secrecy must not be used as a ground to decline mutual legal assistance requests if the case falls within the scope of the Convention, even if such refusal is permitted as a ground for refusal of assistance under the other treaty.[55]

Under Article 18(3)(g), mutual legal assistance may be requested for the purpose of identifying or tracing proceeds of crime, property, instrumentalities, or other things for evidentiary purposes. This provision is closely related to Article 12(2), which deals with measures to enable the identification, tracing, freezing, or seizure of items referred to in Article 12(1). While Article 12 deals with measures 'for the purpose of eventual confiscation', requests under Article 18(3)(g) are made 'for evidentiary purposes', though there may be cases involving both of these purposes. Lastly, Article 18(3)(h) enables States to ask another party to facilitate the voluntary appearance of persons, who may be witnesses, victims, or perpetrators, including persons in custody, in the requesting State.

6.4.2 Refusal and execution of requests under Article 18

Article 18(21) allows States to refuse mutual legal assistance under certain conditions. Requests for mutual legal assistance can be refused if requirements under Article 18 are not met (Article 18(21)(a)) or if the execution of the request would be prejudicial to the essential interests of the requested State (Article 18(21)(b)). Assistance, however, cannot be refused on the grounds of bank secrecy (Article 18(8), discussed above) or for offences considered to involve fiscal matters (Article 18(22)). Where a request for mutual legal assistance is refused, reasons must be given.

There is an obligation to consult with the requesting State Party to consider whether a request may be granted, subject to terms and conditions. Otherwise, States must execute requests expeditiously and take into account possible deadlines facing the requesting authorities (for example, expiration of a statute of limitation).

Article 18(4) and (5) of the UNTOC provide a legal basis for a State Party to forward information or evidence it believes is important for combating the offences covered by the Convention to another State Party without a prior request (sometimes referred to as 'spontaneous transmission of information').[56] There is, however, no obligation to do so in a particular case.[57]

55 Ibid., 187, 200; UNODC, *Legislative Guide* (n 9) [563].
56 Joutsen (n 12) 364, 382.
57 UNODC, *Legislative Guide* (n 9) [570].

6.4.3 *Regional treaties*

6.4.3.1 *European Convention on Mutual Legal Assistance in Criminal Matters*

The *European Convention on Mutual Assistance in Criminal Matters*[58] was adopted by the Council of Europe in 1959. This Convention has been referred to as the 'oldest, most widely applied, and arguably most influential' multilateral mutual legal assistance arrangement.[59]

Article 1(1) provides that States Parties to the treaty

> undertake to afford each other, in accordance with the provisions of this Convention, the widest measure of mutual assistance in proceedings in respect of offences the punishment of which, at the time of the request for assistance, falls within the jurisdiction of the judicial authorities of the requesting Party.

This provision is interpreted broadly to extend to all kinds of mutual legal assistance and is not restricted to the assistance specifically covered by the Convention.[60] The Convention is not limited to serious offences and also applies to minor offences.[61] The Convention notably relates to assistance 'within the jurisdiction of the judicial authorities', and requests are generally to originate from 'judicial authorities'.[62] This contrasts with other international arrangements, such as the UNTOC, which allow assistance in earlier stages before proceedings have been commenced.[63] Article 2 of the European Convention provides that assistance may be refused for political or fiscal offences or if the requested State considers that the assistance is likely to prejudice the 'sovereignty, security, *ordre public* or other essential interests of its country'.[64]

6.4.3.2 *Inter-American Convention on Mutual Legal Assistance*

The *Inter-American Convention on Mutual Legal Assistance in Criminal Matters*,[65] adopted in Nassau in 1992, was developed by the OAS.[66] Article

58 Opened for signature on 20 April 1959, ETS No 30 (entered into force 12 June 1962).
59 Joutsen (n 2) 364, 378.
60 David McClean, *International Co-operation in Civil and Criminal Matters* (Oxford University Press, 3rd edn 2012) 172.
61 Council of Europe, *Explanatory Report to the European Convention on Mutual Assistance in Criminal Matters* (Council of Europe, 1959) 3.
62 *European Convention on Mutual Assistance in Criminal Matters*, Articles 1(1), 15; McClean (n 60) 174.
63 Ibid.
64 Ibid., Article 2.
65 Opened for signature 23 May 1992, OAS Treaty Series No 75 (entered into force 14 April 1996).
66 The development and content of this Convention are outlined in Marian Nash, 'Contemporary Practice of the United States Relating to International Law' (1998) 92 *American Journal of International Law* 48–54.

2 of this Convention creates an obligation for the parties 'to render to one another mutual assistance in investigations, prosecutions, and proceedings that pertain to crimes over which the requesting State has jurisdiction at the time the assistance is requested'. The assistance that may be sought and provided under the Convention includes, *inter alia*, (Article 7):

a. notification of rulings and judgments;
b. taking of testimony or statements from persons;
c. summoning of witnesses and expert witnesses to provide testimony;
d. immobilisation and sequestration of property, freezing of assets, and assistance in procedures related to seizures;
e. searches or seizures;
f. examination of objects and places;
g. service of judicial documents;
h. transmittal of documents, reports, information, and evidence;
i. transfer of detained persons for the purpose of this convention; and
j. any other procedure provided there is an agreement between the requesting State and the requested State.

Article 2 further provides that States Parties 'shall render to one another mutual assistance in investigations, prosecutions, and proceedings that pertain to crimes over which the requesting state has jurisdiction'.[67] States Parties are not authorised to exercise jurisdiction or perform functions which are in the exclusive purview of the requested State's authority under its domestic law. Article 4 acknowledges the diverse legal systems of participating States and specifies that assistance through the Convention is to be based upon requests from criminal investigation or prosecution authorities. Article 5 dismisses the principle of dual criminality, allowing assistance to be rendered even if the offence is not punishable under the domestic law of the requested State. However, Article 5 allows States to decline cooperation because of the absence of dual criminality where the request for assistance relates to the immobilisation and sequestration of property and searches and seizures.

In order to make a valid request, the relevant offence must be punishable by at least one year of imprisonment in the requesting State.[68] The Convention does not apply to military offences and provides six grounds of refusal a State may exercise, including if the offence is a political offence or where 'public policy ... sovereignty, security or basic public interests' would be prejudiced.[69]

In addition to this Convention, the *Agreement to Promote Cooperation and Mutual Legal Assistance* has been developed by the Ibero-American Association of Public Prosecutors and provides a framework for international

67 *Inter-American Convention on Mutual Legal Assistance*, Article 2.
68 Ibid., Article 6.
69 Ibid., Articles 8, 9.

cooperation in criminal matters between the member prosecution authorities. It was signed in Quito on 4 December 2003.

6.4.3.3 ASEAN Treaty on Mutual Legal Assistance in Criminal Matters

The Association of Southeast Asian Nations' (ASEAN) *Treaty on Mutual Legal Assistance in Criminal Matters* was a 'crucial step for ASEAN cooperation in response to transnational crime' when it was signed in 2004.[70] Article 1(1) provides that the parties shall 'render to one another the widest possible measure of mutual legal assistance in criminal matters, namely investigations, prosecutions, and resulting proceedings'. Assistance is limited on 11 grounds, including where the relevant offence is of a political nature, is a military offence, or where assistance would affect the 'sovereignty, security, public order, public interest or essential interests of the Requested Party'.[71] Article 3(2) provides three further conditions under which assistance may be refused, including if the provision of assistance would impose an 'excessive burden on the resources of the Requested Party'.[72]

The ASEAN treaty has been notably impeded by incompatible legislation of Member States. For example, it has been noted that disparities in the criminalisation of money laundering hinder the implementation of the treaty and its effectiveness in combating transnational crime because of the consequent inability of States to meet the requirements of dual criminality.[73] Because the absence of dual criminality is a ground on which a State may refuse to provide assistance under Article 3(1)(e), this limitation is substantial.

6.5 Transfer of criminal proceedings

The transfer of criminal proceedings is the process in which the jurisdiction of the proceedings is transferred to another State and the substantive and procedural laws of the transferred State apply. It generally involves transferring the record, evidence, and anything else relating to the judicial proceedings but not the accused (for which extradition is required).[74] The fact that the proceedings can be transferred implies that the proceedings have commenced and the

70 Chat Le Nguyen, 'Towards the Effective ASEAN Mutual Legal Assistance in Combating Money Laundering' (2012) 15(4) *Journal of Money Laundering Control* 383, 384; *Treaty on Mutual Legal Assistance in Criminal Matters*, opened for signature 29 November 2004 (entered into force on various dates from 28 April 2005).

71 *Treaty on Mutual Legal Assistance in Criminal Matters*, Article 3(1).

72 Ibid., Article 3(2)(c).

73 Nguyen (n 70) 389.

74 M Cherif Bassiouni, 'Introduction to Transfer of Criminal Proceedings' in M Cherif Bassiouni (ed), *International Criminal Law, Volume 2 Multilateral and Bilateral Enforcement Mechanisms* (Brill, 3rd edn 2008) 515, 518.

accused has been identified; however, it is also possible to transfer proceedings at the trial stage or when a judgment has been given but not enforced.[75]

The possibility of transferring criminal proceedings from one State to another can increase the likelihood of the success of a prosecution when, for instance, another State appears to be in a better position to conduct the proceedings. It can also be used to increase the efficiency and effectiveness of the prosecution in a State that is initiating proceedings in lieu of extradition. Furthermore, it can be a useful method of concentrating the prosecution in one jurisdiction, thereby increasing its efficiency and the likelihood of its success in cases involving several jurisdictions.[76] A jurisdictional basis is required for the transferred State to accept the transfer of proceedings and cannot be created through a treaty; however, treaties are required to 'amend or supplement the national jurisdictional laws'.[77]

6.5.1 Article 21 UNTOC

Article 21 of the UNTOC is designed to encourage the transfer of criminal proceedings for the prosecution of offences under the Convention. In order to transfer criminal proceedings, the involved States first need to evaluate whether the State in which the proceedings are to be held has jurisdiction over the principal issues of the case. To effectively transfer the prosecution to another State, two further steps may be required. First, the two States would need to share and transfer information and evidence. Article 15(5) of the UNTOC provides that, where two States are involved in the investigation, prosecution, or judicial proceedings with respect to the same conduct, they shall, as appropriate, consult one another with a view to coordinate actions. Secondly, if the matter had already reached the courts in one State, it would be necessary to 'stay' or suspend the prosecution, pending resolution in the other State.[78] In 1990, the UN General Assembly adopted the *Model Treaty on the Transfer of Proceedings in Criminal Matters* to assist States requiring legislative provisions in developing agreements to enable the transfer of criminal proceedings.[79]

75 UN Conference of the Parties to the United Nations Convention against Transnational Organized Crime, Working Group on International Cooperation, *Practical Considerations, Good Practices and Challenges Encountered in the Area of Transfer of Criminal Proceedings as a Separate form of International Cooperation in Criminal Matters, Background Paper Prepared by the Secretariat*, UN Doc CTOC/WG.3/2017/2 (7 August 2017) [5].

76 UNODC, *Criminal Justice Toolkit* (n 13) 13.

77 Bassiouni (n 74) 516.

78 UNODC, *Legislative Guide* (n 9) [606].

79 UN General Assembly, *Model Treaty on the Transfer of Proceedings in Criminal Matters*, UN Doc A/RES/45/118 (14 December 1990).

6.5.2 *Regional treaties*

The *European Convention on the Transfer of Proceedings in Criminal Matters*[80] allows a State in which a crime is suspected to have been committed to request another State to take prosecutorial action on its behalf. The requested State does so under its domestic law. Article 8 of this Convention sets out eight circumstances in which a State can request another to take proceedings, including if the suspected offender is ordinarily a resident in the requested State.

The Convention creates jurisdiction by conferring competence on the transferred State if that State has issued a formal request in accordance with the Convention and by creating a 'legal fiction allowing the transferred State to treat the offence as if it had been committed in its own territory'.[81] If the requirements of dual criminality and *ne bis in idem* are met, the requested State is obliged to accept a request for the transfer of proceedings unless a prescribed ground of refusal can be relied upon.[82] However, it is relevant to note that while the list of grounds for refusal is limited, the first ground allows the requested State to refuse the request 'if it considers the grounds on which the request is based under Article 8 are not justified'.[83] Therefore, a transfer of proceedings can only occur when both the requesting and requested States consent.[84]

6.6 Transfer of sentenced persons

The transfer of sentenced persons enables a person who is convicted and sentenced to a term of imprisonment involving deprivation of liberty in one State (the sentencing State) to serve their sentence in another State (the administering State). This may be done at the request of the person who has been sentenced so that they may be able to serve their sentence in a State in which they have social ties, usually by virtue of being a national of that State. A further point of consideration is that rehabilitation and reintegration are generally more likely to occur in a State in which the person has family and friends. The decision to transfer a sentenced person may also be made on the basis of humanitarian or compassionate grounds, including medical or mental health needs, or where the conditions in the institution in which the person was convicted and sentenced fall below minimum international standards. In addition,

80 Opened for signature 15 May 1972, ETS 73 (entered into force 30 March 1978).

81 Bassiouni (n 74) 516; *European Convention on the Transfer of Proceedings in Criminal Matters*, Articles 2, 7.

82 Bassiouni (n 74) 516; *European Convention on the Transfer of Proceedings in Criminal Matters*, Article 7(1).

83 *European Convention on the Transfer of Proceedings in Criminal Matters*, Article 11(a).

84 Boudewijn de Jonge, 'Transfer of Criminal Proceedings: From Stumbling Block to Cornerstone of Cooperation in Criminal Matters in the EU' (2020) 21(3) *ERA Forum* 449, 451.

international relations may play a role in cases involving the transfer of sentenced persons.[85]

6.6.1 Article 17 UNTOC

Article 17 of the UNTOC merely encourages States Parties to enter into bilateral or multilateral agreements or arrangements on the transfer to their territory of persons sentenced to imprisonment or other forms of deprivation of liberty for offences established in accordance with the Convention. A model agreement providing simple procedures for the transfer of sentenced persons was adopted in 1985 by the United Nations Congress on the Prevention of Crime and the Treatment of Offenders with the *Model Agreement on the Transfer of Foreign Prisoners and Recommendations on the Treatment of Foreign Prisoners* [*Sentenced Persons*].[86]

6.6.2 Regional treaties

Specialised legal instruments that enable the transfer of sentenced persons are a relatively recent development. Some bilateral and regional agreements of the late 1950s and early 1960s permit States with similar laws to enforce each other's sentences and to transfer sentenced persons (then referred to as prisoners) for the purpose of enforcement. The first multilateral treaty, the *European Convention on the Supervision of Conditionally Sentenced or Conditionally Released Offenders* of 1964,[87] as its name suggests, does not deal directly with sentenced persons but it does provide for the original prison sentence to be carried out in the State to which the sentenced person has been transferred.[88]

6.6.2.1 European Convention on the Transfer of Sentenced Persons

Deemed the '[m]ost prominent of the multilateral instruments' on the transfer of sentenced persons,[89] the *European Convention on the Transfer of Sentenced Persons* of 1983 allows either the sentencing State or the administering State to request a transfer.[90] Article 2(2) provides that '[a] person sentenced in the territory of a Party may be transferred to the territory of another Party'. The

85 UNODC, *Legislative Guide* (n 9) [600]; see further, UNODC, *Handbook on the International Transfer of Sentenced Persons* (United Nations, 2012) 9–15 (UNODC, *Transfer of Sentenced Persons Handbook*).

86 See further, Mohamed Abdul-Aziz, 'International Perspective on Transfer of Prisoners and Execution of Foreign Penal Judgements', in M Cherif Bassiouni (ed), *International Criminal Law, Volume 2: Multilateral and Bilateral Enforcement Mechanisms* (Brill, 3rd edn 2008) 529, 530–536.

87 Opened for signature 30 November 1964, ETS No 51 (entered into force 22 August 1975).

88 See further, UNODC, *Transfer of Sentenced Persons Handbook* (n 85) 17.

89 Ibid., 19.

90 Opened for signature 21 March 1983, ETS 112 (entered into force 1 July 1985), Article 2(3).

Convention provides detailed procedures for transfer, such as Article 5, which specifies that requests and replies are to be made in writing and addressed to the relevant Ministry of Justice.[91]

In order for a person to be transferred, they (or a legal representative) must consent to the transfer.[92] This requirement has been modified to allow a transfer to occur without the consent of the sentenced person where they have fled the territory of a State where they are not a national for the purpose of avoiding the completion of their sentence, or where the sentence includes an expulsion or deportation order.[93]

6.6.2.2 *Inter-American Convention on Serving Criminal Sentences Abroad*

The *Inter-American Convention on Serving Criminal Sentences Abroad*, which entered into force in 1996, provides a similar model to the European Convention.[94] Article 2(a) provides that 'a sentence imposed in one state party upon a national of another state party may be served by the sentenced person in the state of which [they] are a national' and requires the sentenced person's consent to the transfer.[95] A procedure for transfer is provided in Article 5, and provides that a request may be made by the sentencing State, receiving State, or the sentenced person and is to be processed through central authorities or consular or diplomatic channels.[96]

6.7 Observations

This chapter has shown that the UNTOC provides a range of mechanisms to enable and enhance international cooperation in cases involving transnational organised crime. Some of these mechanisms are established tools that can also be found in a range of other multilateral and—not further discussed here—bilateral treaties. Others are more innovative measures that require more comprehensive and sophisticated cooperation, along with greater levels of trust.

If implemented and executed properly, the international cooperation provisions under the UNTOC enable countries to seek legal assistance, extradition, transfer of prisoners, transfer of proceedings in criminal matters, and cooperation for the purposes of confiscation of criminal proceeds and asset recovery.[97]

91 Ibid., Article 5(1), (2).

92 UNODC, *Transfer of Sentenced Persons Handbook* (n 85) 19; *European Convention on the Transfer of Sentenced Persons*, Article 3(1)(d).

93 *Additional Protocol to the Convention on the Transfer of Sentenced Persons*, opened for signature 18 December 1997, ETS 167 (entered into force 1 June 2000) Articles 2, 3.

94 UNODC, *Transfer of Sentenced Persons Handbook* (n 85) 20.

95 Signed 10 January 1995, OAS Treaty Series 76 (entered into force 12 April 1996), Article 3(2).

96 Ibid., Article 5(1), (2).

97 UNODC, *Criminal Justice Toolkit* (n 13) 1.

They open avenues to obtain additional evidence, access information, recover assets, freeze funds, confiscate property, and arrest and return fugitives that would otherwise be immune to prosecution.

Research has shown that many State Parties have put the international cooperation measures under the UNTOC to good use and employed them in relation to a myriad of crime types involving a diverse range of States.[98] Unsurprisingly, the more traditional tools of mutual legal assistance and extradition are more commonly employed than, for instance, the transfer of proceedings or the transfer of sentenced persons.

The cooperation measures under the UNTOC do not exist in isolation; they are built on and complement other international conventions and, importantly, regional agreements for specific types of cooperation in criminal justice matters. These are particularly common among States in Europe and the Americas. In practice, it is not unusual to use the UNTOC provisions alongside other international, regional, or bilateral agreements. In many instances, these agreements reiterate or complement the provisions under the UNTOC and can thus be used as an additional legal basis for the request.[99]

Based on the available cases,[100] it appears that UNTOC is used alongside other international or regional agreements in one of two circumstances. The first involves situations where the investigation or proceedings involve more than one crime type, for example, cases in which an organised criminal group is involved in drug trafficking or money laundering. The second category broadly involves situations in which the UNTOC and the other agreement provide the same or similar tools to request international cooperation and thus offer an additional avenue to request extradition or mutual legal assistance.

International cooperation has many advantages and faces many challenges. But despite these challenges, for the purpose of fighting organised crime, international cooperation should be seen as an opportunity rather than an obstacle. 'Transnational crimes', notes Stefano Betti, 'should be perceived as increasingly affecting the substantial, not simply marginal interests, of several

98 UNODC, *Digest of Cases: International Cooperation in Criminal Matters Involving the United Nations Convention against Transnational Organized Crime as a Legal Basis* (UNODC, 2021) 121 ('UNODC, *Digest of Cases*'); and Andreas Schloenhardt, 'International Cooperation under the United Nations Convention against Transnational Organized Crime: Expectations and Experiences' (2019) 3(4) *Brll Research Papers on Transnational Crime* 3–25.

99 UNODC, *Digest of Cases* (n 98) 117–118.

100 Ibid., 96–110.

States simultaneously. Correspondingly, their investigation and punishment by the authority of one State should be regarded as immediately beneficial to the others'.[101] This rationale, he adds, is embodied in the UNTOC, as it is in the *United Nations Convention against Illicit Traffic in Narcotic Drugs and Psychotropic Substances* and the UNCAC.[102]

101 Stefano Betti, 'New Prospects for Inter-state Co-operation in Criminal Matters: The Palermo Convention' (2003) 3 *International Criminal Law Review* 151, 160.

102 Ibid.

7 The European Arrest Warrant

A model for use in the global fight against organised crime?

Lena Wasser

7.1 Introduction

Transnational organised crime is perceived as a major threat in many parts of the world. In the face of increasing globalisation, it seems obvious that the fight against organised crime can only be a global effort, requiring a high degree of international cooperation. A typical form of international cooperation in criminal matters is the extradition of fugitive persons. Extradition can be defined as

> a cooperative law enforcement process by which the physical custody of a person: (i) charged with committing a crime or (ii) convicted of a crime whose punishment has not yet been determined or fully served, is formally transferred … by authorities of one State to those of another at the request of the latter for the purpose of prosecution or punishment.[1]

When organised criminal groups operate across borders, it is almost inevitable that their crimes will be prosecuted in one country while suspects are located in another. If the persons concerned are not extradited or prosecuted in such circumstances, their country of stay turns into a safe haven where they can continue their criminal activities largely unthreatened by punishment. Operating in well-networked transnational structures makes it even easier for criminals to evade prosecution. Therefore, extradition is indispensable for the successful prosecution of transnational organised crime.

Traditional extradition procedures are, however, often slow, bureaucratic, and the outcome unpredictable.[2] Existing laws and regulations place numerous obstacles in the way of extradition. This is especially unsatisfying when swift and intense cooperation is needed due to complicated cross-border structures

1 David A Sadoff, *Bringing International Fugitives to Justice—Extradition and Its Alternatives* (Cambridge University Press, 2016) 43.

2 Philip B Heymann and Stephen P Heymann, *Challenging Organized Crime in the Western Hemisphere: A Game of Moves and Countermoves* (Routledge, 2019) 95.

DOI: 10.4324/9781003519317-9

in transnational organised crime investigations.[3] In 2002, the European Union (EU) started an attempt to radically simplify the extradition process by creating the European Arrest Warrant (EAW), an EU-specific extradition mechanism that in many respects deviates greatly from established extradition law.

This chapter examines the extent to which the EAW could serve as a model for potential global extradition agreements to combat transnational organised crime. For this purpose, the EAW is first presented in more detail (Section 7.2) and then compared to traditional extradition law (Section 7.3). Next, the EAW is compared to the extradition provisions of the *United Nations Convention against Transnational Organized Crime* (UNTOC),[4] the most important international treaty in the field of organised crime (Section 7.4). Section 7.5 then determines whether and to what extent the three most prominent features of the EAW could be transferred to the global level to enhance the fight against transnational organised crime.

7.2 The European Arrest Warrant: from extradition to surrender

On 13 June 2002—just nine months after the European Commission submitted a first proposal for a Council Framework Decision on this issue[5]—the Council of the European Union adopted the *Council Framework Decision on the European Arrest Warrant and the Surrender Procedures between Member States* and thus the legal basis for the EAW (hereafter 'Framework Decision').[6] This rapid development was not least a consequence of the terrorist attacks on 11 September 2001 in the United States, which provided the 'necessary political momentum'[7] to quickly follow through with the idea of the EAW.

Even though the 9/11 events contributed to the acceleration of the process, these events were by no means the first trigger. Organised crime had become a prominent problem in Europe in the 1990s. The abolition of border controls

3 Ibid.

4 Opened for signature 15 November 2000, 2225 UNTS 209 (entry into force 29 September 2003).

5 *Proposal for a Council Framework Decision on the European Arrest Warrant and the Surrender Procedures between the Member States* [2001] OJ C 332 E/305.

6 *Council Framework Decision of 13 June 2002 on the European Arrest Warrant and the Surrender Procedures between Member States* [2002] OJ L 190/1. The Framework Decision was amended in 2009 by the *Council Framework Decision 2009/299/JHA of 26 February 2009 amending Framework Decisions 2002/584/JHA, 2005/214/JHA, 2006/783/JHA, 2008/909/JHA, and 2008/947/JHA, thereby enhancing the procedural rights of persons and fostering the application of the principle of mutual recognition to decisions rendered in the absence of the person concerned at the trial* [2009] OJ L 81/24. Whenever regulations of the Framework Decision are cited in this chapter, they are taken from the current version. The provisions of the Framework Decision do not apply directly in the Member States but must be implemented by the States into their national law.

7 Michael Plachta, 'European Arrest Warrant: Revolution in Extradition?' (2003) 11(2) *European Journal of Crime, Criminal Law and Criminal Justice* 178, 179.

and the free movement of goods, services, and persons within the Schengen Zone were increasingly exploited by organised criminal groups, as were the growing opportunities offered by new technologies.[8] The key approach to addressing this development was closer judicial cooperation, including improvements to existing extradition agreements.[9] At a special meeting held in Tampere in October 1999, the European Council suggested replacing the formal extradition procedure regarding persons who had already been convicted with an automated surrender procedure and to considerably speed up the extradition of persons who had not yet been convicted.[10] The EAW was the culmination of this development, intended to serve as a step toward the realisation of the 'Area of Freedom, Security and Justice' envisioned by the Member States.[11]

The EAW is defined in Article 1(1) of the Framework Decision to mean

> a judicial decision issued by a Member State with a view to the arrest and surrender by another Member State of a requested person, for the purposes of conducting a criminal prosecution or executing a custodial sentence or detention order.

Contrary to what its name suggests, the EAW is not an arrest warrant issued at the European level, but an instrument used by one State to arrange for the arrest and surrender of a wanted person by another State.[12] The desired automation of processes is noticeable in the change of terminology: The Framework Decision uses the term 'surrender' rather than 'extradition'; instead of 'requesting' and 'requested State', it refers to 'issuing judicial authority' and 'executing judicial authority'.[13]

According to the Framework Decision, the surrender procedure involves the following steps:

8 *Action Plan to combat Organized Crime* [1997] OJ C 251/1, 1 [1].

9 *Action Plan of the Council and the Commission on how best to implement the provisions of the Treaty of Amsterdam on an Area of Freedom, Security and Justice* [1999] OJ C 19/1, 14 [49a].

10 Council of the European Union, *Presidency Conclusions, Tampere European Council, 15–16 October 1999*, 16 October 1999 [35]. This is also reflected in recital 1 of the Framework Decision.

11 Framework Decision, recital 5.

12 Johannes N Henke, *Der Europäische Haftbefehl: Entwicklung und Schwierigkeiten* (AVM, 2008) 4.

13 Cf. Otto Lagodny, '"Extradition" Without a Granting Procedure: The Concept of "Surrender"', in Rob Blekxtoon and Wouter van Ballegooij (eds), *Handbook on the European Arrest Warrant* (TMC Asser Press, 2005) 39, 39–40; Elies van Sliedregt, 'The Dual Criminality Requirement' in Nico Keijzer and Elies van Sliedregt (eds), *The European Arrest Warrant in Practice* (TMC Asser Press, 2009) 51, 51. Plachta (n 7) at 190–194 heavily criticises this new terminology.

First, after a national arrest warrant has been issued,[14] the issuing judicial authority issues an EAW and transmits it to the executing judicial authority of the other State. The EAW may be issued for offences punishable under the national law of the issuing State by a custodial sentence or a detention order for a maximum period of at least 12 months or to enforce an already imposed sentence of at least four months (Article 2(1) Framework Decision). The executing judicial authority is obliged to execute the EAW unless one of the grounds for refusal set out in Articles 3, 4, and 4a applies. In principle, the executing judicial authority does not examine more than the possible existence of one of these (mandatory or optional) grounds for refusal. Neither the issuing State's underlying legal decision nor its expected treatment of the requested person after the surrender are reviewed, as the EAW is based on the principles of mutual recognition of legal decisions[15] and mutual trust in the States' respective legal systems.[16]

For its decision, the executing judicial authority must adhere to a time limit of 60 days from the arrest of the requested person (Article 17(3)). In cases where the requested person consents to their surrender, the time limit is reduced to ten days from the granting of that consent (Article 17(2)). As soon as the executing authority has made its decision, it must inform the issuing judicial authority (Article 22). Reasons must be given in the event of a refusal (Article 17(6)). In case of an affirmative decision, the concerned authorities agree on the earliest possible date for the surrender of the requested person. This should be within the first ten days from the decision (Article 23(1), (2)).

After the requested person has been transferred to the custody of the issuing State, they can be put on trial there or, in cases where the person's surrender was requested for the execution of a sentence already imposed in the issuing State, the sentence can be enforced. If the surrendered person was in custody in the executing State, this time must be deducted from the sentence in the issuing State (Article 26).

The available data shows that the EAW is frequently used in practice. From 2005, when data on the use of the EAW was first collected, to 2021, 236,528 EAWs have been issued; 71,478 of which have been successfully executed.[17] The introduction of the EAW has also led to a significant shortening of the extradition process. While the extradition procedure took, on average, one year under pre-existing extradition regimes,[18] the average time between the arrest of the requested person and the decision on surrender as of 2021 was

14 Cf. *Criminal Proceedings against MM* (Court of Justice of the European Union, C-414/20 PPU, ECLI:EU:C:2021:4, 13 January 2021) [57].

15 Framework Decision, recital 6.

16 Framework Decision, recital 10.

17 Cf. European Commission, *Commission Staff Working Document: Statistics on the practical operation of the European arrest warrant 2021* (SWD(2023) 262 final, 20 July 2023) 54.

18 Wouter van Ballegooij and Ivana Kiendl-Kristo, *European Arrest Warrant: Framework for Analysis and Preliminary Findings on its Implementation* (PE 642.814, European Parliamen-

approximately 54 days.[19] In cases where the requested person consented to their surrender, it was only 20 days.[20]

There is no separate data on the use of the EAW in connection with organised crime cases. Consequently, it is not possible to provide any statistical evidence of how successful the EAW has been in this area. However, it is clear from the general data shown above that the introduction of the EAW has led to much closer cooperation on extradition and the surrender of fugitives in the EU, which addresses a long-standing obstacle in the fight against organised crime.

7.3 Comparison to traditional extradition law

The EAW differs in many respects from established extradition law and procedures. Even though there is no single or universal model of extradition law (extradition is regulated somewhat differently, in different legal sources, and administered differently in different jurisdictions), there are nevertheless some basic principles that can be found in most treaties and national laws on extradition.[21] Not all of the EAW's deviations from these established principles can be discussed here in detail.[22] Rather, the following sections focus on three very prominent differences: (1) the underlying principles of mutual trust and mutual recognition, (2) the partial abolition of the double criminality requirement, and (3) the exclusion of the executive from the extradition/surrender procedure.

7.3.1 Mutual trust and mutual recognition

Several differences between the EAW and traditional extradition law stem from the fact that the European system is based on the principles of mutual trust and mutual recognition. 'Mutual trust' means the trust of EU Member States in each other's legal systems. The existence of this trust is presupposed in recital 10 of the Framework Decision. It is based on the assumption that Member States share the same fundamental values—in particular, the respect for human dignity, human rights, and the rule of law—and that all Member States will equally respect and protect individual rights.[23] One result of this

tary, February 2020) I; Auke Willems, *The Principle of Mutual Trust in EU Criminal Law* (Hart, 2021) 60.

19 European Commission (n 17) 14.

20 Ibid.

21 Geoff Gilbert, *Transnational Fugitive Offenders in International Law—Extradition and other Mechanisms* (Martinus Nijhoff, 1998) 2.

22 For a concise list of all the deviations, see Willems (n 18) 58–59.

23 Tony P Marguery 'Towards the End of Mutual Trust? Prison Conditions in the Context of the European Arrest Warrant and the Transfer of Prisoners Framework Decision' (2018) 25(6) *Maastricht Journal of European and Comparative Law* 704, 707.

mutual trust is the principle of 'mutual recognition', which is considered to be the cornerstone of judicial cooperation within the EU.[24] 'Mutual recognition' means that Member States recognise and, if necessary, enforce the judicial decisions of other Member States 'without many questions being asked'.[25] The decisions of one State are accepted and have effect in the other State, even if that State would have handled the situation differently.[26] In relation to the EAW, this means that surrender takes place without a closer examination of the facts or circumstances in the issuing State. For example, it is, in principle, not examined whether allegations of discrimination are associated with the issuance of the EAW[27] or whether the person sought might be facing human rights violations or violations of the fair trial principle after their surrender. Questions and concerns of this kind are seen as unnecessary and therefore, in most cases, omitted.[28] This level of trust and mutual recognition goes well beyond the standards found in conventional extradition treaties.[29]

7.3.2 Double criminality

A central feature of most extradition laws and treaties is the principle of double (or dual) criminality.[30] Double criminality means that the conduct for which the person is sought is punishable by the law of the requesting State and by the law of the requested State.[31] According to the European Commission's original draft,[32] the double criminality requirement was to be abolished by the

24 Council of the European Union, *Presidency Conclusions, Tampere European Council, 15–16 October 1999*, 16 October 1999 [33]; Framework Decision, recital 6.

25 Valsamis Mitsilegas, 'The Symbiotic Relationship between Mutual Trust and Fundamental Rights in Europe's Area of Criminal Justice' (2015) 6(4) *New Journal of European Criminal Law* 457, 465.

26 Eva-Maria Unger, *Schutzlos ausgeliefert? Der Europäische Haftbefehl—Ein Beispiel für die Missachtung europäischer Bürgerrechte* (Peter Lang, 2005) 91.

27 Recital 12 of the Framework Decision does make clear, however, that '[n]othing in this Framework Decision may be interpreted as prohibiting refusal to surrender a person for whom a European arrest warrant has been issued when there are reasons to believe, on the basis of objective elements, that the said arrest warrant has been issued for the purpose of prosecuting or punishing a person on the grounds of his or her sex, race, religion, ethnic origin, nationality, language, political opinions or sexual orientation, or that that person's position may be prejudiced for any of these reasons'.

28 Daniel Rohlff, *Der Europäische Haftbefehl* (Peter Lang, 2003) 34–35.

29 Ibid., 33–34.

30 Cf. UNODC, *Report of the Informal Expert Working Group on Effective Extradition Casework Practice* (2004) <https://www.unodc.org/pdf/ewg_report_extraditions_2004.pdf> 10 [33]. It is also included as a requirement for extradition in the UN General Assembly, *Model Treaty on Extradition*, UN Doc A/RES/45/116 (14 December 1990) annex, Article 2(1).

31 M Cherif Bassiouni, *International Extradition—United States Law and Practice* (Oxford University Press, 6th ed 2014) 500; Neil Boister, *An Introduction to Transnational Criminal Law* (Oxford University Press, 2nd ed 2018) 359.

32 *Proposal for a Council Framework Decision on the European Arrest Warrant and the Surrender Procedures between the Member States* [2001] OJ C 332 E/305, recital 14.

Framework Decision. The draft merely provided that Member States should be given the possibility to draw up a list of offences with regard to which they would refuse surrender because this would conflict with their fundamental legal principles. This proposal did not make it into the final text. In the end, it was agreed not to abolish the double criminality requirement altogether, but instead diminish its significance.

Under the Framework Decision, double criminality is not a mandatory requirement for extradition, but a lack of double criminality can, in principle, be invoked as a ground for refusal (Article 2(4)). This is at the discretion of the executing State. Double criminality is, however, expressly not required for the offences listed in Article 2(2) of the Framework Decision. For these offences, and as long as they are punishable in the issuing State by a custodial sentence or a detention order for a maximum period of at least three years, criminalisation in the executing State is irrelevant, and the EAW must be executed. Among the offences listed in Article 2(2) are, for instance, those covered by the UNTOC and its additional protocols: participation in a criminal organisation, trafficking in persons, trafficking in firearms and ammunition, corruption, laundering of proceeds of crime, and facilitation of unauthorised entry and residence.

7.3.3 Ministerial level of review

Another major difference between the EAW and traditional extradition law is the fact that the executive is not involved in the issuing or execution of the EAW; this may indeed be the most important difference in procedural terms.[33] Traditionally, the extradition decision is a two-step process, involving, first, a judicial, and, second, an administrative decision. Just which issues are part of the judicial or part of the administrative decision varies from State to State. In general, the judiciary examines whether the legal requirements for extradition are met, whereas the executive decision is of a more political nature.[34]

Article 6 of the Framework Decision, in contrast, assigns the decision-making power exclusively to the 'judicial authorities' in both the issuing and the executing State. The usual division into judicial and political review is thus abolished; instead, the surrender procedure only involves judicial cooperation between the two States.[35] By this, the Commission intended to expedite the

33 Verena Murschetz, 'Das "Übergabe"-Verfahren nach dem Europäischen Haftbefehl im Vergleich mit dem herkömmlichen Auslieferungsverfahren' in Otto Lagodny, Ewald Wiederin, and Roland Winkler (eds), *Probleme des Rahmenbeschlusses am Beispiel des Europäischen Haftbefehls—Ein neues Instrument der europäischen Integration aus Sicht von Europarecht, Strafrecht, Verfassungsrecht und Völkerrecht* (NWV, 2007) 85, 85; Rohlff (n 28) 40.

34 Boister (n 31) 383.

35 Murschetz (n 33) 85.

process and increase its effectiveness.[36] This also fits the principle of mutual recognition enshrined in the EAW, which leaves no room for politically opportune decisions.[37]

In the past, the term 'judicial authority' has been the subject of much debate. In its jurisprudence, the Court of Justice of the European Union (CJEU) stated that while the issuing judicial authority does not have to be a Court and that involvement in the administration of justice would suffice, the authority has to be independent from the executive branch of government.[38] It must be clear that the issuing judicial authority performs its duties objectively and without political influence, and that its decision is not ultimately made by the Executive.[39] In a judgment of 24 November 2020, the CJEU also applied these principles to the executing judicial authority.[40]

7.4 Extradition under the UNTOC

In international law, the UNTOC contains, inter alia, an elaborate framework to enable and facilitate extradition in cases involving organised crime, which also applies to the three protocols supplementing the Convention. Although Article 16 of the UNTOC includes very detailed provisions, its purpose is 'not to set out all the requirements and conditions, but rather to establish a broad legal framework' for extradition.[41] Instead, Article 16 'relies heavily on the domestic laws of the States Parties'.[42] If a State Party seeks extradition of a person from another Party, the extradition process and decision will be primarily determined by extradition treaties, if any, between the States involved and the national law of the requested State.

Article 16 of the UNTOC may serve as a ground for extradition in three scenarios:

36 Commission of the European Union, *Proposal for a Council Framework Decision on the European arrest warrant and the surrender procedures between the Member States—Explanatory Memorandum* (COM(2001) 522 final/2, 25 September 2001) [4.5.4].

37 Rohlff (n 28) 41–42.

38 Cf. *Openbaar Ministerie v Poltorak* (Court of Justice of the European Union, C-452/16 PPU, ECLI:EU:C:2016:858, 10 November 2016) [33], [35]; *Openbaar Ministerie v Kovalkovas* (Court of Justice of the European Union, C-477/16 PPU, ECLI:EU:C:2016:861, 10 November 2016) [34], [36]; *Minister for Justice and Equality v OG and PI (Public Prosecutor's Office in Lübeck and in Zwickau)* (Court of Justice of the European Union, C-508/18 and C-82/19 PPU, ECLI:EU:C:2019:456, 27 May 2019) [50].

39 *Minister for Justice and Equality v OG and PI (Public Prosecutor's Office in Lübeck and in Zwickau)* (Court of Justice of the European Union, C-508/18 and C-82/19 PPU, ECLI:EU:C:2019:456, 27 May 2019) [73].

40 *Criminal Proceedings against AZ (Forgery of Documents)* (Court of Justice of the European Union, C-510/19, ECLI:EU:C:953, 24 November 2020) [40]–[56].

41 Stefano Betti, *The European Union and the United Nations Convention against Transnational Organised Crime*, Working Paper PE 311.427 (European Parliament, 2001) 42.

42 Ibid.

If an extradition treaty exists between the States involved, but the offence for which extradition is requested is not considered an extraditable offence by that treaty, Article 16(3) provides that 'each of the offences to which this article applies shall be deemed to be included as an extraditable offence in any extradition treaty existing between States Parties'.[43]

If no extradition treaty between the requesting and the requested State exists, but the requested State makes extradition conditional on the existence of such a treaty, the UNTOC can serve as the legal basis for extradition (Article 16(4)). Subparagraph (5)(a) obliges States Parties to inform the UN Secretary-General if they will make use of this option.[44]

If no extradition treaty between the requesting and the requested State exists and the States involved do not make extradition conditional on the existence of a treaty, they 'shall recognize offences to which this article applies as extraditable offences between themselves' (Article 16(6)).

The most fundamental difference between Article 16 of the UNTOC and the EU Framework Decision is the obligation to extradite. Although States Parties to the UNTOC are asked (to seek) to conclude new extradition arrangements with other States Parties under Article 16 (5)(b) and (17), they are neither obliged to do so nor are they obliged to grant extradition on the grounds of the UNTOC in cases of paragraph 4.[45] 'Given the very limited number of bilateral and multilateral extradition treaties and the strong reservations of many countries to surrender suspected offenders to foreign jurisdictions', notes Andreas Schloenhardt, it is 'unlikely that Article 16 will find frequent use unless bilateral and multilateral extradition treaties between the two countries already exist'.[46] States Parties may thus refuse extradition without violating the terms of the treaty. If, however, extradition is refused solely on the ground that the person sought is a national of the requested State, Article 16(10) obliges the requested State, if the requesting State so demands, to 'submit the case without undue delay to its competent authorities

43 Article 16 applies to 'the offences covered by this Convention or in cases where an offence referred to in article 3, paragraph 1 (a) or (b), involves an organized criminal group' (Article 16(1) UNTOC). For a critical analysis of this wording, cf. David McClean, *Transnational Organized Crime: A Commentary on the UN Convention and its Protocols* (Oxford University Press, 2007) 177.

44 For the notifications the States Parties have made so far, see United Nations Treaty Collection, Chapter XVIII Penal Matters, 12. United Nations Convention against Transnational Organized Crime (United Nations, Treaty Section) <treaties.un.org/pages/ViewDetails.aspx?src=TREATY&mtdsg_no=XVIII-12&chapter=18&clang=_en>.

45 For an overview of the nature of the UNTOC's different provisions, cf. Patrick M Pintaske, *Das Palermo-Übereinkommen und sein Einfluss auf das deutsche Strafrecht: Eine Untersuchung der UN-Konvention gegen grenzüberschreitende organisierte Kriminalität und ihrer Zusatzprotokolle* (Universitätsverlag Osnabrück, 2014) 71–77.

46 Andreas Schloenhardt, 'Transnational Organised Crime and International Law: The Palermo Convention' (2005) 29(6) *Criminal Law Journal* 340, 350.

for the purpose of prosecution'. This corresponds to the aut dedere aut judicare (extradite or prosecute) principle.[47]

Compared to the Framework Decision, Article 16 contains few specifications regarding the conditions of extradition. Article 16(1) stipulates that the offence for which extradition is sought must be 'punishable under the domestic law of both the requesting State Party and the requested State Party', thus restating the double criminality requirement. Article 16(15) states that Parties 'may not refuse a request for extradition on the sole ground that the offence is also considered to involve fiscal matters'. Apart from this, States are largely free to determine the conditions of extradition in their domestic laws and in separate treaties (Article 16(7)). Regarding the extradition procedure, States Parties are asked to expedite the proceedings in their national law and to simplify evidentiary requirements (Article 16(8)). The only specific obligations Article 16 imposes on the Parties with regard to the conduct of the proceedings are the duties to treat the person concerned fairly at all stages of the procedure and to grant them all the rights to which they are entitled under the State's domestic law (Article 16(13)), and the duty to, where appropriate, contact the requesting State and give it the opportunity to state its opinion and provide more information before refusing an extradition request (Article 16(16)).

It is difficult to comment on the uptake of Article 16 in practice and its use as a legal basis in actual extradition cases. A *Digest of Cases of International Cooperation in Criminal Matters Involving the United Nations Convention against Transnational Organized Crime as a Legal Basis* published by the United Nations Office on Drugs and Crime (UNODC) in 2021 identified 16 confirmed cases of successful or attempted extraditions between States Parties based solely on the UNTOC, in addition to 20 cases where extradition was based on the UNTOC together with other (regional) treaties. The Digest acknowledges that this is not the full record and number of cases and that no statistics are kept on the use of the UNTOC in this (and other) contexts.[48]

Given the diversity of States and legal systems that are Parties to the UNTOC, the legal and practical obstacles of extradition, and the lack of mutual trust and recognition between States Parties, it can, however, be safely

47 Article 16(10) does not impose a strict obligation to extradite or prosecute, but merely obliges States Parties to submit the case to their prosecution authorities, which then examine it and may prosecute. Cf. Banuelos Mejía, 'The United Nations Convention against Transnational Organized Crime 20 Years from Its Adoption: Strengths, Achievements and Challenges Ahead' in Serena Forlati (ed), *The Palermo Convention at Twenty—Institutional and Substantive Challenges* (Brill, 2021) 3, 10. For more information on the principle in general, see M Cherif Bassiouni and Edward M Wise, *Aut Dedere, Aut Judicare: The Duty to Extradite or Prosecute in International Law* (Martinus Nijhoff, 1995).

48 UNODC, *Digest of Cases of International Cooperation in Criminal Matters Involving the United Nations Convention against Transnational Organized Crime as a Legal Basis* (UNODC, 2021), 12, 128–158.

assumed that extradition under the UNTOC and other transnational criminal law treaties occurs far less frequently than within the EU on the basis of the EAW. This is despite the fact that the requirements of Article 16 are much more rudimentary than those of the EAW and provide much greater leeway to States and their national sovereignty. Since nearly 25 years have passed since the adoption of the UNTOC in the year 2000, it remains doubtful whether Article 16 will ever be used to its full potential and whether it can address the gaps and obstacles in extradition practice in organised crime cases. This then begs the question of whether new and more comprehensive mechanisms, such as the EAW, may be needed and suitable to fight organised crime at the global level.

7.5 From Europe to the world: a model for future extradition agreements at the global level?

The legal analysis and practical experience outlined above demonstrates that the EAW greatly simplifies and accelerates extradition proceedings between EU Member States. Outside the EU, no comparable mechanism exists. At first glance, a global extradition arrangement similar to the EAW—a 'global arrest warrant' system—thus seems appealing, especially as a much-needed tool to fight organised crime.

It remains, however, questionable whether the introduction of such a global instrument would be feasible in practice and whether it would entail too many risks. The three most striking deviations of the EAW from traditional extradition law are examined more closely in the following sections in order to determine whether a transfer of the idea and ingredients of the EAW to the global level is both feasible and desirable. The following reflections are generally made with the scope, offences, and Parties of UNTOC and its Protocols in mind, in the sense that a 'global arrest warrant system' would be complementary to this existing international regime.

7.5.1 The problem with mutual trust

As explained earlier, mutual recognition refers to the recognition of legal decisions of one State by another even though this may differ from what would have been decided in that State in a comparable situation. This represents a renouncement of the strict sovereignty principle that characterises traditional extradition law, in particular, the assumption that the State's own legal system always provides the best guarantee for the conduct of fair proceedings.[49] This assumption is the source of many obstacles in extradition proceedings, and includes by extension the double criminality requirement. Such duality

49 Thomas Weigend, 'Grundsätze und Probleme des deutschen Auslieferungsrechts' [2000] *Juristische Schulung* 105, 110.

requirements make the extradition process slow and bureaucratic and carry the risk that extradition requests may fail.

Evidently, the principle of mutual recognition greatly reduces these obstacles. Its consistent enforcement is linked to two key points: (1) For interstate cooperation, it is not mandatory that the legal system and its practical application meet the same standards in the involved States, but only that a minimum standard of rule of law and human rights guarantees is met in both States. (2) If it can safely and generally be assumed that the other State complies with these minimum standards, then its decisions in the specific case need not and may not be questioned and reviewed.[50] Mutual recognition presupposes mutual trust as to the compliance with these standards. If foreign decisions are recognised without question and review, the entire responsibility for the legitimacy of the extradition proceedings rests with the requesting State.[51] Extradition arrangements based on the principle of mutual recognition thus require extensive mutual trust between all participating States.

Such trust, and some desistance from the prerogative of national sovereignty, emerges more easily between States that share close and long-standing cultural, economic, and political ties[52] and similar legal cultures and traditions.[53] Herein lies the first and principal problem of closer international cooperation in criminal justice matters at the supra-regional and global levels: The more States Parties, the greater the diversity of legal systems and political cultures between them. This is evident in the case of the UNTOC, which presently brings together 192 Parties from around the world, rather than just 27 States covered by the Framework Decision that governs the EAW. The similarity in legal cultures and political systems which provides the mutual trust basis for the EAW among EU Member States is lacking at the global level to enable a worldwide arrest warrant treaty.

A different foundation of mutual trust could be, however, the firm commitment to human rights and civil liberties, along with the associated procedural fairness, transparency, and accountability. Within the EU, mutual trust, as presupposed in recital 10 of the Framework Decision, is based, above all, on the Member States' shared commitment to the values listed in Article 2 of the *Treaty on the European Union*[54] (including respect for human dignity, freedom, equality, the rule of law, respect for human rights) and their ratification of and compliance with the *European Convention on Human Rights* (ECHR).[55]

50 Mitsilegas (n 25) 472.
51 Rohlff (n 28) 66.
52 Ibid., 33.
53 Weigend (n 49) 110.
54 *Consolidated Version of the Treaty on European Union* [2012] OJ C 326/13.
55 Susie Alegre and Marisa Leaf, 'Mutual Recognition in European Judicial Cooperation: A Step Too Far Too Soon? Case Study—the European Arrest Warrant' (2004) 10(2) *European Law Journal* 200, 201; Marguery (n 23) 707; Rohlff (n 28) 34–35; Willems (n 18) 64.

The same cannot be said about the 192 States Parties of the UNTOC. Although many of them are Parties to regional human rights treaties in Europe, the Americas, Africa, or the Arab region, and/or have signed international human rights law treaties, chief among them the *International Covenant on Civil and Political Rights*,[56] the standards set by these treaties differ greatly, as does the commitment by their Parties to implement, enforce, and adhere to them. Suspicion, rather than trust, is warranted in this environment and mutual recognition of judicial, legal, and administrative decisions is a distant illusion.

Even within the EU, some scholars doubt that mutual trust between Member States truly exists. For example, it has been said that intergovernmental trust in the application of laws that sufficiently protect the rights of the person concerned is only weakly developed in the EU, especially since the expansion to include Eastern European States.[57] The assumption that all Member States will abide by the obligations to which they have signed up has been called 'questionable, if not naïve',[58] especially given the large number of judgments against various Member States by the European Court of Human Rights (ECtHR). Others have called the presumed mutual trust no more than a 'legal fiction'.[59] Indeed, the EU itself has adopted measures to address Member States' lack of trust in each other.[60]

Despite these recognised problems, the CJEU initially upheld the principle of mutual recognition as recognised in the Framework Decision. In various judgments, the Court affirmed that the execution of the EAW could, in fact, be refused solely on the grounds expressly set out in Articles 3, 4, and 4a of the Framework Decision.[61]

The Court has since moved away from this approach. In its more recent case law, it 'raised the thresholds' for the execution of an EAW.[62] In 2016

56 Opened for signature 16 December 1966, 999 UNTS 171 (entry into force 23 March 1976).

57 Eckhart von Bubnoff, *Der Europäische Haftbefehl—Ein Leitfaden für die Auslieferungspraxis* (C.F. Müller, 2005) 51.

58 Nicola Vennemann, 'The European Arrest Warrant and Its Human Rights Implications' (2003) 63 *Zeitschrift für ausländisches öffentliches Recht und Völkerrecht* 103, 118; cf. Alegre and Leaf (n 55) 201.

59 Marguery (n 23) 705.

60 For example, *The Hague Programme: Strengthening Freedom, Security and Justice in the European Union* [2005] OJ C 53/1; *The Stockholm Programme—An Open and Secure Europe Serving and Protecting Citizens* [2010] OJ C115/1; European Commission, *Strengthening mutual trust in the European judicial area—A Green paper on the application of EU criminal justice legislation in the field of detention* (COM(2011) 327 final (14 June 2011)).

61 Cf. *Ministerul Public v Radu* (Court of Justice of the European Union, C-396/11, ECLI:EU:C:2013:39, 29 January 2013) [36]; *Criminal Proceedings against Stefano Melloni* (Court of Justice of the European Union, C-399/11, ECLI:EU:C:2013:107, 26 February 2013) [63].

62 André Klip, 'The European Arrest Warrant, from Mutual Recognition to Mutual Supervision?' (2022) 12(1) *European Criminal Law Review* 82, 82.

and again in 2018, the CJEU faced two cases in which one Member State wanted to refuse the execution of an EAW on the basis of the human rights and rule of law standards in the issuing State. In *Aranyosi and Caldararu* (2016), Germany sought to refuse the surrender of requested persons to the issuing States (Hungary and Romania) because the ECtHR had previously found these States to be in violation of, inter alia, Article 3 of the ECHR (prohibition of torture) by reason of their overcrowded prisons.[63] Germany feared imminent human rights violations in the event of a transfer and referred to the CJEU the question of whether it was possible to refuse to execute the EAW on this background. Similarly, in *LM* (2018), Ireland asked the CJEU whether it was permissible to refuse to execute EAWs if it was feared that the requested person would not receive due process of law in the issuing State, in this case Poland.[64] In these cases the Court held that if there are serious suspicions that the issuing State would not respect human rights or the rule of law in the specific circumstances, this had to be carefully examined by the executing State and, in case of doubt, the EAW does not have to be executed.[65]

With these judgments, the CJEU confirms that efficiency in extradition and prosecution must not come at the expense of fundamental human rights or rule of law guarantees. The cases also demonstrate that mutual trust between EU Members is not absolute when it comes to the observance of fundamental human rights and the rule of law. Indeed, the CJEU seems to acknowledge that mistrust may be justified in some circumstances.

It thus appears that what follows is that neither geographical proximity, nor a shared legal culture and a commitment to human rights have led the EU Member States to trust each other just enough to fully adopt the principle of mutual recognition. In light of the so-called European 'rule of law crisis',[66] no improvement on this matter can be expected in the near future.

This then also begs the question: If the principles of mutual trust and mutual recognition already do not fully work in the current EU conditions—which compare favourably to the rest of the world—how could an integrated global arrest warrant system involving many more and more diverse States ever become operational? In a world where, sadly, torture in prisons and disappearances and deaths of detainees are a reality, mutual trust and mutual recognition as envisioned by the EAW remain unthinkable.

63 *Aranyosi and Caldararu* (Court of Justice of the European Union, C-404/15 and C-659/15 PPU, ECLI:EU:C:2016:198, 5 April 2016).

64 *LM (Deficiencies in the system of justice)* (Court of Justice of the European Union, C-216/18 PPU, ECLI:EU:C:2018:586, 25 July 2018).

65 Ibid., [73]–[79]; *Aranyosi and Caldararu* (n 63) [104].

66 Cf. Luuk van Middelaar, 'Europe's Existential Crisis', *Politico* (10 December 2020) <www.politico.eu/article/europe-existential-crisis-rule-of-law-hungary-poland/>; Steven Erlanger and Monika Panczuk, 'E.U. Slams Poland and Hungary on Rule of Law, but to Little Effect', *New York Times* (20 July 2021, updated 26 October 2021) <www.nytimes.com/2021/07/20/world/europe/eu-poland-hungary-rule-of-law.html>.

7.5.2 The problem with double criminality

Double criminality, as mentioned, requires criminalisation in both the requesting and requested State before extradition can be considered. This requirement can be interpreted in different ways. A broad interpretation suggests that the requirement is met when the conduct of which the requested person is accused falls under any offence in the requested State.[67] A slightly narrower approach taken by some States requires that the relevant offences in the requesting and the requested State, at a minimum, protect the same legal interest or fall into the same category of offences.[68] Narrower still is the requirement that the offences have to be largely identical or at least very similar, and that all of their preconditions are met. Some States also take into account factors such as justifications and excuses, statutes of limitations, amnesties, etc., applicable in the specific case.[69]

While some international conventions prescribe how the double criminality requirement is to be interpreted, the UNTOC contains no such guidance.[70] Rather, States Parties determine under their own existing extradition treaties or national laws how widely or narrowly they interpret this requirement and what criteria need to be met. Stefano Betti thus fears that the double criminality requirement of the UNTOC could become a 'mere pretext to get around the obligations posed by the Palermo Convention'.[71] Seen this way, it seems attractive to abolish the double criminality requirement within the framework of a global extradition treaty or at least to set a very low threshold. However, whether this is desirable and feasible is a separate question.

Two main arguments could be put forward in support of the double criminality requirement: first, the principle of legality would not permit States to enter into an extradition treaty under which they have to extradite persons for conduct that is not punishable under their own law; second, given the serious restrictions extradition inflicts on the rights of the person concerned, there would be no justifiable reason for a State to enable the prosecution abroad of conduct which from its perspective does not constitute a wrong worthy of sanctioning.

67 See, for example, UN General Assembly, *Model Treaty on Extradition*, UN Doc A/RES/45/116 (14 December 1990), Article 2(2).

68 This approach is taken in US law, cf. Bassiouni (n 31) 506.

69 This is often called 'double criminality in concreto', cf. Shneuer-Zalman Feller, 'The Significance of the Requirement of Double Criminality in the Law of Extradition—*Steven Ivan Ross v. State of Israel*' (1975) 10(1) *Israel Law Review* 51, 71; Michal Plachta, 'The Role of Double Criminality in International Cooperation in Penal Matters' (1989) 76(5) *Nordisk Tidsskrift for Kriminalvidenskrab* 84, 109.

70 Cf. McClean (n 43) 177–178.

71 Stefano Betti, 'New Prospects for Inter-state Co-operation in Criminal Matters: The Palermo Convention' (2003) 3(2) *International Criminal Law Review* 151, 162.

The principle of legality is anchored in the constitutions of many States and also recognised in international law.[72] It holds that a person can only be punished or prosecuted for conduct that, at the time of the Commission, is criminalised by law (*nullum crimen sine lege, nulla poena sine lege*).[73] Due to the principle of legality, extradition may not take place in cases where the conduct in question is not punishable in the requesting State. It is more difficult, however, in cases where the act is not punishable in the requested State. May a State enter into an extradition treaty which permits or even requires extradition in these circumstances, or does the principle of legality prohibit this? On the one hand, it can be argued that, strictly speaking, extradition as such does not constitute punishment and does not constitute a criminal prosecution by and in the requested State. Therefore, the principle of legality would not stand in the way of granting extradition.[74] On the other hand, this view seems rather simplistic. Extradition takes place for the purpose of enabling prosecution or the execution of a sentence in the requesting State. It is a 'help-procedure' within the criminal process and associated with restrictions on human rights.[75] From the perspective of the rule of law, it therefore does not seem appropriate to reject the applicability of the *nulla poena*-principle with the purely formal argument that extradition as such does not constitute punishment in and of itself. The deciding factor should rather be whether the rationale behind the principle of legality is violated if extradition for an act that is not punishable in the extraditing (requested) State is granted.

The principle of legality is intended to offer predictability and legal certainty. People should be able to adapt their behaviour accordingly, knowing what the consequences of doing otherwise would be.[76] This means that if persons choose to act in ways that they have no reason to believe could be prohibited or punishable, they should be able to do so without fear of later being prosecuted for this behaviour. It also means, in turn, that if persons know or could have known that their conduct is punishable and nevertheless chose to engage in that conduct, they may be extradited to the State where that conduct took place. The principle of legality is not intended to protect persons from prosecution and extradition who flee from a jurisdiction where

72 Gerhard Werle and Florian Jeßberger, *Principles of International Criminal Law* (Oxford University Press, 4th ed, 2020) 48.

73 Ibid., 48–49.

74 Joachim Vogel, 'Abschaffung der Auslieferung? Kritische Anmerkungen zur Reform des Auslieferungsrechts in der Europäischen Union' (2001) 56(19) *Juristenzeitung* 937, 942.

75 Van Sliedregt (n 13) 53.

76 Van Sliedregt (n 13) at 60 argues that foreseeability might be difficult regarding foreign law and therefore is only guaranteed by double criminality. Here, however, a distinction must be made: If foreseeability is not given because the foreign law is not sufficiently determined, the principle of legality is already not adequately observed by the requesting State and extradition can therefore be refused. If, on the other hand, the criminal liability was unforeseeable only for the specific person to be extradited (e.g. due to language barriers), then in my opinion this is not a problem of the principle of legality, but a possible excuse.

they consciously 'broke the law' to a place where their conduct is not criminalised.[77] For this reason, the principle of legality, without more, does not prohibit States from concluding extradition treaties with no double criminality requirement.

It is a separate question whether, from a human rights perspective, it is permissible for one State to support another in the prosecution of an act, which is not an offence under the first State's laws.[78] Extradition generally severely encroaches on the rights of the person concerned, not least because it is often preceded by detention in the requested State while the extradition request is still pending. Lech Gardocki notes that it would be 'very difficult' for the requested State to convey to the person concerned that the person may be arrested and extradited 'because the requested [S]tate, though not criminalizing the alleged act, was simply interested in maintaining good relations with the requesting [S]tate'.[79] In this context, double criminality seems to be an essential requirement to protect basic human rights and civil liberties.

Indeed, if the double criminality requirement was removed entirely from extradition law, this could severely compromise human rights in a range of situations. This would be the case, for instance, where one State requests extradition to prosecute a person for 'homosexual acts'. Here, the double criminality requirement can serve to protect fundamental human rights. However, it is not the lack of double criminality that is the decisive factor in such cases—although this requirement may appear to be an easy way to refuse an extradition request.[80] Instead, the important point here is whether prosecution and punishment of the conduct would be compatible with fundamental human rights. To address this issue, it may be more suitable to include a human rights-related ground of refusal in extradition treaties.

It must be noted at this point that these concerns go far beyond the limited scope of and concerns associated with the extradition provisions found in Article 16 of the UNTOC. Their application is limited to the offences established pursuant to the Convention and its Protocols. Given the large number of States Parties to these treaties around the world, it is rather unlikely that any of their core offences are not criminalised or are not considered punishable in one of the requesting and requested States. In other words, a lack of double criminality is less likely to arise except, perhaps, in cases involving one or more States that have thus far failed to comply with the criminalisation obligations under the UNTOC and its Protocols, or in situations where that

77 See also Harmen van der Wilt, *The Law and Practice of Extradition* (Routledge, 2022) 27–28.

78 Cf. Unger (n 26) 39–41.

79 Lech Gardocki, 'Double Criminality in Extradition Law' (1993) 27(1–2) *Israel Law Review* 288, 295.

80 Bert AHJ Swart, 'Human Rights and the Abolition of Traditional Principles' in Albin Eser and Otto Lagodny (eds), *Principles and Procedures for a New Transnational Criminal Law: Documentation of an International Workshop in Freiburg, May 1991* (Eigenverlag des Max-Planck-Instituts, 1992) 505, 521.

criminalisation departs substantially from the design and spirit of the treaty provisions (and where one State prefers a very narrow interpretation of double criminality). Neither could be attributed to the fact that the States have not recognised the conduct at issue as worthy of criminalisation, and therefore should not prevent them from extraditing. In the author's opinion, the double criminality requirement could therefore be waived within a global extradition treaty, provided that the treaty's scope of application is limited to offences that a large number of States have already committed themselves to criminalising in other international treaties, such as the UNTOC and its protocols.

It is, however, questionable whether this would be politically feasible. During the negotiations on the EAW, double criminality was one of the most controversial topics, so much so that the negotiations nearly collapsed on this point.[81] Similarly, during the drafting of the UNTOC, the double criminality requirement was the subject of debate, and after earlier drafts did not contain the requirement, it was later included.[82] As the double criminality requirement has shown to be a controversial issue in both contexts, it seems unlikely that its abolition would be politically feasible even with regard to extradition treaties with a limited scope of application.

7.5.3 The problem with ministerial review

The EU's decision to make the EAW a purely judicial procedure was aimed at speeding up and simplifying the extradition process.[83] Diplomatic considerations of public authorities (the Executive) were seen as the main factor delaying extradition proceedings and were thus excluded from the EAW process.[84] Based on the information provided above, it appears that this aim has been accomplished.

Even beyond the argument of speed, on the surface, it seems sensible and appealing to exclude (or as far as possible limit) policy and political considerations from extradition decisions. The extradition cases involving Messrs Assange, Puigdemont, and the late Pinochet best illustrate how politics and policies can both cause and complicate extradition proceedings. One way to de-politicise the extradition process is to remove ministerial review and discretion from that process. However, it is hardly possible to make general statements about what consequences it would have to remove the executive from the extradition process. In some States the Executive examines exclusively

81 Rohlff (n 28) 83.

82 UN General Assembly, Ad Hoc Committee on the Elaboration of a Convention against Transnational Organized Crime, *Revised Draft United Nations Convention against Transnational Organized Crime*, UN Doc A/AC.254/4/Rev. 8 (7 April 2000) 14 fn 40.

83 Commission of the European Union, Proposal for a Council Framework Decision on the European Arrest Warrant and the Surrender Procedures between the Member States—Explanatory Memorandum (COM(2001) 522 final/2, 25 September 2001 [4.5.4]).

84 Cf. Rohlff (n 28) 41.

aspects of state policy. Here, the elimination of ministerial review represents a pure de-politicisation of the proceedings. In other States, however, the executive may be the only body to examine the human rights and rule of law situation in the requesting State.[85] Here, excluding the executive branch from the extradition process without substitution would come at the expense of human rights protection. If there is insufficient mutual trust between States in the overall compliance with human rights and rule of law standards, there must necessarily be some mechanism to check and ensure this compliance in the specific case before extradition can be granted.

Whether the executive branch of government is best suited for this task remains debatable, especially if it is preoccupied with diplomatic (and perhaps economic, military, or other) considerations. In most States there is no judicial way for the requesting State to enforce an extradition request.[86] For the most part, it has to rely on the exercise of diplomatic pressure to defend its interests against those of the requested State.[87] If the requesting State does not have many diplomatic means of pressure at its disposal, or if the interests of a more powerful third State are also involved, it is possible that even a justified and reasonable extradition request may come to nothing. Likewise, if the requesting State has a strong diplomatic influence on the requested State, there is a risk that extradition may be granted that would not have been granted under other, less politically charged circumstances.

In sum, if foreign policy considerations play an overly prominent role in extradition proceedings, this can be problematic for both the person to be extradited and the requesting State. To prevent politicisation, extradition proceedings should be placed entirely in the hands of the courts, which, at least in principle, should be free from political interference and base their decisions purely on the application and interpretation of the current law. This must, however, also include an inquiry into the human rights and rule of law standards of the requesting State, both in general and in the particular case.

It remains highly questionable, though, whether it is feasible to propose that, like the EAW, extradition proceedings for organised crime offences under an international treaty such as the UNTOC could be conducted solely between judicial authorities and with no involvement of the executive branch of government.

Although the crimes covered by the UNTOC are not political offences, the problems described above may nevertheless arise here due to general foreign policy considerations. For this reason, from a practical point of view, a

85 This is the case, for instance, in the USA, cf. Bassiouni (n 31) 632–633.

86 Exceptions include, for instance, Italy, Spain, and the UK; cf. William Julie, Sophie Menegon, and Juliette Fauvarque, 'From a Political to a Judicial Approach to Extradition: A Case for the Consolidation of the Requesting State's Rights in Domestic Extradition Procedures' (2021) 12(3) *New Journal of European Criminal Law* 464, 467–468.

87 Ibid., 466.

reduction or abolition of ministerial review may be desirable but appears too difficult to implement and enforce. The history, interpretation, and use of the UNTOC demonstrates that there are, rightly or wrongly, many political considerations, agendas, and sensitivities associated with the topic of organised crime. Furthermore, among the large number of Parties to the UNTOC are many States with difficult, if not hostile, relations, between which simple, de-politicised extradition proceedings are inconceivable. At least in the current global political situation, extradition without the involvement of the executive branch of government, as practiced by the EAW, is not a feasible suggestion.

7.6 Conclusion

At first sight, it seems very tempting to promote and develop global extradition frameworks that mirror the system set up among EU Member States with the EAW; a system that within a relatively short time has proven to be fast and efficient. This experience begs the question of whether such a model can be used globally to further advance the fight against transnational organised crime, perhaps as part of or complementary to the extradition procedures set out in Article 16 of the UNTOC.

This chapter has, however, shown that there are significant obstacles to this idea and that, in sum, a global extradition mechanism similar to the EAW may neither be suitable nor feasible from the supra-regional level. There is, at present, little hope and support for an automatic surrender procedure and a global arrest warrant of an EAW-style, even if such a mechanism would be limited to organised crime-related offences only, such as those covered under the UNTOC and its Protocols. A lack of mutual trust, problems associated with the double criminality requirement, and various arguments relating to the involvement of the executive branch of government in extradition proceedings have been identified as some of the greatest of many hurdles.

Although a 'GAW', a global arrest warrant, seems to be distant and fanciful, the discussion in this chapter leads to two further suggestions. First, the practical and political problems associated with conventional extradition treaties are long-standing, and organised criminal groups benefit greatly from the well-documented gaps and obstacles in international criminal justice cooperation, including extradition. In the quest to prevent and suppress transnational organised crime, more needs to be done to speed up and simplify extradition proceedings, and the EAW provides some new and innovative elements worthy of further consideration and analysis. Second, the EAW model may be suitable for adoption by other regional organisations and at the bilateral level. Further research is needed to examine where and how this may be feasible, always taking into account relevant human rights considerations.

8 Joint Investigation Teams in transnational organised crime cases and their potential impact on human rights

Marilù Porchia

8.1 Introduction

Transnational organised crime is a global phenomenon that can have severe implications for States, economies, and individuals. Given its cross-border nature, States cannot on their own effectively prevent and combat such crime. For this reason, States are strengthening their cooperation to provide better operational responses and involve competent authorities from multiple jurisdictions in the investigation and prosecution.[1]

Joint investigations are one way to maximise direct personal contacts between law enforcement authorities of multiple States[2] and are widely seen as an important step to enhance the capacity to investigate and prosecute transnational organised crime.[3] According to some experts, joint investigations constitute one of the most promising forms of international cooperation, offering the possibility to share an investigative approach of the criminal phenomenon under investigation.[4]

In international law, references to joint investigations can be found in several global and regional treaties. The origin can be traced to Article 9(1)(c) of the *Convention against Illicit Traffic in Narcotic Drugs and Psychotropic*

1 Guido Colaiacovo, 'Nuove prospettive in tema di coordinamento delle indagini e cooperazione giudiziaria alla luce della disciplina delle squadre investigative comuni' (2017) 1 *Diritto penale contemporaneo* 169, 173; Fulvia Staiano, *Transnational Organized Crime: Challenging International Law Principles on State Jurisdiction* (Elgar, 2022) 14.

2 Andreas Schloenhardt, 'UNTOC Article 19: Joint Investigations', in Andreas Schloenhardt et al. (eds), *UN Convention against Transnational Organized Crime: A Commentary* (Oxford University Press, 2023) 217, 217.

3 UN, Conference of the Parties to the United Nations Convention against Transnational Organized Crime, Working Group on International Cooperation, *The Use and Role of Joint Investigative Bodies in Combating Transnational Organized Crime*, UN Doc CTOC/COP.WG.3/2020/2 (12 May 2020) 1 (hereafter 'CTOC/COP.WG.3/2020/2').

4 Gianluca Varraso, 'Ordine europeo di indagine penale e squadre investigative comuni' in Anna Maria Maugeri (ed), *Stati generali della lotta alle mafie tavolo XV—'Mafie e Europa'* (Diritto Penale Contemporaneo, 2019) 181–202.

DOI: 10.4324/9781003519317-10

Substances of 1988.[5] The concept was further developed in Article 19 of the *United Nations Convention against Transnational Organized Crime* (*UNTOC*),[6] which is replicated in Article 49 of the *United Nations Convention against Corruption* (*UNCAC*).[7] At the regional European level, provisions can be found in Article 20 of the *Second Additional Protocol to the European Convention on Mutual Assistance in Criminal Matters* of 2001,[8] and in Article 27 of the *Convention on Police Cooperation in South East Europe*, and the *Police Cooperation Convention for Southeast Europe*.[9] The European Union's (EU) legal framework establishing Joint Investigation Teams (JITs) between Member States consists of Article 13 of the *European Union Convention on Mutual Assistance in Criminal Matters*,[10] and the Council Framework Decision of 13 June 2002 on Joint Investigation Teams.[11]

Although the most comprehensive guidance on the establishment and operation of JITs is offered by the Council of Europe and EU instruments, in line with the theme of the present volume, the focus of this chapter is on the UNTOC provisions since it suggests the use of JITs specifically for the purpose of investigating organised crime; the other instruments do not make this express connection.

While some view joint investigations and other forms of international cooperation as the panacea to fight organised crime, others have expressed concerns over the 'overall moribund level of protection' of human rights in transnational criminal law instruments.[12] It has been argued that, at best, these treaties require States Parties to adhere to their pre-existing international human rights law obligations when engaging in cross-border criminal cooperation.[13] The UNTOC, however, was drafted when the awareness of the need to address human rights issues within the sphere of international cooperation in criminal matters was growing.[14] Consequently, the UNTOC

5 Opened for signature 20 December 1988, 1582 UNTS 95 (entry into force 11 November 1990).
6 Opened for signature 15 November 2000, 2225 UNTS 209 (entry into force 29 September 2003).
7 Opened for signature 31 October 2003, 2349 UNTS 41 (entry into force 14 December 2005).
8 Done at Strasbourg 8 November 2001, ETS 182.
9 Done at Vienna, 5 May 2006.
10 [2000] OJ L 197/01.
11 [2002] OJ L 300.
12 Robert J Currie, 'The Protection of Human Rights in the Suppression of Transnational Crime', in Neil Boister and Robert J Currie (eds), *Routledge Handbook of Transnational Criminal Law* (Routledge, 2015) 27, 34.
13 Robert J. Currie and Sarah Douglas, 'Human Rights and the Policing of Transnational Organized Crime' in Felia Allum and Stan Gilmour (eds), *Routledge Handbook of Transnational Organized Crime* (Routledge, 2nd ed 2021) 388–408, 392.
14 UNODC, *The United Nations Convention against Transnational Organized Crime and International Human Rights Law*, Issue Paper (UNODC, 2022) 11.

contains numerous instances where the imperative of upholding human rights is expressly acknowledged.[15]

Nevertheless, joint investigations involve a high risk of creating gaps in or encroaching on the protection of fundamental human rights and civil liberties. The purpose of this chapter is to identify these issues and shed light on aspects of cooperation that may unjustifiably undermine internationally protected human rights in the investigation of transnational organised crime. Ultimately, this chapter attempts to make some recommendations that assist in preventing human rights violations that may occur during the various stages of a joint investigation.

8.2 Structure, content, and scope of Article 19 UNTOC

Under Article 19 of the UNTOC:

> States Parties shall consider concluding bilateral or multilateral agreements or arrangements whereby, in relation to matters that are the subject of investigations, prosecutions or judicial proceedings in one or more States, the competent authorities concerned may establish joint investigative bodies. In the absence of such agreements or arrangements, joint investigations may be undertaken by agreement on a case-by-case basis. The States Parties involved shall ensure that the sovereignty of the State Party in whose territory such investigation is to take place is fully respected.

Although the UNTOC entered into force more than 20 years ago, it is only recently that its utility in transnational criminal investigations has started to be acknowledged and its wider use for this purpose explored.[16] When the UNTOC was adopted in 2000, some States feared that its call for comprehensive law enforcement cooperation could foster cooperation between investigative authorities at the expense of greater judicial cooperation.[17]

Recent times have seen growing interest in and an increased willingness to use the law enforcement cooperation tools under the UNTOC, of which joint investigations are the most far-reaching. Article 19, however, offers little guidance and contains no detailed regulations concerning the setting up and

15 UNTOC, Articles 11(3), 12 (8), 13(8), 16(13), 24(2), and 25(2).

16 Neil Boister 'The Cooperation Provisions of the UN Convention against Transnational Organised Crime: A "Toolbox" Rarely Used?' (2016) 16(1) *International Criminal Law Review* 39, 39.

17 Ibid., citing Hans-Jörg Albrecht, 'Introduction' in Hans-Jörg Albrecht and Cyrille Fijnaut (eds), *The Containment of Transnational Organised Crime: Comments on the UN Convention of December 2000*, (Edition Iuscrim, 2002) 17–18. For the negotiating history of Article 19, see Schloenhardt (n 2) 221–222.

operation of joint investigations.[18] States Parties have full discretion whether to implement laws and regulations on joint investigations and, if they do, how to design them.[19]

8.2.1 Scope and conditions

Article 19 stipulates that States Parties may conclude multilateral or bilateral agreements or arrangements 'in relation to matters that are the subject of investigations, prosecutions or judicial proceedings in one or more State'. This allows for one State Party to engage in joint investigations with another, even if there are no prosecutions pending in either of the two States; joint investigations may be instigated at any stage of the criminal proceedings.[20]

Some of the international and regional multilateral agreements with provisions on joint investigations have already been identified in the introduction to this chapter. Examples of bilateral agreements with provisions on joint investigations mostly involve States in close geographic proximity or with close historical ties, such as Italy and Switzerland,[21] Italy and Albania,[22] Spain and Cape Verde,[23] and Spain and Colombia.[24]

In addition to or in lieu of agreements and arrangements, Article 19 of the UNTOC encourages States Parties to set up joint investigations on a case-by-case basis. Some States have a legal basis for joint investigations in their national laws, such as criminal procedure legislation. Elsewhere, it can be found in standard operating procedures or as part of long-standing cooperation practices. In States where domestic laws or other rules do not already permit joint investigations, this provision can serve as a source of legal authority

18 Mark Mackarel, 'Procedural Aspects of the Convention against Transnational Organized Crime', in Hans-Jörg Albrecht and Cyrille Fijnaut (eds), *The Containment of Transnational Organised Crime: Comments on the UN Convention of December 2000* (Edition Iuscrim 2002) 145, 153.

19 Cf. UNODC, *Digest of Cases of International Cooperation in Criminal Matters Involving the United Nations Convention Against Transnational Organized Crime as a Legal Basis* (UNODC, 2021) 57.

20 CTOC/COP.WG.3/2020/2 (n 3) [11]–[15].

21 *Accordo tra la Svizzera e l'Italia che completa la Convenzione europea di assistenza giudiziaria in materia penale del 20 aprile 1959 e ne agevola l'applicazione*, signed 10 September 1998, RU 2003 2005 (entry into force 1 June 2003) Article XXI.

22 *Accordo tra la Repubblica italiana e la Repubblica di Albania, aggiuntivo alla Convenzione europea di estradizione del 1957 ed alla Convenzione europea di assistenza giudiziaria in materia penale del 1959*, signed 3 December 2007, OJ (entry into force 7 July 2011) Article X.

23 *Convenio entre el Reino de España y la República de Cabo Verde relativo a la asistencia judicial en materia penal, hecho ad referendum*, signed 20 March 2007, [2009] BOE 224 (entry into force 1 August 2008) Article 21(1).

24 *Instrumento de Ratificación del Protocolo Adicional al Convenio de Cooperación Judicial en materia penal entre el Reino de España y la República de Colombia*, signed 12 July 2005, [2010] BOE 149 (entry into force 1 July 2010) Article 8.

for joint investigations on a case-by-case basis.[25] Whether or not to engage in such cooperation is left, of course, to the discretion of the States.[26]

While Article 3(1) of the UNTOC limits the scope of the Convention to certain categories of offences relating to organised and serious crime, the content of Article 19 is not limited in this way. In the context of Article 49 of the UNCAC, which uses the same wording as Article 19 of the UNTOC, it has been remarked that joint investigations set up pursuant to this provision may have a broader field of application.[27]

The final sentence of Article 19 mandates the full preservation of the sovereignty of the State on whose territory the joint investigation will be carried out.[28] Particular issues that may arise in this context concern the selection of the applicable law, the extent of powers conferred upon foreign officers, including the exercise of public authority, and the extent of other activities that are subject to legal constraints, such as the right to bear arms.[29]

Concerns about intrusions on national sovereignty have marred support for the UNTOC since the early days of its development. This is because national sovereignty represents 'for many smaller developing countries and countries with economies in transition (or emerging democracies) the last bastion of national integrity and identity'.[30] This view also explains the long-standing reluctance by States Parties to engage in joint investigations in the manner envisaged by Article 19.[31] Paolo Ferrua has described the conferral and exercise of law enforcement and procedural powers as the 'forbidden garden' of national sovereignty.[32] The fact that joint investigations have recently caught the eye of States Parties to the UNTOC and received noticeably more attention by the Conference of the Parties marks a pivotal change and may demonstrate a subtle shift from exclusive to shared sovereignty.[33]

25 UNODC, *Legislative Guide for the Implementation of the United Nations Convention against Transnational Organized Crime* (UNODC, 2nd ed 2017) [596].

26 David McClean, *Transnational Organized Crime: A Commentary on the UN Convention and its Protocols* (Oxford University Press, 2007) 238.

27 Frank Zimmermann 'Article 49: Joint Investigations' in Cecily Rose, Michael Kubiciel, and Oliver Landwehr (eds), *The United Nations Convention Against Corruption; A Commentary* (Oxford University Press, 2019) 496, 498.

28 Ibid.

29 Ibid., 499.

30 Dimitri Vlassis, 'The United Nations Convention against Transnational Organized Crime and its Protocols: A New Era in International Cooperation' in *The Changing Face of International Criminal Law* (International Centre for Criminal Law Reform and Criminal Justice, 2002) 76, 90–100.

31 Neil Boister, *An Introduction to Transnational Criminal Law* (Oxford University Press, 2nd ed 2018) 291.

32 Paolo Ferrua, 'Un giardino proibito per il legislatore: la valutazione delle prove' (1998) 3 *Questione Giustizia* 587, 587.

33 Andrea Scella, *Investigazioni e prove transnazionali* (Giuffrè, 2017) 151. See also Otto Lagodny, 'Implementation of the Convention: The Sovereignty Issue' in Hans-Jörg Albrecht

8.2.2 Joint investigations, teams, and bodies

It is worth noting that the first sentence of Article 19, which encourages the conclusion of agreements and arrangements, refers to the establishment of 'joint investigative bodies' whereas the second sentence, which concerns arrangements on a case-by-case basis, uses the term 'joint investigations' (which is also used in the title of Article 19). On the surface, there thus appears to be a difference or, perhaps, 'mismatch'[34] between the content of the two sentences. The United Nations Office on Drugs and Crime (UNODC), the 'guardian' of the UNTOC and its Protocols, suggests that the two need to be read in combination as encouraging States Parties 'to establish a new entity only based on general agreements and to resort to the lesser measure of coordinated investigations when such agreements do not exist'.[35] Further confusion may arise from the use of the term 'joint investigative bodies' rather than the more common term 'joint investigation teams',[36] though it appears that these terms can be used interchangeably and that, in sum, the concept of 'joint investigations' under Article 19 can be interpreted broadly to encompass a range of collaborative, cooperative approaches and joint investigative practices.[37]

The available literature generally refers to two models of joint investigations that can serve as a basis for implementing Article 19:[38]

(1) The first model entails two separate yet parallel coordinated investigations conducted in two different States to achieve a common objective. These investigations are supported by networks of liaison officers or contact persons, supplemented by formal mutual legal assistance requests to acquire evidence.[39] Depending on the legal system(s) involved, the officers may work collaboratively based on established cooperative practices and/or existing mutual legal assistance legislation, often relocating as needed.[40]

(2) The second model involves Joint Investigation Teams, or JITs for short. This is an established international cooperation tool based on an agreement between competent law enforcement or judicial authorities of two or more

---

and Cyrille Fijnaut (eds), *The Containment of Transnational Organised Crime: Comments on the UN Convention of December 2000* (Edition Iuscrim 2002) 165, 165–166.

34 Antonio Balsamo, Andrea Mattarella, and Roberto Tartaglia, *La Convenzione di Palermo: il futuro della lotta alla criminalità organizzata transnazionale* (Giappichelli, 2020) 358, 371 n 10.

35 UNODC, *Digest of Organized Crime Cases: A Compilation of Cases with Commentaries and Lessons Learned* (United Nations, 2012) 79.

36 Ibid., 80.

37 UN, Conference of the Parties to the United Nations Convention against Transnational Organized Crime, *Informal Expert Working Group on Joint Investigations: Conclusions and Recommendations, Draft*, UN Doc CTOC/COP/2008/CRP.5 (2 October 2008) 7 (hereafter 'CTOC/COP/2008/CRP.5').

38 See, among many, Schloenhardt (n 2) 224; UNODC (n 19) 57; Boister (n 16) 50.

39 CTOC/COP/2008/CRP.5 (n 37) 7.

40 UNODC (n 19) 58.

States. JITs are formed for a specific duration and purpose, aimed at carrying out criminal investigations in one or more of the States involved. Setting up a JIT entails creating a distinct entity, equipped with specified investigative functions and powers, 'even if these powers are to be exercised in a non-exclusive way, leaving intact the rights of national law enforcement agencies and prosecutorial offices, and in full respect of national rules governing investigation and prosecution'.[41]

JITs can be further differentiated between integrated and active teams depending on the operational powers of their members. An integrated team would include, for example, a foreign law enforcement officer integrated with officers from the host State, serving in an advisory, consultancy, or supportive capacity as dictated by the technical assistance provisions in the host State. Such teams are usually co-located and are built either on national law concerning the use of foreign officials or on technical assistance agreements.[42] An active team involves officers from another jurisdiction equipped with the ability to exercise equivalent operational powers (or parts thereof) in the operational territory or jurisdiction under the control of the host State.

Article 19 of the UNTOC, as mentioned, also refers to 'joint investigative bodies', a term with no official definition or interpretation in the Convention and the *Travaux Préparatoires*.[43] What is unclear is whether joint investigative bodies encompass structures distinct from JITs and joint parallel investigations. An Informal Expert Group on Joint Investigations set up by the Conference of the Parties to the UNTOC concluded in 2008 that the term 'joint investigative body' 'was intended to be a more permanent structure formed on the basis of a bilateral agreement'.[44] The Group further remarked that

> inspiration for the structure of such a body could be drawn from the existing long term multi agency task forced established in the domestic context to deal with a particular threat or areas of criminal activity and in the international context from the pilot projects conducted by Canada and USA to explore a long term cross-border law enforcement programme, the programme being based on a bi-lateral agreement between Canada and USA and operational agreements between the agencies involved (incorporating law enforcement, customs, coast guard and immigration) on both sides.[45]

A common understanding of the term remains, however, lacking.

41 Ibid., 72.
42 CTOC/COP/2008/CRP.5 (n 37) 11.
43 UNODC, *Travaux Préparatoires of the Negotiations of the United Nations Convention against Transnational Organized Crime and the Protocols thereto* (United Nations, 2006).
44 CTOC/COP/2008/CRP.5 (n 37) 7.
45 Ibid., 13.

8.3 Setting up a Joint Investigation Team

The use of the UNTOC as the legal basis for joint investigations has gained international support, but there is ongoing debate about whether Article 19 is a sufficient and autonomous legal basis. This debate also reflects the fact that some States, such as Switzerland for instance, have noted that Article 19 (as well as Article 49 of the UNCAC) is not sufficiently clear to be directly applied, i.e. it is not a self-executing provision.[46] Eurojust, the EU Agency for Criminal Justice Cooperation, further suggests that Article 19 of the UNTOC should be used in combination with other legal instruments where no other legal basis exists.[47]

Indeed, examples of situations in which Article 19 has been cited as the basis for joint investigations are difficult to find. The UNODC's 2021 *Digest of Cases of International Cooperation in Criminal Matters Involving the United Nations Convention Against Transnational Organized Crime* merely found '[o]ne example of joint investigations carried out on the basis of article 19 of the Organized Crime Convention', which 'involved a collaboration between Brazilian, Portuguese and Spanish authorities in the investigation of an organised criminal group engaged in trafficking cocaine from Brazil through Portugal to Spain'.[48]

In the absence of other regional frameworks and domestic laws and regulations on joint investigations, the first step in setting up a JIT pursuant to Article 19 involves identifying those national agency (or agencies) in the States concerned that have the authority to establish such teams and transmit an official request for investigation cooperation to that agency.[49] Next, a shared interest or common purpose in the investigation of the case needs to be identified, especially with regard to factors such as the complexity of the criminal network, the nature of the activities under investigation, and the interconnections between the various investigations among the States involved.[50]

As a next step a meeting involving prosecutors, investigative judges, and investigators should be convened. This phase serves as an opportunity to discuss the modi operandi, the suspects involved, and the investigative plans. This meeting constitutes a pivotal stage where 'pre-legal' considerations of the criminal phenomenon under investigation are shared.[51] This exchange is particularly valuable for authorities unfamiliar with a certain type of organised

46 Eurojust, JITs Network, *Guidelines on Joint Investigation Teams Involving Third Countries* (Eurojust, June 2022) 27.
47 Ibid., 6.
48 UNODC (n 19) 58.
49 CTOC/COP.WG.3/2020/2 (n 3) 12.
50 Ibid., 11.
51 Varraso (n 4) 181–202.

crime, as it imparts an understanding of the exact dimension of the criminal phenomenon and its forms of manifestation.[52]

At the end of the meeting, if sufficient common ground has been found, a JIT agreement will be drafted. The status and legal nature of such agreements can take many forms depending on who is authorised to draft and conclude them and depending on their content and intended consequences. In some States, domestic law may stipulate which authorities can develop and enter into such agreements. The agreement may merely constitute a technical understanding between competent authorities (investigation, judicial, or other law enforcement authorities) or it may evolve into fully fledged bilateral treaties. The latter scenario will require the involvement of senior government authorities with the power to bind the State on the international level. Irrespective of its form, the JIT agreement becomes valid once all participating parties sign it. Furthermore, it should be amended by mutual consent if its content undergoes any change, such as the modification of the crimes under investigation or the involvement of a new party.[53]

Several issues need to be addressed in JIT agreements, none of which are mentioned or otherwise specified in Article 19 of the UNTOC. First, the agreement needs to set out the composition of the team and its (hierarchical) structure or levels of seniority.[54] As the appointment of participants to the JIT hinges on the legal systems of the States concerned, the agreement should explicitly designate the leader in charge of supervising the team's activities. It should also outline the framework governing the leader's operational control, as well as define the operational roles and tasks of other team members.[55] The JIT agreement should also include a description of how the investigation will be managed and conducted, as well as the special operations and investigative techniques that will be employed during the investigation.[56] Special attention should be paid to identifying the limits that national laws impose on investigative powers, particularly in terms of special investigative techniques and operational constraints.[57] The JIT agreement also needs to address relevant administrative, equipment, resources, and cost issues.[58]

52 Ibid.
53 CTOC/COP.WG.3/2020/2 (n 3) 12.
54 UN, Conference of the Parties to the United Nations Convention against Transnational Organized Crime, Working Group on Trafficking in Persons, *Best Practices in Joint Investigations and Specialized Prosecutions*, UN Doc CTOC/COP/WG.4/2020/3 (26 June 2020) 17 (hereafter 'CTOC/COP/WG.4/2020/3').
55 CTOC/COP.WG.3/2020/2 (n 3) 12.
56 Council Recommendation of 8 May 2003 on a Model Agreement for Setting up a Joint Investigation Team (JIT), OJ C121 of 23 May 2003, Appendix IV 'Proposal for a Check List for the Operational Action Plan (OAP)'.
57 Varraso (n 4) 181–202.
58 Rositsa Zaharieva, 'The European Investigation Order and the Joint Investigation Team—Which Road to Take' (2017) 18 *ERA Forum* 397, 403.

Next, the agreement needs to address issues pertaining to the civil and/or criminal liability of JIT members for conduct authorised under the agreement.[59]

Furthermore, the parties to the agreement should articulate confidentiality rules.[60] Trust between the authorities involved in the investigation lies at the heart of cross-border information exchange. This trust can be undermined by corruption or fear of corruption. In situations where corruption exists inside one State, national authorities could refuse to provide information to the State involved in the JIT. This reluctance stems from the understanding that shared information would subsequently become accessible to other domestic authorities. Therefore, the JIT agreement should precisely regulate the extent to which information received by the team can be incorporated into legal proceedings and be admissible in court, how it may or must be disclosed to interested parties, and the stage of the proceedings when such disclosure is due to take place.[61] Decisions on all those procedural aspects should take into account, on the one hand, the due process rights of the suspect and, on the other, the risk of jeopardising investigations in one State Party to the JIT if the disclosure takes place too early or earlier than in other States.[62]

The JIT agreement should also consider which jurisdiction is best suited to prosecute criminal matters that are, directly or indirectly, revealed by or related to the investigation.[63] In this context, a review of the scope of the various proceedings, extradition, sharing, and/or possible transfer of proceedings may be required to prevent and support the resolution of conflicts of jurisdiction[64] that may result in a violation of the *ne bis in idem* principle.[65] Furthermore, extradition of one State's own nationals to another State may be prohibited by domestic law. Determining the jurisdiction also has an impact on victims' rights, and should thus take into account victims' interests and protection.[66] For example, in the case of JITs dealing with trafficking in persons cases, when designing the JIT, States Parties should consider which of them is best placed in terms of resources and services to provide victims of trafficking with access

59 CTOC/COP.WG.3/2020/2 (n 3) 9. See also UNODC, *Model Legislative Provisions against Organized Crime* (UNODC, 2nd ed 2021) 94.

60 Eurojust, JITs Network (n 46) 12.

61 CTOC/COP.WG.3/2020/2 (n 3) 13.

62 Eurojust, JITs Network, *Conclusion of the Ninth Annual Meeting of National Experts on Joint Investigation Teams (JITs)* (Eurojust, 2013) 9.

63 CTOC/COP.WG.3/2020/2 (n 3) 14.

64 Ibid.; Eurojust, JITs Network (n 46) 11.

65 Eurojust, JITs Network, *Joint Investigation Teams Practical Guide* (Eurojust, 2021) 99; Eurojust, JITs Network (n 46) 13.

66 *Velasquez-Rodriguez v Honduras (Judgement)* (Inter-American Court of Human Rights, Series C No 4, 29 July 1988) [166]–[167], [1740]; UN Human Rights Committee, *General Comment No 31 [80]: The nature of the general legal obligation imposed on States Parties to the Covenant*, UN Doc CCPR/C/21/Rev.1/Add. 13 (26 May 2004) [8]; *Zongo v Burkina Faso (Judgement)* (African Court on Human and Peoples' Rights, App No 013/2011, 28 March 2014) [150]–[156].

to protection (shelters, change of identity, physical protection) and recovery programmes (health and mental health care) during the investigation, and is eventually able to grant them a residence permit.

8.4 Potential human rights issues

Having explained the scope of Article 19 of the UNTOC and the process of setting up a JIT, it is now necessary to consider human rights issues associated with the implementation of Article 19 and the operation of JITs in practice. In this context, UNODC stresses that

> the human rights safeguards set out in the Convention evince an intention that the prevention and combating of transnational organised crime should not be pursued at all costs, but rather in a manner consistent with States' obligations under international human rights law.[67]

UNODC further notes that the protection of human rights is inherently woven into the drafting history of the UNTOC and its Protocols[68] and the Conference of the Parties to the Convention has repeatedly emphasised the relationship between the UNTOC and human rights.[69]

8.4.1 Information and evidence sharing

Since Article 19 is not explicitly limited to offences under the UNTOC, the question may be raised as to whether the speciality principle applies to the operation of JITs. The speciality principle, which was originally developed in the area of extradition law,[70] can be understood in the present context as precluding investigation authorities from using the evidence gathered by the JIT

67 UNODC (n 14) 20.

68 Ibid.

69 See, inter alia, UN, Conference of the Parties to the United Nations Convention against Transnational Organized Crime, *Report of the Conference of the Partes to the United Nations Convention against Transnational Organized Crime on its Fifth Session, Held in Vienna from 18 to 22 October 2010*, UN Doc CTOC/COP/2010/17 (2 December 2010) 6–7 [11]; UN, Conference of the Parties to the United Nations Convention against Transnational Organized Crime, *Report of the Conference of the Partes to the United Nations Convention against Transnational Organized Crime on its Tenth Session, Held in Vienna from 15 to 19 October 2018*, UN Doc CTOC/COP/2018/13 (1 November 2018) 26; UN, Conference of the Parties to the United Nations Convention against Transnational Organized Crime, *Report of the Conference of the Partes to the United Nations Convention against Transnational Organized Crime on its Tenth Session, Held in Vienna from 12 to 16 October 2020*, UN Doc CTOC/COP/2020/10 (3 November 2020) 116–117.

70 See John Dugard and Christine Van den Wyngaert, 'Reconciling extradition with human rights' (1998) 92(2) *American Journal of International Law* 187, 188; Kenneth E Levit, 'International Extradition, the Principle of Speciality, and Effective Treaty Enforcement' (1992) 76(4) *Minnesota Law Review* 1017, 1025.

for any purposes and legal proceedings beyond those for which the JIT was originally set up, unless explicit authorisation is granted by the States Parties.

In relation to extradition, it has been discussed whether the speciality principle is a customary international law principle that binds States even in the absence of a treaty or legislative provisions expressly recognising it. While M Cherif Bassiouni found that this 'is unclear' in relation to the United States' extradition law and practice,[71] for the Italian Court of Cassation (*Corte di Cassazione*) it is 'a principle of customary origin enjoying primacy in the internal legal order'.[72]

This debate is crucial for the scope of JIT operations. If the specific law does not provide protection, can broader principles be invoked in its place? The answer to this question will differ depending on whether the speciality principle is seen as serving only the interests of State sovereignty or whether it also serves to protect individuals.[73] While the Swiss Federal Court (*Tribunale federale*), for instance, has found that the principle of speciality protects both the individual's and the State's prerogatives,[74] the question remains a vexed issue according to the literature.[75]

The Working Group on International Cooperation established by the Conference of the Parties to the UNTOC appears to take a different view, noting that the absence of a reference in Article 19 to the scope of applicable offences could be due to the fact that States

> will normally not limit the scope of such agreements to Convention offences, but include other offences linked to them that need to be investigated as elements of the overall criminal case under scrutiny for purposes of the proper administration of justice.[76]

On the surface and without further clarification, it thus seems that official UNTOC bodies generally take the view that, at least for the time being, the wording of Article 19 permits a more extensive and flexible use of information obtained through the JIT process. This view creates a potential risk that information obtained by JITs may be used for domestic purposes by the authorities involved or in cooperation matters with other States for crimes other than those originally identified in the JIT agreement.[77] This risk is amplified by

71 M Cherif Bassiouni, *International Extradition: United States Law and Practice* (Oxford University Press, 2014) 546.

72 Corte di Cassazione, Sezioni Unite, No 11971, 18 March 2008.

73 See Alex Tinsley, 'Specialty: Arresting an Elusive "Right" in European Extradition Law', (2021) 12(1) *New Journal of European Criminal Law* [s.p].

74 Cour de Cassation Penale, ATF 123 IV 42, 3 December 1996.

75 Jonathan George, 'Toward a More Principled Approach to the Principle of Specialty' (1979) 12(2) *Cornell International Law Journal* 309.

76 CTOC/COP.WG.3/2020/2 (n 3) 4.

77 Balsamo, Mattarella, and Tartaglia (n 34) 371.

the fact that in the work of JITs, oftentimes no distinction is made between information and evidence in the modalities of exchange or in the permitted use, and thus evidence for use in court is, wittingly and unwittingly transferred through the JIT.[78] This practice may result in a separate *notitia criminis* and may thus be used to start new and further investigations, but may also be directly used at trial as evidence.

On the one hand, it could be argued that the further use of information gathered by a JIT set up for investigating one set of offences constitutes a useful opportunity to also investigate other crimes and thus to acquire information to combat transnational organised crime more broadly. For example, the Office of the Prosecutor of the International Criminal Court used the information gathered by a JIT created for the purpose of investigating crimes committed against migrants in Libya to arrest two key suspects of crimes against victims of trafficking in persons and smuggling of migrants.[79]

On the other hand, this practice may open the door for the potential misuse of the information gathered by a JIT and can raise concerns relating to the dual criminality principle, especially where the States participating in the JIT have adopted different criminal offences and associated policies. Such a situation would arise where information gathered by a JIT is used to investigate and prosecute conduct that is not criminalised in some of the States involved in the JIT. In such circumstances, fundamental human rights may be at stake, especially where the information is used in proceedings involving political offences or other crimes relating to a person's opinion.[80] Similar concerns can be raised in relation to offences criminalising consensual sexual relations between adults outside marriage or same-sex relationships.[81]

These concerns are not limited to the types of offences for which information derived from JIT investigations may be used but also concern the penalties associated with the offences under investigation. This is, of course, particularly relevant for offences that attract the death penalty under the laws of one of the States involved in the JIT. In this regard, the UN Human Rights Committee stressed that Parties to the *International Covenant on Civil and Political Rights* (ICCPR)[82] must take appropriate measures to protect individuals against the deprivation of life by other States operating inside their territory or in other areas subject to their jurisdiction. They must also ensure that

78 Eurojust, JITs Network, *Joint Investigation Teams Practical Guide* (Eurojust, 2021) 30; CTOC/COP.WG.3/2020/2 (n 3) 2.

79 ICC, The Office of the Prosecutor, *Towards a more just world every day, Annual Report of the Office of the Prosecutor—2022* (ICC, 2022) 34.

80 Such offences may violate the rights protected by Articles 19 and 22 of the *International Covenant of Civil and Political Rights* (ICCPR) and Article 10 of the *European Convention on Human Rights* (ECHR, opened for signature 4 November 1950, ETS 5 (entry into force 3 September 1953)).

81 Violating ICCPR Articles 2, 26, 28; ECHR 8, 14.

82 Opened for signature 16 December 1966, 999 UNTS 171 (entry into force 23 March 1976).

all activities occurring wholly or partly inside their territory, as well as in other places subject to their jurisdiction, and which have a direct and reasonably foreseeable impact on the right to life of individuals outside their territory, are consistent with Article 6 of the ICCPR, which protects the right to life.[83]

The debate about international cooperation in criminal justice matters in cases involving offences that may attract the death penalty is long-standing and goes beyond the scope of the present chapter.[84] It suffices to note here that the protection of human life should, of course, be paramount and absolute. But it also needs to be noted that insisting on a commitment against using the evidence and information gathered by the JIT in proceedings involving offences that carry the death penalty in one or more States can severely hamper the ability of States to collaborate effectively in combating transnational organised crime.[85]

8.4.2 Sharing of personal data

A further issue relates to the protection of personal data when it is transmitted among participating JIT agencies. Sharing information about individuals outside of any legal framework and without sufficient oversight may result in an unjustified interference with the right to private life/privacy.[86]

While in its jurisprudence the European Court of Human Rights (ECtHR) has accepted, for instance, that in criminal investigations involving wiretapping restrictions to the right to privacy may be necessary. The Court also noted that to avoid abuse of power, precautions to be taken when communicating the

83 UN Human Rights Committee, *General comment No 36: Article 6: right to life*, UN Doc CCPR/C/GC/36 (3 September 2019) [22].

84 See, for example, Lorraine Finlay, 'Exporting the Death Penalty? Reconciling International Police Cooperation and the Abolition of the Death Penalty in Australia' (2011) 33 *Sydney Law Review* 95–117; Miguel Beltrán de Felipe and Adán Nieto Martín, 'Post 9/11 Trends in International Judicial Cooperation: Human Rights as a Constraint on Extradition in Death Penalty Cases' (2012) 10(3) *Journal of International Criminal Justice* 581–604; Bharat Malkani, 'The Obligation to Refrain from Assisting the Use of the Death Penalty' (2013) 62(3) *International and Comparative Law Quarterly* 523–556; Eef Vandebroek and Frank Verbruggen, 'The EU and Death Penalty Abolition: The Limited Prospects of Judicial Cooperation in Criminal Matters as an External Policy Tool' (2013) 4(4) *New Journal of European Criminal Law* 481–505.

85 See generally, Kate Westmoreland, 'Sharing the Evidence across Borders: The Human Rights Challenge' (2012) 30 *Australian Year Book of International Law* 161–200.

86 Article 17 of the ICCPR obliges States not to subject individuals to 'arbitrary and unlawful interference' with privacy, meaning that lawful and non-arbitrary interference is permitted. Article 8(2) of the ECHR States further that the right to privacy can be restricted in the name of, among others, national security, the economic well-being of the country, and prevention of disorder and crime.

data to other parties should be set out in law, even in cases where the wiretapping is done for national security reasons.[87]

Since bulk wiretapping may also be used by JITs in the context of organised and other serious crime, the recent decision by the ECtHR in *Big Brother Watch and Others v United Kingdom* (2021) is of particular significance.[88] In this decision, the Court addressed the issue of compatibility with Article 8 of the ECHR in a case involving the sharing of wiretapped data intercepted by foreign intelligence services. Here, the Court stressed that the exchange of such data

> needed to be governed by precise, definite rules, able to offer reliable safeguards against using this power to circumvent domestic law and/or the obligations of the States under the [ECHR]. The State receiving the intercepted material shall have in place sufficient safeguards to ensure the assessment, usage, and secure storage of the received material, as well as for its subsequent transmission, erasure, and destruction.[89]

Additionally, in the context of the right to privacy, the UN Human Rights Committee has interpreted the concept of 'justifiable restriction'[90] to indicate that 'any interference with privacy must be proportional to the end sought and be necessary in the circumstances of any given case'.[91] The Committee further emphasised that the human rights risks presented by information-sharing arrangements are exacerbated by a lack of transparency, accountability, and oversight.[92]

In the case of JITs set up between EU Member States and third countries, the processing and transmission of personal data is subject to the application of Directive (EU) 2016/680 (also known as the LED or Law Enforcement

87 *Huvig v France* [1990] 176 ECHR (ser A) [34]; *Kruslin v France* [1990] 176 ECHR (ser A) [35]; *Valenzuela Contreras v Spain* [1998] V ECHR [46].

88 *Big Brother Watch and Others v United Kingdom* (ECHR, Grand Chamber, Application No 58170/13, 25 May 2021).

89 Ibid., [498].

90 ICCPR, Article 17; ECHR, Article 8.

91 UN Human Rights Committee, *Communication No 488/1992: Views of the Human Rights Committee under Article 5, paragraph 4, of the Optional Protocol to the International Covenant on Civil and Political Rights*, UN Doc CCPR/C/50/D/488/1992 (4 April 1994) [8.3]; UN Human Rights Committee, *Communication No 903/1999: Views of the Human Rights Committee under the Optional Protocol to the International Covenant on Civil and Political Rights*, UN Doc CCPR/C/82/D/903/1999 (15 November 2004) [7.3].

92 UN Human Rights Committee, *Concluding observations on the Seventh Periodic Report of the United Kingdom of Great Britain and Northern Ireland*, UN Doc CCPR/C/GBR/CO/7 (17 August 2015) [24]; and UN Human Rights Committee, *Concluding observations on the Seventh Periodic Report of Sweden*, UN Doc CCPR/C/SWE/CO/7 (28 April 2016) [36].

Directive).[93] This Directive requires that for the purposes of preventing, investigating, detecting, or prosecuting criminal offences or executing criminal penalties, personal information may only be transmitted if the EU Commission has decided that the recipient ensures an 'adequate' level of protection.[94] The concept of an 'adequate level' of protection has been developed[95] by the Court of Justice of the European Union (CJEU), inter alia, in the *Schrems* cases.[96] It requires the third country to ensure, by reason of its domestic law or its international commitments, a level of protection of fundamental rights and freedoms that is essentially equivalent to that guaranteed within the European Union. The Court has also stated that the EU Commission's discretion as to the adequacy of the level of protection ensured by a third country should be limited, considering, first, the important role played by the protection of personal data in the light of the fundamental right to respect for private life and, second, the large number of persons whose fundamental rights are at risk of being infringed where personal data is transferred to a third country without ensuring an adequate level of protection.[97] In the absence of an 'adequacy decision', transmission of personal data may only take place based on the procedures and mechanisms provided by a legally binding instrument (such as a mutual legal assistance treaty). Thus far, only one decision under the Directive on the adequate protection of data has been adopted; it involves law enforce-

93 *Directive (EU) 2016/680 of the European Parliament and of the Council of 27 April 2016 on the protection of natural persons with regard to the processing of personal data by competent authorities for the purposes of the prevention, investigation, detection or prosecution of criminal offences or the execution of criminal penalties, and on the free movement of such data, and repealing Council Framework Decision 2008/977/JHA* [2016] OJ L 119/89.

94 The Commission is also tasked with monitoring adopted decisions and to amend, suspend or repeal them if the level of protection no longer fulfils the adequate fundamental rights standard; see *Directive (EU) 2016/680 of the European Parliament and of the Council of 27 April 2016 on the protection of natural persons with regard to the processing of personal data by competent authorities for the purposes of the prevention, investigation, detection or prosecution of criminal offences or the execution of criminal penalties, and on the free movement of such data, and repealing Council Framework Decision 2008/977/JHA* [2016] OJ L 119/89, Article 36(3), (4), (5), and (6).

95 The concept of 'adequate level of protection' already existed under *Directive 95/46/EC of the European Parliament and of the Council of 24 October 1995 on the protection of individuals with regard to the processing of personal data and on the free movement of such data* [1995] OJ L 281/31 and *Council Framework Decision 2008/977/JHA of 27 November 2008 on the protection of personal data processed in the framework of police and judicial cooperation in criminal matters* [2008] OJ L 350/60.

96 *Maximillian Schrems v Data Protection Commissioner* (Court of Justice of the European Union, Grand Chamber, C-362/14, ECLI:EU:C:2015:650), 6 October 2015; *Data Protection Commissioner v Facebook Ireland Ltd and Maximillian Schrems* (Court of Justice of the European Union, Grand Chamber, C-311/18, ECLI:EU:C:2020:559), 16 July 2020.

97 *Data Protection Commissioner v Facebook Ireland Ltd and Maximillian Schrems* (Court of Justice of the European Union, Grand Chamber, C-311/18, ECLI:EU:C:2020:559), 16 July 2020 [92] (Schrems II); see Maria Helen Murphy, 'Assessing the Implications of Schrems II for EU–US Data Flow' (2022) 71(1) *International & Comparative Law Quarterly* 245–262.

ment cooperation with the United Kingdom,[98] which was once a Member State of the European Union.

8.4.3 *Admissibility of evidence*

To respect the sovereignty of the State Party in whose territory the investigation is to be conducted, the general rule is that the authorities involved in a JIT conduct all investigative activities in accordance with that State's national law (*lex loci*). An exception may apply only where the host State's laws specifically allow for the application of foreign law.[99] One example of this can be found in an agreement between Italy and Switzerland,[100] which instead required compliance with the *lex fori*.[101]

When *lex loci* applies, the national laws of the State Party in whose territory the investigation is to be conducted may not necessarily be the same as those of the State in which the trial will be held. Procedural admissibility of evidence gathered abroad traditionally constitutes the main issue concerning the circulation of criminal evidence collected in the context of judicial cooperation.[102] But in the case of JITs, the parties are free to decide whether evidence collected in full compliance with one State's national laws is admissible in their jurisdiction.

For example, because most special investigative techniques are highly intrusive and may raise concerns regarding their compatibility with basic rights and freedoms, the laws of some States do not allow them to be used. However, within the framework of a JIT, the same States may mutually consent to admit evidence gathered through such techniques within the territory of another State, provided that the national law of that State permits their use. JITs parties may also agree to admit evidence gathered by acts carried out without a lawyer present in the territory of a State where national law does not require this, even if it is mandatory under the law of the State where the trial takes place. Alternatively, they may even decide to indiscriminately admit to national

98 *Commission Implementing Decision of 28.6.2021 Pursuant to Directive (EU) 2016/680 of the European Parliament and of the Council on the Adequate Protection of Personal Data by the United Kingdom* [2021] OJ L 360/69.

99 CTOC/COP.WG.3/2020/2 (n 3) 6 [26].

100 *Accordo tra la Svizzera e l'Italia che completa la Convenzione europea di assistenza giudiziaria in materia penale del 20 aprile 1959 e ne agevola l'applicazione*, signed 10 September 1998 (entry into force 1 June 2003).

101 See Colaiacovo (n 1) 173 citing Chiara M Paolucci, *Cooperazione giudiziaria e di polizia in materia penale* (Utet Giuridica, 2011) 476; Gaetano De Amicis, 'Cooperazione orizzontale', AA.VV., *Manuale di procedura penale europea* (Giuffrè Editore, 2017) 301.

102 Simona Di Monte, 'Le squadre investigative comuni' in Fabiana Falato (ed), *Appunti di cooperazione giudiziaria penale* (Edizioni Scientifiche Italiane, 2019) 210.

proceedings all evidence gathered by investigative acts carried out abroad that cannot be performed again.[103]

In its case law, the ECtHR has repeatedly stated that the admissibility of evidence is primarily a matter to be regulated under national law.[104] In general, it is not the Court's prerogative to rule on the admissibility of specific types of evidence, such as evidence obtained unlawfully under domestic law. The Court's role is limited to assessing whether the proceedings as a whole, including the manner in which the evidence was obtained, were fair.[105] A look at the ECtHR's case law can help in identifying to what extent evidence gathered in a manner inconsistent with national rules can be considered either a mere procedural violation or a violation of the right to a fair trial and thus in determining whether such evidence is admissible in Court.

For example, in the case of *Salduz*, the ECtHR examined the question of whether a restriction on access to a lawyer is compatible with the right to a fair trial.[106] Here, the Court articulated the principle that every suspect has the right to access a lawyer from the time of the first police interview and held that a systematic restriction on access to a lawyer results in an automatic violation of Article 6(1) and (3)(c) of the ECHR.[107] According to Dimitros Giannoulopoulos, this means that the use of confession evidence obtained during a police interview in custody without access to a lawyer inevitably breaches the right to a fair trial and amounts to an automatic violation of Article 6(3)(c).[108] Consequently, the exclusionary rule (the judge-made rule preventing the use of evidence obtained in breach of the defendant's rights) should be applied unless there exists a compelling and exceptional reason for the inter-

103 For example, the Italian Legislative Decree No 43 of 15 February 2016, implementing EU Council Framework Decision 2002/465/JHA of 13 June 2002 on Joint Investigation Teams, regulates the admissibility of evidence by distinguishing between investigative acts carried out abroad into those that can be performed again (*atti ripetibili*) and those that cannot be performed again (*atti irripetibili*). While evidence gathered by *atti ripetibili* may be admitted to a national criminal trial according to the ordinary procedural rules concerning evidence gathering, States may agree that evidence gathered abroad by *atti irripetibili* may be 'automatically' used in Court.

104 *Schenk v Switzerland* (ECtHR, Application No 10862/84, 12 July 1988) [45]–[46]; *Moreira Ferreira v Portugal (no 2)* (ECtHR, Grand Chamber, Application No 19867/12, 11 July 2017) [83]; *Heglas v Czech Republic* (ECtHR, Application No 5935/0, 21 March 2007) [84].

105 *Ayetullah Ay v Turkey* (ECtHR, Second Section, Application No 29084/07, 1191/08, 27 October 2020) [123]–[130]; *Bykov v Russia* (ECtHR, Grand Chamber, Application No 4378/02, 10 March 2009) [88]; *Schenk v Switzerland* (n 104) [45]–[46]; *Moreira Ferreira v Portugal (no 2)* (n 104) [83]; *Heglas v Czech Republic* (n 104) [84].

106 *Salduz v Turkey* (ECtHR, Grand Chamber, Application No 36391/02, 27 November 2008) [59]; see also UN Human Rights Committee, *Ahment Gunan v Kyrgystan, Communication No 1545/2007*, UN DOC CCPR/C/102/D/1545/2007 (25 July 2011) [6.3].

107 *Salduz v Turkey* (n 106) [53]–[55].

108 Dimitrios Giannoulopoulos, *Improperly Obtained Evidence in Anglo-American and Continental Law* (Hart, 2019) 172.

view.[109] In *Ibrahim and Others*, the ECtHR set out a non-exhaustive list of factors concerning the lack of a lawyer to be taken into account when assessing the overall fairness of the proceedings.[110] In sum, it follows that where national law prohibits contact with a lawyer in certain phases of the proceedings, this restriction may be considered systematic. Consequently, if within the context of a JIT information is obtained in a State under such circumstances, ECtHR case law suggests that it should not be admissible as evidence in trials in any JIT State Party that is bound by the ECHR.

Regarding the use of special investigative techniques, States Parties to the UNTOC are encouraged by Article 20 to deploy measures such as surveillance, wiretapping of communications, and undercover operations 'if permitted by the basic principles of its domestic legal system'. The UN Human Rights Committee and the ECtHR have accepted that special investigative techniques, despite their intrusive nature, may be needed and justified to prevent and suppress transnational organised crime.[111] Both have, however, also stressed that States must specify in detail in their national law the circumstances in which the use of special investigative techniques and the associated interferences may be permitted.[112] In its case law addressing wiretapping of communications in criminal investigations, the ECtHR has stated that, to avoid abuses of power, certain safeguards must be established in law. These include: specifying the nature of offences that may give rise to a wiretapping order, defining the categories of people who may have their communications wiretapped, and imposing a legally defined timeframe for the duration of such

109 Some scholars say that *Salduz v Turkey* (n 106) is not clear on this point: Annemarieke Beijer, 'False Confessions during Police Interrogations and Measures to Prevent Them' (2010) 18 *European Journal of Crime, Criminal Law & Criminal Justice* 311, 312–313; Anna Ogorodova and Taru Spronken, 'Legal Advice in Police Custody: From Europe to a Local Police Station' (2014) 4 *Erasmus Law Review* 191–205. *Salduz v Turkey* was confirmed in *Tikhonov v Ukraine* (ECtHR, Fifth Section, Application No 17969/09, 10 December 2015) [50]–[52]; *Płonka v Poland* (ECtHR, Fourth Section, Application No 20310/02, 31 March 2009) [42]; and *Pishchalnikov v Russia* (ECtHR, First Section, Application No 7025/04, 24 September 2009) [79].

110 *Ibrahim and Others v United Kingdom* (ECtHR, Grand Chamber, Application Nos 50541/08, 50571/08, 50573/08, 40351/09, 13 September 2016) [274]. See also, *Beuze v Belgium* (ECtHR, Grand Chamber, Application no 71409/10, 9 November 2018) and the comment by Ergul Celiksoy, 'Overruling "*the Salduz Doctrine*" in *Beuze v Belgium*: The ECtHR's further retreat from the *Salduz* principles on the right to access to lawyer' (2019) 10(4) *New Journal of European Criminal Law*, 342–362.

111 *Malone v United Kingdom* (ECtHR, Application No 8691/79, 2 August 1984) [81]; *Bannikova v Russia* (ECtHR, First Section, Application No 18757/06, 4 November 2010) [33].

112 UN Human Rights Committee, *General Comment No 16: Article 17 (Right to Privacy), The Right to Respect of Privacy, Family, Home and Correspondence, and Protection of Honour and Reputation*, UN Doc HRI/GEN/1/Rev.1 (8 April 1988) [8]; UN Human Rights Committee, *Concluding Observations on the Fourth Periodic Report of the United States of America*, UN Doc CCPR/C/USA/CO/4 (23 April 2014), [22]; *Leander v Sweden* (ECtHR, Application No 9248/81, 26 March 1987) [50]–[51].

wiretapping.[113] Such laws must be accessible[114] and predictable in the sense that States must specify clear circumstances under which wiretapping can be used.[115]

For evidence obtained through special investigative techniques to be admissible in judicial proceedings, most jurisdictions require strict adherence to several safeguards. These safeguards commonly involve judicial or independent oversight of the use of those techniques as well as adherence to the principles of legality, subsidiarity, and proportionality,[116] in accordance with the trial State's own domestic law and sometimes in that of other States participating in the investigation. Although neither Article 19 nor Article 20(1) of the UNTOC expressly require States Parties to set and observe such safeguards, the supporting material to the Convention clearly advocates that.[117] To ensure the admissibility in Court of evidence obtained through special investigative techniques in the context of JITs, it is thus necessary that all participating States have mechanisms for supervisory control of such techniques—not least also to prevent abuse of special investigative techniques by the JITs themselves. While this principle has emerged mainly in Europe, the UN Human Rights Committee has made similar remarks on various occasions,[118] which lends support to the view that these considerations also apply at the global level. In sum, information obtained through special investigative techniques that are not authorised or supervised by JIT parties should also not be admissible as evidence in the trials held by any participating JIT State.

A further aspect to consider is that of evidence gathered from other States where there is doubt or concern about the possibility that such evidence may have been obtained by means involving torture or other cruel, inhuman, or degrading treatment. In this case, where no explicit exclusion of such evidence is provided in the domestic law of States or in a specific clause of the JIT agreement, such evidence is in any case impermissible because of the exclusionary

113 *Huvig v France* (ECtHR, Application No 11105/84, 24 April 1990) [34]; *Kruslin v France* (ECtHR, Application No 11801/85, 24 April 1990) [35]; *Roman Zakharov v Russia* (ECTHR, Grand Chamber, Application No 47143/06, 4 December 2015) [231].

114 *Rotaru v Romania* (ECtHR, Application No 28341/95, 4 May 2000) 109 [52]; *Kennedy v United Kingdom* (ECtHR, Fourth Section, Application No 26839/05, 18 May 2010) [151].

115 *Malone v United Kingdom* (n 111) [67]; *Rotaru v Romania* (n 114) [229].

116 Dimosthenis Chrysikos, 'Special Investigative Techniques', in Cecily Rose, Michael Kubiciel, and Oliver Landwehr (eds), *The United Nations Convention against Corruption: A Commentary* (Oxford University Press, 2019) 507.

117 See, for example, UNODC (n 59) 60–61.

118 UN Human Rights Committee, *Concluding Observation on the Fifth Periodic Report of France, 71*st sess, UN Doc CCPR/C/FRA/CO/5 (23 February 2016) [12]; UN Human Rights Committee, *Concluding Observations on the Second Periodic Report of Honduras*, 120th sess, UN DOC CCPR/C/HND/2 (22 August 2017) [39]; UN Human Rights Committee, *Concluding Observations on the Initial Report of Pakistan*, UN Doc CCPR/C/PAK/1 (23 August 2017) [36].

rule under Article 15 of the *Convention against Torture and Other Cruel, Inhuman or Degrading Treatment or Punishment*,[119] which is said to have customary law status.[120] The relevant standard of proof varies between jurisdictions, ranging from those requiring a 'real risk' that the evidence was obtained by torture or other maltreatment,[121] to those applying a 'balance of probabilities' standard.[122] A related issue is the exclusion of derivative evidence, that is, evidence stemming directly or indirectly from confessions or statements obtained through torture or other maltreatment.[123] Some States exclude such evidence entirely while others apply a balancing test.[124] Under the ECHR, the use of such evidence, obtained as a result of a violation of one of the core and absolute rights guaranteed by the Convention, always raises serious issues as to the fairness of the proceedings.[125] The use in criminal proceedings of statements obtained as a result of a violation of Article 3 of the ECHR (prohibition of torture) thus renders the proceedings as a whole unfair because of the breach of Article 6 (right to a fair trial).[126]

In a similar vein, Gaetano de Amicis and Andrea Scella further argue that a trial may also be unfair if the JIT was established not for real investigative and/or procedural needs but instead to circumvent national laws on the gathering and admissibility of evidence.[127] The latter may be described as 'investigation forum shopping' whereby the State where the investigative activity is to be carried out is chosen based on the leniency of evidentiary rules and low human rights safeguards.[128] Moreover, the possibility of deciding jurisdiction at any time during the investigation allows JIT members to engage in 'jurisdiction

119 Opened for signature 10 December 1984, 1465 UNTS 85 (entry into force 26 June 1987).

120 UN Committee against Torture, *Decision adopted by the Committee under Article 22 of the Convention, concerning Communication No 857/2017*, UN Doc CAT/C/67/D/857/2017 (2 September 2019) [9].

121 *Police and Criminal Evidence Act 1984* (England and Wales), s 76.

122 *Australian Evidence Act 1995* (Cth), s 84(1).

123 *Teodoro Cabrera García and Rodolfo Montiel Flores v Mexico (Judgment)* (Inter-American Court of Human Rights, Case No 12, 449, 26 November 2010) [167].

124 UN Convention against Torture Initiative, 'Non-admission of Evidence Obtained by Torture and Ill-treatment: Procedures and Practices', Exclusionary Rule Tool 8/2020 (2020) <https://cti2024.org/wp-content/uploads/2021/01/CTI-Exclusionary_Rule_Tool_8-2020_FINAL_.pdf> 11.

125 *Jalloh v Germany* (ECtHR, Grand Chamber, Application No 54810/00, 11 July 2006) 281, [99], [105]; *Harutyunyan v Armenia* (ECtHR, Third Section, Application No 36549/03, 28 June 2007) [63].

126 *Gäfgen v Germany* (ECtHR, Grand Chamber, Application No 22978/05, 1 June 2010) 247, [166]; *Ibrahim and Others v United Kingdom* (n 110) [254]; *Haski v Belgium* (ECtHR, Second Section, Application No 649/08, 25 September 2012) [85]; *Cēsnieks v Latvia* (ECtHR, Fourth Section, Application No 9278/06, 11 February 2014) [67]–[70].

127 Gaetano De Amicis, 'Cooperazione orizzontale', AA.VV., *Manuale di procedura penale europea* (Giuffrè Editore, 2017) 301; Scella (n 33) 145.

128 Colaiacovo (n 1) 169–174.

forum shopping'.[129] Indeed, the decision where to conduct the trial may be driven by the type of evidence, the circumstances of the evidence gathering, and the applicable evidence admissibility standards (and the consequence if these were not observed).[130] This practice can undermine and jeopardise the accused's legal position and the accused's right to an effective defence.

8.4.4 JIT officers operating in another jurisdiction

Article 19 of the UNTOC leaves it to States Parties to determine the legal standing, powers, and liability of JIT officers operating in another jurisdiction.[131] Because of the sovereignty principle, the investigation should be carried out under the supervision of the national authority and the guidance of one of its representatives (the JIT's leader) of the State in which the investigation is taking place. Foreign officials may then be allowed to be present during the investigation and, with the consent of the State conducting the investigation and the sending State, may be permitted and tasked by national authorities to carry out certain investigative measures.[132]

On the one hand, the benefits of enabling seconded members to play an active role in the investigation in this manner are among the main rationale for setting of JITs in the first place. For example, if witnesses and victims are from the same State as the seconded officers, they may be willing and able to engage with the investigators more openly and, importantly, in their own language.[133] Moreover, it provides seconded officers with an opportunity to personally gather evidence in a way best suited for the needs and requirements of their domestic investigation and future trial.

On the other hand, the use of seconded officers from the same country as the victims and witnesses they engage with and interview may place those victims and witnesses in fear; this is especially the case in the context of trafficking in persons and smuggling of migrants investigations, where victims and smuggled migrants may fear return and repatriation if they encounter officials from the country of origin or former residence.[134] They may also be in fear of retaliation by organised criminal groups from their former homes if they provide evidence against them. The creation of JITs to counter trafficking in

129 Eurojust JITs Network, *Third JIT Evaluation Report* (Eurojust, 2020) 13.

130 Sabine Gless, 'Birds-Eye View and Worm's Eye View: Towards a Defendant-Based Approach in Transnational Criminal Law' (2015) 6(1) *Transnational Legal Theory* 117–129.

131 UNODC (n 59) Article 17.

132 Stefano Betti, 'New Prospects for Inter-state Co-operation in Criminal Matters: the Palermo Convention' (2003) 3(2) *International Criminal Law Review* 151, 157–158.

133 Krasimira Ipokratova et al., 'Using the Joint Investigation Team as a Legal Tool for Investigating Human Trafficking for Sexual Exploitation within the EU', European Judicial Training Network ([s.d.]) 13 <http://ejtn6r2.episerverhosting.com/PageFiles/17290/WR%20TH-2018-01%20BG.pdf>.

134 CTOC/COP/WG.4/2020/3 (n 54) 11 [44].

persons and smuggling of migrants is not uncommon and usually serves to bring together countries of origin, transit, and/or destination. If victims of trafficking or smuggled migrants left their country of origin in fear of persecution, torture, or other cruel, degrading, or inhumane treatment, JITs can create a real risk that victims and witnesses re-encounter authorities and the kind of officials they fled from. Such circumstances may conflict with principles of international refugee and human rights law, which are expressly recognised by Article 14 of the *Trafficking in Persons Protocol* and Article 19 of the *Smuggling of Migrants Protocol.*

8.5 Conclusion

Joint investigations, including the creation of Joint Investigation Teams, offer a promising form of international cooperation and mark a significant development in international law and law enforcement, especially when compared to letters rogatory and parallel investigations. In the context of organised crime investigations, JITs may be seen as the ideal tool to prevent, detect, and suppress cross-border crime, as the collaboration of multiple agencies and officials somewhat mimics a key feature of international criminal syndicates. JITs are thus uniquely well positioned to investigate the structure, operations, methods, means, and locations used by organised criminal groups. It is not surprising that the UNTOC, the chief international instrument to fight organised crime, advocates the greater use of JITs and other forms of joint investigations.

This chapter has, however, also shown that there are valid concerns about the composition and activities of JITs, especially in relation to information sharing, the use and admissibility of evidence, and the deployment and powers of JIT officers working abroad. The gist of this chapter is that there are important human rights implications that need to be considered when planning, setting up, and conducting joint investigations as advocated by Article 19 of the UNTOC. As a first point, the use of information and sharing of evidence obtained through joint investigations need to be clearly defined and limited from the outset. States should also provide for a specific agreement on personal data protection.

In particular, the parties to a JIT should limit the admissibility of information acquired through JIT operations to the crimes that prompted the establishment of the JIT in the first place or, at most, to the specific purposes agreed upon when drafting the JIT agreement. It is also appropriate for States to place clear limitations on the sharing of information between the JIT partners in order to ensure that such information is not used in violation of domestic or international laws and to establish procedures to monitor adherence to and address breaches of such limitations. Importantly, specific guarantees should be given by the States permitting the use of the death penalty to ensure that any information and evidence provided by the parties to the JIT will not be used to seek, impose, or execute the death penalty. Moreover, authorities should prevent information sharing with States where there is a credible risk that such sharing will contribute to or facilitate any violation of the prohibition of torture.

Furthermore, in line with their international obligations, States should have procedures in place to assess any risk that information may have been obtained by torture or other cruel, degrading, or inhumane treatment and to articulate clear restrictions to the scope of cooperation if that risk cannot be ruled out. As a further layer of protection, it would also be beneficial for the participating authorities to maintain internal mechanisms by which JIT officers can disclose any concerns about information sharing. To make such systems work, States should provide adequate police training and establish mechanisms to minimise the risk of, and to detect and report, corruption by the agencies and officials involved.

Regarding the admissibility of evidence, it is important that States establish a clear basis to avoid so-called forum shopping, a practice that systematically circumvents national rules on evidence gathering. Moreover, States should provide information about the criteria used to choose the jurisdiction and location to prosecute and try offenders.

Lastly, concerning the legal standing and powers of officials operating in another jurisdiction, States should make sure that the participation of seconded members in investigations does not conflict with the rights and principles of international refugee and human rights law and the right to seek asylum from persecution, torture, and armed conflict. JIT agreements should take note of these issues, just as they should clearly determine and delineate the type and extent of powers that foreign officials may (and may not) use when seconded to another jurisdiction.

Part 3

Organised crime and prisons

9 Organised crime and prisons

Andreas Schloenhardt and Monika Stempkowski

9.1 Introduction

The detention of members of organised criminal groups poses unique challenges to the prison system. There is a real risk that leading members maintain their ties to the organisation whilst in prison, using their position to direct further offences or to threaten or eliminate their rivals. They may also use their wealth to fund further criminal operations or to bribe lawyers, witnesses, and criminal justice officials within and outside the prison. Furthermore, there is a risk that they recruit new members or collaborate with existing members and engage in threats, violence, and other criminal activities within the prison. Lower-ranking members of organised criminal groups may equally continue their affiliation with the group whilst in prison, executing jobs and crimes for the group, and returning to their criminal activities upon release from gaol. For these reasons, members of organised criminal groups are usually regarded as 'high-risk prisoners'.[1] Affiliations with organised criminal groups can also make detainees the target of reprisals and revenge acts by other inmates. The safety of prisoners thus poses a further challenge for correctional authorities.

International legal frameworks, chief among them the *United Nations Convention against Transnational Organized Crime* (UNTOC),[2] provide no guidance to States on how best to address the challenges associated with detaining members of organised criminal groups (hereafter 'organised crime prisoners') and mitigate the risks of them recruiting new members or engaging in criminal activities within or outside the prison environment. Similarly, regional organisations such as the European Union, the Council of Europe, and the Organization for American States, do not provide much advice or articulate standards on these points. International prison standards and human

1 UNODC, *Handbook on the Management of High-Risk Prisoners* (United Nations, 2016) 2 ('*Handbook High Risk Prisoners*'); UNODC, *The United Nations Convention against Corruption Handbook on Anti-Corruption Measures in Prisons* (United Nations, 2017) 9 ('*UNCAC Handbook*').

2 Opened for signature 15 November 2000, 2225 UNTS 209 (entry into force 29 September 2003).

DOI: 10.4324/9781003519317-12

rights law merely set some parameters to ensure humane prison conditions and prohibit cruel detention methods, such as prolonged solitary confinement or denying contact to close relatives and lawyers. This dearth of material stands in sharp contrast to other crime types, especially terrorism-related offences, for which a myriad of recommendations, handbooks, and other guidelines articulating options and limitations of detaining sentenced persons exist.

On this background, it is not surprising that prison laws and corrections authorities around the world differ greatly in their approach to the detention of organised crime prisoners. Some States have developed elaborate laws and built designated facilities to detain leading members of organised criminal groups in complete isolation, closely monitoring all their communication. Some have introduced controversial schemes to prolong the detention of organised crime members beyond the original sentence.[3] Elsewhere, however, measures to address the challenges associated with the detention of members of organised criminal groups are only in their infancy, if they exist at all. On the surface, it appears that most States have not devoted much attention to this question, or, if they have, they have merely adopted ad hoc, case-based solutions.

This chapter serves to identify and contextualise the challenges for the criminal justice system concerning the detention of organised crime prisoners. This is achieved by utilising open-source reports and case examples, focusing solely on the post-sentencing phase, excluding considerations of police arrest, remand, and the post-release phase. Moreover, the paper explores the (limited) relevant international frameworks setting out parameters to be observed when detaining organised crime prisoners.

The focus here is on organised criminal groups that (pre)exist and operate predominantly outside prisons, not on prison gangs that operate within prisons. It is, of course, acknowledged that there are many synergies and similarities between prison gangs and organised criminal groups and that several notorious groups such as the Camorra,[4] the Russian Mafia,[5] the Primeiro Comando da Capital (PCC) in Brazil,[6] and the Big Circle Boys (大圈仔) or Big Circle Gang (大圈幫)[7] originated in prisons.

3 See the example of Italy discussed in the following chapter in this volume.

4 George W Knox, Gregg W Etter, and Carter F Smith, *Gangs and Organized Crime* (Taylor & Francis, 2019) 340; Paul Lunde, *Organized Crime: An Inside Guide into the World's Most Successful Industry* (Dorling Kindersley, 2004).

5 Knox, Etter, and Smith (n 4) 350–352.

6 Benjamin Lessing and Graham D Willis, 'Legitimacy in Criminal Governance: Managing a Drug Empire from Behind Bars' (2019) 113 *American Political Science Review* 584, 587.

7 LaVerle B Berry et al., *Transnational Activities of Chinese Crime Organizations* (Bureau of Justice Statistics, US Department of Justice, 2003) 63.

9.2 Context and challenges

Organised crime poses a myriad of challenges to the criminal justice system. These challenges, in summary, can stem from the scale and spread of their criminal activities, the size and structure of the organised criminal group, their accumulated wealth, and their affiliations with private enterprises, government officials, and the community. These challenges are all the greater if organised criminal groups engage in corruption or intimidation of those working in the criminal justice sector. Organised crime members 'need not be many in number, but their impact on a prison can be severe if their efforts to condition, manipulate and corrupt others and to canvass networks both inside and outside the prisons are successful'.[8] For example, a 2012 publication examining 13 cases of organised crime prisoners in two Dutch prisons revealed:

> Not only did they continue with existing lines of business, but new enterprises were also set up, in some cases in cooperation with fellow inmates or former fellow inmates. Several crime entrepreneurs attempted to arrange, from prison, for debts to be collected from fellow perpetrators, suppliers, or customers. Attempts were also made to unlawfully influence their own criminal procedures, for instance by putting pressure on witnesses or victims. In most cases, accomplices on the outside were deployed.[9]

Much has been said and written about the laws, skills, powers, and resources needed to criminalise, investigate, and prosecute the activities of such organised criminal groups and to shield the criminal justice process, including law enforcement, prosecutors, and the judiciary, from undue influence. In international law, the UNTOC sets out a range of measures to enhance criminal laws and criminal procedure. However, scant attention has been paid to the problems faced by those responsible for detaining members of organised criminal groups; most available laws and literature end with the sentencing of offenders but fail to address the risks associated with the detention of organised crime figures.[10] For this reason, most prison laws and regulations lack specific security regimes for organised crime prisoners.

The challenges associated with the detention of organised crime members can be broadly divided between risks inside the prison system and those outside. The risks explored in the following sections are merely an illustrative collection; they are not an exhaustive list. Furthermore, it needs to be stressed that organised criminal groups exist in many shapes, structures, and sizes. Not

8 UNODC, *UNCAC Handbook* (n 1) 10.

9 Franca van der Laan, '"Prison Doesn't Stop Them" Orchestrating Criminal Acts from Behind Bars' (2012) 15 *Trends in Organised Crime* 130, 132.

10 See also, Kate Gooch and James Treadwell, '"It Doesn't Stop at the Prison Gate": Understanding Organised Crime in Prison' (2021) 252 *Prison Service Journal* 15, 16.

all have a cohesive culture and associations that amount to membership. Ad hoc, opportunistic networks may form if and when opportunities or needs arise. They may meet the definition of 'organised criminal group'[11] but may not have any bonds that last beyond the immediate or serial commission of offences. Even where structured groups exist, individuals may occupy different roles and may have different levels of seniority and loyalty to the groups.

Not further discussed here are the risks associated with the release of organised crime members from prison, or with sanctions such as house arrest, electronic tracking devices, day-release, or open correctional facilities.

9.2.1 Risks inside prisons

In a 2021 paper on organised crime in English prisons, Kate Gooch and James Treadwell note that 'prisons are places where some individuals continue to offend and where organised crime can be initiated and become embedded in the very routine activities of prison life'.[12] The authors argue

> that organised criminal networks and activities have become an embedded feature of prison life over the last decade, primarily because more sophisticated groups have been able to take advantage of the market opportunities created by a flourishing prison illicit economy, by exploiting weaknesses in State governance, and by accessing digital technology to communicate, trade and organise themselves (often without necessarily leaving the prison cell).[13]

9.2.1.1 Cohabitation and collaboration with other members inside

The most obvious risk arises if members of organised criminal groups are detained in the same facility, perhaps even in the same ward, cell, or another environment which is conducive to easier communication, collaboration, and continued association between members. Cohabitation and collaboration heighten the risk that organised crime prisoners will continue to engage in criminal activities, 'including bringing drugs or other illegal items into prison and running an underground economy in prisons'.[14]

While corrections authorities would (and should) normally avoid the cohabitation of members of the same group and prevent contact between them, strict separation may not be possible in some prisons, especially when prisons are overcrowded or where the building facilities are such that physical separation is not achievable. The risk of ongoing collaboration inside the

11 UNTOC, Article 3(a).
12 Gooch and Treadwell (n 10) 15.
13 Ibid., 16.
14 UNODC, *Handbook High-Risk Prisoners* (n 1) 39.

prison is all the greater if corrections authorities are unaware of the affiliations of their inmates and the associations between them. The risks are greater still if persons are detained in facilities used or built specifically to detain large numbers of organised crime members in the same place. On the other hand, research from Brazil shows that it may not be advisable to separate organised crime members between multiple prisons as this can risk spreading their influence across these facilities.[15]

9.2.1.2 Recruitment

Prisons provide unique opportunities to establish ties with other offenders.[16] Persons associated with organised criminal groups may use their standing and connections to recruit new members among fellow inmates. They may do so by promising to provide them with money, income, or other opportunities upon release, which may include access to accommodation, social networks, jobs, etc., or by offering to assist and support family and others whilst in prison. Franca van der Laan adds that 'prisoners can also benefit from one another's criminal networks, and by doing so, they can broaden the markets for their illegal goods, or they can establish contacts with new drug suppliers'.[17]

9.2.1.3 Influence and intimidation

Beyond the specific risk of recruitment, there are further concerns about how members of organised criminal groups may influence or intimidate other inmates by way of promising benefits or other favours, or by threatening or coercing other inmates. Within the prison, influence and intimidation is not limited to other inmates but may also involve prison staff, other officials, service providers, and perhaps lawyers and visitors to the prison. The UNODC *Handbook on the Management of High-Risk Prisoners* notes:

> A feature of prison life is that prisoners endeavour to manipulate staff. They may do this for malicious reasons or as a game played for psychological domination. Whatever the motivation, the consequences are always serious. In manipulating staff, prisoners seek to take control from them and this threatens safe custody, leaving staff anxious and uncertain. Manipulation involves causing a person to think, feel or behave in a way that is ultimately not in their best interests. This may be done consciously by bullying or coercion; or subtly through lying

15 Stephanie G Stalberg, 'From Prison Gangs to Transnational Mafia: The Expansion of Organized Crime in Brazil' (2022) 25 *Trends in Organized Crime* 443, 451.

16 Russell G Smith, *Responding to Organised Crime through Intervention in recruitment pathways*, Trends & Issues in Crime and Criminal Justice No 473 (Australian Institute of Criminology, October 2014) 5.

17 Van der Laan (n 9) 140.

> or deception. Psychological manipulation can take many forms, from distraction to exploitation of relationships and conditioning. Obvious violations include having a personal relationship with a prisoner; trafficking goods; disclosing classified information; and bypassing procedures for any reason. However, manipulation is often subtle and can take time to engineer.[18]
>
> Prisoners are particularly good at conditioning prison staff ... Within the prison context, it is how prisoners impose their will upon staff and how some staff impose their will on other members of staff. Prisoners can adopt a number of methods to identify potential staff targets for conditioning and exploitation. Once identified, the target is singled out, which may take some time and include several prisoners over many months collecting information about the target. The potential target will then be tested to identify how tolerant they are (how far can they be pushed, will they turn a blind eye when faced with confrontation, if they allow prisoners to get away with breaking the rules).[19]

Van der Laan adds:

> Having a high status seems to serve individuals well in their attempts to set up or maintain a criminal organisation from prison. A number of cases show that high-status prisoners were offered privileges by fellow prisoners and prison employees alike. These included things like additional telephone privileges, extra time with visitors, or a popular prison job. It is not always clear if it is the high criminal status itself that helps criminal leaders to arrange these privileges; it can also be their underlying personal skills, such as good social capabilities.[20]

In the case of officials (and, by extension, lawyers), there is the additional risk that organised crime prisoners may try to bribe them or, in turn, that officials solicit bribes if they are aware of the inmate's wealth, standing, and connections. Prisons are considered to be particularly vulnerable to corruption, partly because of their closed nature and the risk of insufficient public scrutiny. In such circumstances, prison staff may retreat into a passive role and 'turn a blind eye' to the prisoner's interactions, ceasing to enforce prison rules. This, in turn, increases the influence of organised crime in prisons and can lead to a loss of control.[21]

18 UNODC, *Handbook High-Risk Prisoners* (n 1) 28.
19 Ibid.
20 Van der Laan (n 9) 139.
21 UNODC, *UNCAC Handbook* (n 1) 1, 14.

9.2.1.4 Safety

Members of organised criminal groups, especially those with a record of violent offending, may pose particular risks to the physical safety of others. By extension, safety also relates to the heightened risk of escape of members of organised criminal groups from prison.[22]

In turn, the safety of such members may be at particular risk if they become the targets of threats and violent attacks within the prison. This risk escalates, especially if they are exposed to members of rival gangs or other inmates who were victims or otherwise adversely affected by the activities of that group. In some cases, the lives of organised crime members may be at risk if their identity or affiliations become known to other inmates.

This was the case, for instance, with Carl Williams, the 'baby-faced Melbourne gangland killer', 'kingpin of a multimillion-dollar crime empire', and 'one of the most powerful figures in Australia's underworld'. Along with his father, he had been involved in drug trafficking, and in 2007 was sentenced to life imprisonment for his involvement in the murder of three members of a rival clan. In April 2010, aged 38, Williams was bashed to death with part of an exercise bike while he was sitting in a common area outside his cell at a high-security prison near Geelong, Victoria.[23]

Francisco Hélmer Herrera Buitrago, one of the leaders and the chief money launderer of the Cali Cartel, suffered the same fate when he was killed in prison in 1998 by a man posing as a lawyer.[24] Another example is that of James Joseph 'Whitey' Bulger, leader of the Winter Hill Gang, a group of mostly Irish-American and some Italian-American members in Massachusetts, who was killed in October 2018 at a prison in West Virginia. In October 2022, three members from a rival Italian gang were indicted in connection with the beating death of Whitey Bulger.[25] An inquiry by the US Department of Justice in December 2022 identified serious failings by corrections authorities in the staffing of the prison and the management of the case that enabled his rivals

22 UNODC, *Handbook High-Risk Prisoners* (n 1) 39.

23 ABC, AAP, 'Carl Williams Bashed and Killed in Jail', ABC News online (19 April 2010) <https://www.abc.net.au/news/2010-04-19/carl-williams-bashed-and-killed-in-jail/402028>; Ellen Connolly, 'Australia's Baby-faced Killer Carl Williams Dies in Jail', The Guardian online (20 April 2010) <https://www.theguardian.com/world/2010/apr/19/australian-killer-carl-williams-dies>.

24 William Rempel, *At the Devil's Table: The Untold Story of the Insider Who Brought Down the Cali Cartel* (Random House, 2011) 317; Knox, Etter, and Smith (n 4) 397.

25 [s.n.], 'James "Whitey" Bulger: Three Men Charged in Mob Boss Murder', BBC News online (19 August 2022) <https://www.bbc.com/news/world-us-canada-62600194>; Edward Helmore, 'What's the Real Story behind James "Whitey" Bulger's Violent Murder?', The Guardian online (28 August 2022) <https://www.theguardian.com/world/2022/aug/28/james -whitey-bulger-murder-prison-plot>.

to know about the transfer of Bulger, ultimately creating the conditions for him to be killed.[26]

9.2.2 Risks outside prisons

9.2.2.1 Continuing criminal activities

The main concern for criminal justice authorities—and perhaps the public at large—is the risk that members of organised criminal groups will maintain their roles in, and associations with, the group whilst in prison and continue to engage in the group's criminal activities.[27] While the prison environment prevents any direct involvement in crimes committed outside, leaders and other office bearers of organised criminal groups may nevertheless direct, oversee, manage, or instigate criminal activities committed by members on the outside.[28] They may also fund or profit from such activities. '[T]he supervision in prison and the fact that the criminals were kept at a distance from the actual crime scenes [does] not eliminate the possibility of them organising crime', remarks van der Laan.[29]

One of the most infamous examples involves Salvatore (Charlie 'Lucky') Luciano, a leader of the New York Mafia in the 1920s and 1930s, who continued to run his gang from prison after being convicted for promoting prostitution in 1936.[30] Better known to a contemporary audience is the case of Pablo Escobar Gaviria, who set up the Medellin Cartel to traffic cocaine to the United States and, in the early 1990s, became one of the richest people in the world. Escobar briefly served time in prison while still effectively running his cartel, reportedly enjoying other luxuries even during his incarceration.[31]

A 2012 publication from the Netherlands documents a case where an organised crime prisoner directed criminal activities 'using meetings with accomplices in the visitor's room and mobile phones that were smuggled in for him', thereby 'giving other members of the organisation instructions'.[32] In another case mentioned in the same study, '[a]t the instruction of the imprisoned human trafficker, new women were put to work, and forced to hand over most of their earnings'.[33] An article from the UK published in 2021 similarly reports on prisoners who 'were able to orchestrate drone deliveries of drugs,

26 US Department of Justice, Office of the Inspector General, *Investigation and Review of the Federal Bureau of Prisons' Handling of the Transfer of Inmate James 'Whitey' Bulger*, Report 23-007 (December 2022).

27 UNODC, *Handbook High-Risk Prisoners* (n 1) 39.

28 Ibid.; UNODC, *UNCAC Handbook* (n 1) 67.

29 Van der Laan (n 9) 136.

30 Tim Newark, *Lucky Luciano: The Real and the Fake Gangster* (St Martin's Press, 2010) 136–137.

31 Knox, Etter, and Smith (n 4) 390.

32 Van der Laan (n 9) 134.

33 Ibid.

weapons, and mobile phones by drawing on a wider network of accomplices both within prison and the community'[34] and further notes:

> Prison based criminal entrepreneurs require networks and associates beyond the prison walls. Increasingly the smuggling of contraband, the associated transfer and recovery of payments, reflects something more sophisticated than an isolated incident of 'crime that is organised', typically involving criminal networks that spread across the country and into more than one prison.[35]

9.2.2.2 Influence and intimidation

There is a risk that members of organised criminal groups in prison will leverage their role, influence, or wealth to influence or intimidate persons on the outside. This may concern fellow group members, rivals, relatives, persons in connection with these groups and their activities, witnesses, lawyers, as well as officials. In the latter case, there is the additional risk of bribery, which, along with threats and intimidation, may be employed to pervert the course of justice or to influence the decisions of other officials to achieve beneficial outcomes for the inmate, their groups, or their associates.[36]

9.3 International frameworks

9.3.1 UNTOC

In international law, the *United Nations Convention against Transnational Organized Crime* is the chief and sole treaty setting out specific measures to prevent and combat organised crime. Most of its provisions concern criminalisation and international cooperation, with a small number of articles containing measures relating to criminal procedure and prevention. The UNTOC, along with the extensive explanatory material published by the United Nations Office on Drugs and Crime (UNODC)—'guardian' of the Convention and its Protocols—does not contain express provisions or provide specific guidance on the punishment, including imprisonment, of persons convicted for their involvement in organised criminal groups.

9.3.1.1 Sanctions against organised crime

Article 11 contains some rudimentary references to sanctions for offences under the Convention but leaves the interpretation and implementation to States Parties according to their legal traditions and national systems. Article

34 Gooch and Treadwell (n 10) 25.
35 Ibid.
36 See further Chapter 3 of this volume.

11(1) merely obliges them to ensure that offences relating to participation in an organised criminal group, laundering of proceeds of crime, corruption, and obstruction of justice under Articles 5, 6, 8, and 23, are punished with sanctions 'that take into account the gravity of that offence'. This includes, at least theoretically, civil, administrative, and criminal sanctions.[37] The vagueness of Article 11(1) stems from the difficulties of harmonising penalties and sanctions across jurisdictions because of their different legal traditions and constitutional provisions (including admissibility of the death penalty or life imprisonment) as well as different sentencing practices.

Article 11(4) addresses the execution of the sanctions and requires States Parties to ensure that the courts 'bear in mind the serious nature' of the offences when considering early release, parole, or any other decision that may reduce the period of detention.[38] Article 11 contains no further information about the terms and conditions of the sanctions, including requirements concerning the safe imprisonment of organised crime members and the need to separate them from other members of the group.

9.3.1.2 Transfer of sentenced persons

Another provision under the UNTOC that can be of relevance in the context of detaining members of organised criminal groups is Article 17, which calls on States Parties to consider transferring persons sentenced to imprisonment or other forms of deprivation of liberty to another jurisdiction to complete their sentence.[39] Because many organised crime activities are transnational, a considerable number of perpetrators are detained in countries to which they have no personal ties. The transfer of sentenced persons is frequently driven by human rights considerations, enabling individuals to serve their sentence in an environment where the goals of rehabilitation and reintegration can be best achieved.[40] Usually, the transfer is done to a receiving State where the person has social ties, especially by virtue of nationality or family.[41] The decision to transfer a sentenced person may also be made on the basis of humanitarian or compassionate grounds, including the expenses incurred by family visiting and

37 Thea Coventry, 'Article 30: Prosecution, Adjudication, and Sanctions' in Cecily Rose, Michael Kubiciel, and Oliver Landwehr (eds), *The United Nations Convention Against Corruption: A Commentary* (Oxford University Press, 2019) 301, 303.

38 Francesco Calderoni, 'Article 11: Prosecution, Adjudication and Sanctions', in Andreas Schloenhardt et al., *The United Nations Convention against Transnational Organized Crime and its Protocols: A Commentary* (Oxford University Press, 2023) 111, 116.

39 See further, Andreas Schloenhardt, Article 17: 'Transfer of Sentenced Persons', in Andreas Schloenhardt et al., *The United Nations Convention against Transnational Organized Crime and its Protocols: A Commentary* (Oxford University Press, 2023) 179–185.

40 See further, Eveline de Wree, Tom van der Beken, and Gert Vermeulen, 'The Transfer of Sentenced Persons in Europe' (2009) 11(1) *Punishment & Society* 111, 116–117.

41 See further, Michael Plachta, 'Human Rights Aspects of the Prisoner Transfer in a Comparative Perspective' (1993) 53(4) *Louisiana Law Review* 1043, 1045–1046.

supporting relatives imprisoned abroad, medical or mental health needs, complaints of mistreatment, or where the conditions in the institution in which the person was convicted and sentenced fall below minimum international standards.[42]

The motivation to transfer sentenced persons can also have financial and practical considerations. For corrections authorities in the sentencing State, the transfer of sentenced persons provides an avenue to alleviate the burden associated with the detention of foreign nationals convicted by their courts.[43] Difficulties in providing consular services, international relations, and the inability to supervise sentenced persons after their release also play a role in cases involving the transfer of sentenced persons.[44]

The transfer of sentenced persons from one jurisdiction to another is a complex undertaking, and legal requirements, along with the conditions and circumstances of transfers, frequently differ between States. For this reason, Article 17 promotes the creation of mechanisms that permit and facilitate the transfer of sentenced persons from one State to another. It does not set out the purposes, requirements, and modalities for the transfer of sentenced persons or specify the State to which a person may be transferred; it merely encourages States to consider entering into arrangements and agreements on such transfers.

9.3.1.3 Obstruction of justice

Article 23 of the UNTOC, which requires States Parties to criminalise obstruction of justice, plays a role in addressing attempts by organised criminal groups to coerce or otherwise influence prison staff. Article 23(b) specifically concerns the use of coercive means to interfere with law enforcement and justice officials in relation to the commission of offences covered by the UNTOC. The nexus between obstruction of justice and organised crime is further discussed in Chapter 3 of this volume.

9.3.2 International prison rules

While international law provides next to no guidance on how to address the challenges posed by detaining organised crime members, it does articulate a range of standards and limitations to ensure the humane treatment of all

42 Michael Abbell, *International Prisoner Transfer 2010* (Brill, 2010) 7.
43 Ibid., 5.
44 UNODC, *Legislative Guide for the Implementation of the United Nations Convention against Transnational Organized Crime* (2nd ed, UNODC, 2017) [600]; UN, *Commentary on the United Nations Convention against Illicit Traffic in Narcotic Drugs and Psychotropic Substances 1988* (United Nations, 1998) 173 [6.46]; Abbell (n 42) 6–7; see further UNODC *Handbook on the International Transfer of Sentenced Persons* (United Nations, 2012) 9–15.

prisoners and adequate respect for their dignity, human rights, and civil liberties.[45] The detention and management of organised crime prisoners thus requires a careful balancing between, on one hand, security considerations to contain the influence of organised crime in prisons and, on the other hand, fundamental human rights considerations and the duty to support the social reintegration of all prisoners.

Various international instruments establish rights, rules, and principles relating to the humane and respectful treatment of prisoners. None of these instruments make specific mention of organised crime-related measures and considerations. For the most part, these frameworks apply to all prisoners, regardless of the type of their offending. Special consideration is given to prisoners who are young offenders or women, prisoners with special physical or mental health conditions, and recommendations and best practice guidelines have been developed for the detention of high-risk prisoners and persons involved in terrorism or at risk of radicalisation.

The relevant international instruments range from global treaties with binding obligations for States Parties, to regional legal frameworks, and 'soft law' principles and recommendations. At the global level, binding obligations arise, inter alia, from the *International Covenant on Civil and Political Rights*,[46] the *Convention against Torture and Other Cruel, Inhuman or Degrading Treatment or Punishment*,[47] the *Convention on the Rights of the Child*,[48] and, by extension, the *Universal Declaration of Human Rights*.[49]

Chief among the non-binding international frameworks are the *United Nations Standard Minimum Rules for the Treatment of Prisoners* (the *Nelson Mandela Rules*),[50] along with the *Body of Principles for the Protection of All Persons Under Any Form of Detention or Imprisonment*,[51] the *United Nations Standard Minimum Rules for the Administration of Juvenile Justice* (the *Beijing Rules*),[52] the *United Nations Rules for the Protection of Juveniles Deprived of their Liberty*,[53] and the *United Nations Rules for the Treatment*

45 UN General Assembly, *The United Nations Standard Minimum Rules for the Treatment of Prisoners (the Nelson Mandela Rules)*, UN Doc A/RES/70/175 (8 January 2016) ('*Nelson Mandela Rules*') Rule 1.

46 Opened for signature 16 December 1966, 999 UNTS 171 (entry into force 23 March 1976).

47 Opened for signature 10 December 1984, 1465 UNTS 85 (entry into force 26 June 1987).

48 Opened for signature 20 November 1989, 1577 UNTS 3 (entry into force 2 September 1990).

49 UN General Assembly, *Universal Declaration of Human Rights*, Resolution 217 (III) (10 December 1948).

50 *Nelson Mandela Rules* (n 45).

51 UN General Assembly, *Body of Principles for the Protection of All Persons under Any Form of Detention or Imprisonment*, UN Doc A/RES/43/117 (19 March 1989).

52 UN General Assembly, *United Nations Standard Minimum Rules for the Administration of Juvenile Justice ('The Beijing Rules')*, UN Doc A/RES/40/33 (20 December 1985).

53 UN General Assembly, *United Nations Rules for the Protection of Juveniles Deprived of their Liberty*, UN Doc A/RES/45/113 (2 April 1991).

of Women Prisoners and Non-custodial Measures for Women Offenders (the *Bangkok Rules*).[54] Additional rules and best practice guidelines have been developed by regional organisations in Africa, the Americas, and Europe and include, *inter alia*, the *Kampala Declaration on Prison Conditions in Africa*,[55] the *Principles and Best Practices on the Protection of Persons Deprived of Liberty in the Americas*,[56] and the *European Prison Rules*.[57]

While these frameworks may not contain specific recommendations relating to the detention of organised crime members, they set out important mandatory requirements, minimum standards, other rules, and, in some contexts, outright prohibitions that must be considered when general or individualised measures against sentenced persons are adopted. These rules relate to any aspect of imprisonment, from the assessment of prisoners upon admission to the preparation for release. They articulate important parameters relevant, inter alia, to the accommodation and general living conditions, including medical care,[58] contact with the outside world, work and education,[59] recreational activities,[60] safety of the prisoner and the security of the prison, use of force and restraint,[61] prison intelligence, and so forth.

It is critical that these international frameworks, along with relevant regional standards and domestic rules, are consulted and observed when specific laws or practical measures concerning the management of organised crime prisoners are designed, implemented, and enforced. In practice, this will mean that there are, for example, limitations on the time prisoners may spend in solitary confinement,[62] on bans, restrictions, and monitoring of contact with the outside world, including communication with close family members,[63] on the conditions in high-security facilities, restrictions and sanctions imposed on prisoners,[64] and the gathering of prison intelligence. It also means that due consideration needs to be given to the vulnerabilities and special needs of individual prisoners, including women or young offenders.

54 UN General Assembly, *United Nations Rules for the Treatment of Women Prisoners and Non-custodial Measures for Women Offenders (the Bangkok Rules)*, UN Doc A/RES/65/229 (6 October 2010).
55 Reprinted in Christoph Heyns and Morne van der Linde, *Human Rights Law in Africa*, volume 4 (Brill, 1999) 345–346.
56 Inter-American Commission on Human Rights (IACHR), *Principles and Best Practices on the Protection of Persons Deprived of Liberty in the Americas*, Resolution 1/08 (13 March 2008).
57 Council of Europe, Committee of Ministers, *Recommendation Rec(2006)2-rev of the Committee of Ministers to Member States on the European Prison Rules* (1 July 2020).
58 *Nelson Mandela Rules* (n 45) Rules 12–22, 24–35, 41.
59 Ibid., Rules 94–104.
60 Ibid., Rules 23, 64–66, 105.
61 Ibid., 47–49.
62 Ibid., Rules 43–45.
63 Ibid., Rule 58.
64 Ibid., Rules 36–46.

9.3.3 International case law

Further parameters for the detention of organised crime members can be found in international case law, chiefly the jurisprudence by the European Court of Human Rights (ECtHR), which seeks to ensure that the rights and principles enshrined in the *European Convention on Human Rights* (ECHR) extend to prisoners in correctional facilities.[65] For obvious reasons, various fundamental rights, such as the right to liberty or the right to respect for family life, are affected by prison conditions. The prison environment poses a particular risk of exposing inmates to conditions and treatment that might endanger their personal dignity. Therefore, the Court holds that States have the obligation to protect prisoners as vulnerable individuals from all forms of degrading treatment.[66]

As far as the rights of prisoners are concerned, the ECtHR has issued a large number of decisions focusing on whether certain measures of treatment of prisoners violate the ECHR, particularly Articles 3 (prohibition of torture), 5 (right to liberty and security), and 8 (right to respect for private and family life). While only a small number of cases focus directly on organised crime prisoners, the ECtHR case law nonetheless articulates important guidelines on how to reconcile the need to maintain security inside prisons and prevent the commission of further crimes with the guarantee to protect the fundamental rights of all prisoners.

For example, there are several limitations to special prison regimes (such as the Italian '41 bis' system discussed in the following chapter) aimed at severing the ties between organised crime prisoners and their criminal organisation by restricting their contact with other inmates, visitors, and the outside world. Generally, the ECHR does not prohibit the use of special detention regimes if the circumstances deem them to be necessary.[67] But to avoid violations of Articles 3 or 8, respectively, certain requirements must be met.

In each individual case, there must be a justification for the application of the special regime, for example, the dangerousness of the prisoner or their connection to organised crime.[68] Serving a life sentence, by contrast, is usually not a sufficient basis for a special regime.[69] The necessity of such additional measures must be ascertained, documented, and justified in each case

65 *Khodorkovskiy and Lebedev v Russia* (ECtHR, Chamber, Applications Nos 11082/06 and 13772/05, 25 July 2013) [836]; *Klibisz v Poland* (ECtHR, Fourth Section, Application No 2235/02, 4 October 2016) [354].

66 *Rooman v Belgium* (ECtHR, Grand Chamber, Application No 18052/11, 31 January 2019) [143].

67 *Piechowicz v Poland* (ECtHR, Fourth Section, Application No 20071/07, 17 April 2013) [161].

68 *Enea v Italy* (ECtHR, Grand Chamber, Application No 74912/01, 17 September 2009) [125].

69 *Harakchiev and Tomulov v Bulgaria* (ECtHR, Fourth Section, Application Nos 15018/11 and 67799/12, 8 July 2014) [204].

individually. This concerns the first time such measures are imposed and any time they are renewed or extended.[70]

Article 8(2) lists various situations in which public authorities may lawfully interfere with the right to privacy and family life, such as national security, public safety, the prevention of crime, and the protection of the rights and freedoms of others. The reference in Article 8(2) to 'in accordance with the law' has been interpreted by the ECtHR to mean that particular attention must be drawn to ensuring that prisoners are protected against the abuse of a special regime and that they have appropriate rights to be heard in proceedings ordering the imposition of such a regime on them.[71]

In several decisions, the ECtHR has reviewed the rationale and the specific conditions of special regimes in light of the ECHR. In relation to Italy's special regime for the detention of members of the mafia, for instance, the Court has held that additional measures to restrict contact of organised crime prisoners to the outside world are permissible if this reduces their ability to maintain their role in the criminal organisation and instigate further criminal activities. In *Enea v Italy*, the ECtHR noted:

> Before the introduction of the special regime, many dangerous prisoners were able to maintain their positions within the criminal organisations to which they belonged, to exchange information with other prisoners and with the outside world and to organise and procure the commission of criminal offences. In that context the Court considers that, given the specific nature of the phenomenon of organised crime, particularly of the mafia type, and the fact that family visits have frequently served as a means of conveying orders and instructions to the outside, the—admittedly substantial—restrictions on visits, and the accompanying controls, could not be said to be disproportionate to the legitimate aims pursued.[72]

The ECtHR also has in principle approved long-term detention under special regimes so long as this is warranted by the individual circumstances of the case, if this is adequately and regularly (re)assessed, and appropriately justified by State authorities.[73] In determining whether special prison regimes align with the rights protected under the ECHR, regard must be given, inter alia, to the ability of prisoners to contact their family members, socialise with fellow inmates, the frequency and duration of such contacts, their ability to access

70 *Provenzano v Italy* (ECtHR, First Section, Application No 55080/13, 25 October 2018) [147]; *Piechowicz v Poland* (n 67) [165].

71 *Masľák v Slovakia (No 2)* (ECtHR, First Section, Applications Nos 38321/17 and 8 others, 31 March 2022) [137].

72 *Enea v Italy* (n 68) [126].

73 *Ramirez Sanchez v France* (ECtHR, Grand Chamber, Application No 59450/00, 4 July 2006) [136].

television and books, and participate in courses offered inside the prison.[74] Special security measures, such as handcuffs or conducting physical examinations, may only be employed if warranted due to specific threats or safety concerns in individual circumstances; they may not be employed by default or automatically, which would constitute a violation of Article 3.[75]

Similar points must be considered if prisoners are placed in solitary confinement.[76] The ECtHR has held that solitary confinement does not, per se, conflict with the rights afforded by the ECHR, chief among them Article 3.[77] If special prison regimes envisage placing inmates in solitary confinement, such a measure may only be employed if there are compelling reasons[78] which must be properly assessed and documented.[79] The state of health of the inmate must be taken into account and reviewed on an ongoing basis[80] and the person must have an avenue to appeal against the decision to place them in solitary confinement.[81] The ECtHR has not articulated any limits for the period solitary confinement may be imposed; this will depend on the individual case and the conditions of such confinement. Prison authorities have an obligation to mitigate as far as possible the negative effects of solitary confinement through other measures. This includes, for example, granting access to TV, magazines, and other entertainment, outdoor exercise and sports, contact with family members, and providing appropriate care by prison staff for the duration of solitary confinement.[82]

9.4 Summary and observations

This chapter has shown that the challenges posed by organised crime to the criminal justice system do not end with the conviction, sentencing, and detention of members of organised criminal groups. Many organised crime prisoners maintain their ties whilst in prison; some continue in their leading roles and provide instructions for further crimes. Some organised criminal groups recruit new members inside the prison and continue their criminal activities within and outside the facilities. If members of rival groups are detained in the same facility, there is the added risk of retaliation and violence.

74 *Piechowicz v Poland* (n 67) [166].
75 *Horych v Poland* (ECtHR, Fourth Section, Application No 13621/08, 17 April 2012) [93].
76 *Rhode v Denmark* (ECtHR, First Section, Application No 69332/01, 21 July 2005) [93].
77 *Ramirez Sanchez v France* (n 73) [123].
78 *A.T. v Estonia (No 2)* (ECtHR, Second Section, Application No 70465/14, 13 November 2018) [73].
79 *Csüllög v Hungary* (ECtHR, Second Section, Application No 30042/08, 7 June 2011) [31].
80 *Jeanty v Belgium* (ECtHR, Third Section, Application No 82284/17, 31 March 2020) [117]; *Ramirez Sanchez v France* (n 73) [139].
81 *Onoufriou v Cyprus* (ECtHR, First Section, Application No 24407/04, 7 January 2010) [71].
82 *Csüllög v Hungary* (n 79) [37].

On this background, it is surprising and perhaps alarming that international law, guidelines, and the literature provide very little advice to legislators and prison authorities about how best to manage organised crime prisoners and to provide a safe environment for fellow inmates, staff, and the prisoners themselves. Importantly, there is next to no guidance on how to minimise, if not eliminate the contact between inmates and the organised criminal groups they belong to and how to prevent them from directing further crimes, accessing their wealth, and recruiting new members inside the gaol. While international and regional organisations, along with thinktanks and scholars, have produced a plethora of material designed to inform authorities about risks associated with the detention of terrorists and radicalisation in prison, there is to this day no literature setting out the tools and limitations to best manage organised crime prisoners.

This chapter seeks to provide a basic platform on which to conduct further research into this subject matter and on which to develop guidelines and criteria to ensure that organised crime prisoners can be isolated from their criminal groups and their criminal assets whilst ensuring that their fundamental rights are respected and that their safety in gaol can be provided.

As a next step it would be desirable to use international legal instruments, such as the UNTOC, along with international prison rules and case law as a starting point to articulate the basic parameters that need to be observed when detaining organised crime prisoners and when placing them under special prison regimes. Based on these sources, it would also be useful to develop guidelines that set out the options and limitations for prison laws, rules, and practical measures that can be used to manage organised crime prisoners.

As a further step, it would be useful to collect and review information on policies, laws, and practical measures adopted by individual jurisdictions specifically for the detention of organised crime members. Around the world, a myriad of measures are or have been considered or used within various national correctional systems for organised crime prisoners. While not all jurisdictions have employed such measures, those that have, have been very creative—sometimes quite controversial and draconian—in their attempts to segregate organised crime prisoners and to subject them to restrictions not permissible for other prisoners, and in some cases, prohibited under international law.

It is hoped that the present chapter provides the necessary background and context to think more carefully about the detention of organised crime members, their place and conditions of detention, restrictions imposed on their contacts within and outside the prison, the influence they may exercise over fellow inmates and prison staff, their safety in prison, and the measures best suited to address these challenges.

10 Italy's '41 bis' special prison regime for leading organised crime figures in view of European Court of Human Rights' case law and international prison standards

Gianmarco Bondi

10.1 Introduction

The origins of Italy's so-called '41 bis prison regime' can be traced back to the early 1990s and the height of Italy's struggle to suppress the increased violence of mafia-related crime, especially by the Sicilian Cosa Nostra. Article 41 bis(2) of the Italian *Prison Administration Act*,[1] which gave the name to the rigid rules used to detain prominent organised crime figures, was first introduced in 1992.[2] After a series of prorogations of this emergency legislation, in 2002, Article 41 bis became a permanent fixture of Italian prison laws.[3] To this day, the Article has been reformed several times, shifting between the need to safeguard fundamental rights and the desire to combat organised crime. Nevertheless, a prevailing theme of the legislator seems to be making the provision more and more severe.

In essence, under the current law, an order under Article 41 bis is issued by the Minister of Justice against individuals detained (awaiting trial or sentenced) for organised crime-related offences (as listed in Article 4 bis of the *Prison Administration Act*) who are considered to be dangerous because of their connections with mafia-style, terrorist, or subversive criminal groups. The order is initially made to last for a period of four years and can be extended further every two years. The order is subject to review by the Supervisory Court (*Tribunale di sorveglianza*) of Rome. Decisions by the Supervisory Court can be appealed before the Court of Cassation (*Corte di Cassazione*).

The 41 bis prison regime entails a whole range of limitations to restrict interaction with other persons, which are much stricter than those that apply to conventional inmates. The restrictions can be loosely divided into two main

1 Law No 354/1975.
2 Law No 306/1992.
3 Law No 279/2002.

DOI: 10.4324/9781003519317-13

categories: those meant for ordinary participants in organised criminal groups and those applying to leading figures (who are accommodated in designated 'reserved areas'). The limitations imposed under Article 41 bis can be revoked if the person collaborates with the authorities.

Due to its history, the 41 bis prison regime is a very sensitive topic in Italy and the subject of polarised public debate.[4] Among academic experts, there is ongoing discussion about the legitimacy of this special prison regime. Many find this system to be excessive and point to shortcomings, challenging the validity of its purported aim, that is, preventing contact with organised crime elements. Reform is advocated in order to avoid using the 41 bis prison regime merely as a harsher punishment, a 'hard prison regime' (*carcere duro*).

At the national level, the Constitutional Court (*Corte Costituzionale*) has examined Article 41 bis in light of relevant constitutional principles and, on some occasions, has declared certain aspects unconstitutional. The European Court of Human Rights (ECtHR) has faced several cases involving persons detained under Article 41 bis and, in some instances, has found certain elements of 41 bis to be violating the *European Convention on Human Rights* (ECHR).[5] Nonetheless, the Constitutional Court and the ECtHR have never stated that the regime is, *per se*, incompatible with the Italian Constitution and the ECHR, respectively.[6]

10.2 Origins

10.2.1 The underlying rationale

The core reason currently provided for the continuing existence and use of the 41 bis prison regime rests upon the understanding that neither pre-trial detention nor imprisonment are sufficiently effective in severing the ties between inmates accused of or sentenced for organised crime-related offences and their criminal group; in other words, the ordinary prison system provides too many opportunities for such inmates to maintain contact with other people outside and inside the gaol.

This view is supported by empirical evidence showing that in the field of mafia crime, interactions granted to detainees both with the outside world and within prisons enable high-ranking organised crime figures to maintain their

4 See, for example, Maria Chr. Alvanou, 'The ECHR and the 41-Bis Prison Regime in Italy: Weakening the Struggle Against Serious Crime or Strengthening Modern Principles of Prison Law?', *JURISTnews* (16 October 2019) <https://www.jurist.org/commentary/2019/10/maria-chr-alvanou-41-bis/>.

5 Opened for signature 4 November 1950, ETS 5 (entry into force 3 September 1953).

6 For a comparison between the case law of the Constitutional Court and the ECtHR, see Fausto Giunta, Sebastiano Ardita, and Massimo Pavarini, 'Il "carcere duro" tra efficacia e legittimità' [2007] *Criminalia, Annuario di scienze penalistiche* 249, 267–268.

place in the structure of the criminal organisation even whilst incarcerated.[7] This includes committing serious offences such as directing or organising a 'mafia-type criminal organisation' under Article 416 bis of the Italian *Penal Code* (*Codice Penale*).[8] This fact is also documented in the Court of Cassation's case aw which, starting from the late 1980s, has noted that the detention of mafia leaders and other members does not constitute the last act in the commission of the crime of membership of a mafia-type criminal organisation.[9]

In her 2016 publication, Angela Della Bella cites several investigations and trials conducted since the second half of the 20th century, which demonstrate that the regular prison system has been unable to stop detained organised crime members from committing crimes from within the gaol.[10] One prominent example is the killing of the Cosa Nostra boss Pietro Marchese in 1982, whose throat was cut in prison by five other inmates on the orders of his brother-in-law Filippo Marchese.[11] Another example is that of Giuseppe Lipari, who managed the assets of the Corleonesi crime family, which is part of the Cosa Nostra, and who was an advisor to its *de facto* leader Bernardo Provenzano. Whilst imprisoned for the crime of membership of a mafia-type criminal organisation, he kept advising Provenzano by exchanging notes with him using various avenues, such as fellow detainees, his lawyer (who was also his daughter), visits by family members, and hiding messages in laundry bags handed to his relatives for washing.[12]

The official purpose of Article 41 bis is to reduce the frequency of contact between organised crime inmates and the outside and exercise closer control over them; on paper, Article 41 bis is not meant to create a situation of solitary confinement or otherwise aggravate the stresses and pains associated with regular imprisonment.[13] The case of Giuseppe Piromalli demonstrates that 41 bis imprisonment does not necessarily lead to complete incommunicado detention but may only partially (albeit significantly) obstruct communication between organised crime members. Piromalli, the head of the Piromalli crime family (which belongs to the Calabrian 'Ndrangheta), whilst detained under 41 bis, decided to break an alliance with the Molè crime family. Following a feud with this former ally-turned-rival, he issued orders to other *'ndranghetisti* via visits of his family in gaol. Knowing that such in-person conversations could be monitored and recorded under the 41 bis prison regime, he was

7 See further Angela Della Bella, *Il 'carcere duro' tra esigenze di prevenzione e tutela dei diritti fondamentali. Presente e futuro del regime detentivo speciale ex art. 41 bis o.p.* (Giuffré, 2016) 1–74.
8 Ibid., 3.
9 Ibid., 9–11.
10 Ibid., 13–74.
11 Giovanni Falcone and Marcelle Padovani, *Cose di Cosa Nostra* (Rizzoli, 1991) 31.
12 Della Bella (n 7) 13–23.
13 Giunta, Ardita, and Pavarini (n 6) 249–262 and Franco Corleone and Andrea Pugiotto (eds), *Volti e maschere della pena. Opg e carcere duro, muri della pena e giustizia riparativa* (Ediesse, 2013) 211–221.

forced to rely on a complicated coded language, which was at times hard to decode even for his close relatives and ultimately prevented him from giving sufficiently clear instructions.[14]

Academic experts and the courts argue that the effects of Article 41 bis far exceed its purpose. Sergio D'Elia and Maurizio Turco, for instance, equate the 41 bis prison regime with State (or 'democratic') torture.[15] Tullio Padovani compares the regime to the practice of using torture on persons found to be guilty in order for them to testify against their accomplices (*jus commune quaestio in caput sociorum*).[16] In 2007, a judge in Los Angeles cited similar reasons when she refused the extradition of a person detained in California who had served a 22-year prison sentence for drug trafficking because of the likelihood that he might be placed under the 41 bis regime upon return to Italy. The judge remarked that this special prison regime was 'designed to physically and psychologically compel criminals to reveal information about the Sicilian Mafia' and that such 'coercion is not related to any lawfully imposed sanction or punishment and thus constitutes torture'.[17] This decision was, however, successfully appealed by US authorities and the person was eventually extradited to Italy.[18]

The cases, conditions, and circumstances in which Article 41 bis has been applied reveal two further purposes of this regime. The first purpose is to push persons detained under Article 41 bis to become State witnesses by making their prison environment inconvenient and intolerable, both for the detainee and their relatives outside. According to Andrea Pugiotto, this is demonstrated by the fact that Article 4 bis of the *Prison Administration Act* prohibits access to probation measures for prisoners sentenced to life imprisonment with reference to extremely serious offences related to organised crime.[19] Such access will, however, be granted if the prisoner provides evidence to State authorities. Padovani thus speaks of a 'soave inquisition' in relation to the opportunities offered in exchange for such collaboration.[20] Massimo Pavarini asks if 'the alternative between extreme rewards or harsh prison regime is capable

14 Della Bella (n 7) 52–60.

15 Sergio D'Elia and Maurizio Turco, *Tortura Democratica: inchiesta su 'la comunità del 41 bis reale'* (Marsilio, 2002) 30.

16 Tullio Padovani, 'Quaestio in caput sociorum. Alle origini dell'obbligo del reo di collaborare alle indagini', in Luigi Stortoni and Donato Castronuovo (eds), *Nulla è cambiato? Riflessioni sulla tortura* (Bononia University Press, 2019) 76–77.

17 See Giunta, Ardita, and Pavarini (n 6) 262–264.

18 Emanuele Nicosia, 'Il c.d. 41-bis è una forma di tortura o trattamento crudele, inumano o degradante?' (2009) 3 *Rivista italiana di diritto e procedura penale* 1240, 1240–1243.

19 Andrea Pugiotto, 'Quattro interrogativi (e alcune considerazioni) sulla compatibilità costituzionale del 41-bis', in Franco Corleone and Andrea Pugiotto (eds), *Volti e maschere della pena. Opg e carcere duro, muri della pena e giustizia riparativa* (Ediesse, 2013) 206–207.

20 Tullio Padovani, 'La soave inquisizione: Osservazioni e rilievi a proposito delle nuove ipotesi di ravvedimento' (1981) 2 *Rivista italiana di diritto e procedura penale* 529–545.

of "loosening tongues"'.[21] The second purpose relates to deterrence. Article 41 bis seeks to pressure participants of organised criminal groups to give up their criminal activities for fear of being caught and detained under the special prison regime. Mario Canepa and Sergio Merlo argue that Article 41 bis does not serve as a means for better custodial containment of organised crime members (the official purpose) but instead seeks to deter members still on the loose.[22]

10.2.2 Evolution of Article 41 bis

10.2.2.1 Beginnings

The 41 bis prison regime is an example of emergency legislation originally intended to be a temporary measure which, over time, has become a permanent feature of Italian penal law.[23] Article 41 bis was designed in the early 1990s, at the height of Italy's struggle to counter increasingly violent mafia-related crime. This fight not only concerned the Cosa Nostra from Sicily but also the 'Ndrangheta from Calabria and the Camorra from Campania. Article 41 bis was introduced with Law No 306/1992 following the assassination of the then Director General of Penal Affairs of the Ministry of Justice and former investigating judge Giovanni Falcone on 23 May 1992.

The first orders under Article 41 bis were issued on 19 July 1992, the day of the assassination of Paolo Borsellino, Deputy District Prosecutor of Palermo and former investigating judge. The night after the killing, following orders made by the Minister of Justice, 50 members of the Cosa Nostra detained at the Ucciardone Prison in Palermo were taken from their cells and brought by plane and helicopter to the prison on the remote Pianosa Island in the Tyrrhenian Sea. In the subsequent weeks, further orders made by the Department of Prison Administration of the Ministry of Justice brought the number of persons transferred and placed under the 41 bis prison regime to more than 1,000, including many who were taken to the prison on Asinara, an island north of Sardinia.[24]

Quite quickly, allegations of maltreatment of persons detained under the new regime emerged.[25] For example, as early as 1992 it was alleged that detainees endured forms of abuse, such as being forced to run in front of prison guards with their heads held down and in silence, being beaten, having their clothes ripped, glasses trampled on, and their dentures rendered useless,

21 Giunta, Ardita, and Pavarini (n 6) 265.

22 Mario Canepa and Sergio Merlo, *Manuale di diritto penitenziario* (Giuffré, 2010) 210.

23 On the history of the special prison regime, see Della Bella (n 7) 105–163.

24 Ibid., 106–107.

25 For a first-hand experience of what 41 bis was in its early days, as enforced at the Pianosa Island Prison, see Rosario Enzo Indelicato and Cetta Brancato, *L'inferno di Pianosa: L'esperienza del 41 bis nel 1992* (Sensibili alle foglie, 2015).

though these accusations were never proven at trial in Italy.[26] Some of these allegations were later brought before the ECtHR when two prisoners filed an action against Italy for violating the prohibition of torture under Article 3 of the ECHR. The Court found that Italy was in breach of the procedural positive obligation derived from Article 3 mainly because the competent national authorities did not investigate these facts in a thorough, effective, and timely manner.[27]

Since its introduction, the 41 bis prison regime has served as a strong show of force by Italy that it will fight and avenge the kinds of attacks on the State and its representatives that took place, especially the assassinations of two of its most prominent civil servants mentioned above. Later on, the work of supervisory judges (*magistrati di sorveglianza*), Parliament, and human rights groups resulted in modifications and a softening of an otherwise rather draconian regime.[28] When Article 41 bis was first introduced in 1992, orders under this provision could be issued against anyone who was detained for offences under Article 416 of the *Penal Code* and for crimes related to or aiding mafia-type criminal organisations, regardless whether the person was in remand awaiting trial or had already been sentenced. Orders were often not issued against individual inmates but collectively for whole groups of persons. The orders were made indefinite and frequently contained vague instructions about the suspension of general rules relating to the treatment of detainees and ignored—and often violated—fundamental rights. Furthermore, a right to appeal the instructions was not available under Article 41 bis in its original form.[29]

10.2.2.2 2002 reform

As mentioned, Article 41 bis was initially introduced as a temporary measure, meant to operate for three years from the day it passed into law. Accordingly, it would have lapsed on 6 August 1996. After a series of prorogations, Law No 279/2002 elevated Article 41 bis into a permanent feature of the *Prison Administration Act*.[30] This reform had the purpose of updating the special prison regime a decade after its introduction, taking into account the principles stated in the case law of both the Italian Constitutional Court and the ECtHR.[31]

26 See Della Bella (n 7) 110–111.

27 *Labita v Italy* (ECtHR, Grand Chamber, Application No 29772/95, 6 April 2000) [136]; *Indelicato v Italy* [2001] ECHR 599, [37].

28 Della Bella (n 7) 112.

29 Ibid., 108–110.

30 See Alessandro Bernasconi, 'L'emergenza diviene norma: un ambito e discutibile traguardo per il regime ex art. 41-bis comma 2 ord. penit.', in Giuseppe Di Chiara (ed), 2003, *Il processo penale tra politiche della sicurezza e nuovi garantismi* (Giappichelli, 2003) 285–319. On Article 41 bis after 2002, see Sebastiano Ardita, *Il regime detentivo speciale 41 bis* (Giuffré, 2007).

31 Della Bella (n 7) 139.

The 2002 reform also added a statutory statement of purpose of Article 41 bis, expressly mentioning the prevention of connections with organised crime. Furthermore, the scope of offences for which the special prison regime can be imposed was limited to those listed in Article 4 bis of the *Prison Administration Act*, i.e. offences committed within a criminal organisation. To ascertain the inmates' continuing dangerousness, proof of connections between them and the organised criminal group of origin was also mandated. The 2002 reform further introduced a time limit of one to two years for the imposition and renewal of 41 bis orders. It also enhanced the review by the supervisory courts of orders made under Article 41 bis.

Other modifications to Article 41 bis were made in order to reduce possible abuses, provide for more uniformity and consistency of application, and to safeguard the rights of the persons concerned. As a result, the special prison regime became more effective, but the changes also resulted in much wider use of the regime setting. The authority to place persons under the 41 bis prison regime remained in the hands of the Minister of Justice, but it became mandatory to consult prosecution and investigation authorities in that process. This was done to get a better picture of the detainees' connections to organised criminal groups, but it afforded these authorities considerable influence in the decision-making process as well.

10.2.2.3 From 2009 to the present

A further significant reform of Article 41 bis took place in 2009. With Law No 94/2009 the legislator further tightened the rules around the special prison regime.[32] This reform, for the most part, changed the system to the way in which it operates today. The reform was triggered by two interconnected developments. First, with the growing number of top mafia figures being imprisoned, organised crime detainees gained increasing importance for the running and strategies of criminal organisations. Second, and related to the first point, it became clear that organised crime members were able to maintain their roles whilst in prison almost unabated.[33]

As of 27 February 2023, 740 prisoners (including 12 women) were detained in Italian gaols under the 41 bis regime. This is out of a total prison population in Italy of 56,319 persons. The 41 bis detainees were accommodated in 60 sections of 12 different prisons across the country. On the day of the census, 87 inmates were aged 70 years or older, two were hospitalised, and 11 were

32 Carlo Fiorio, 'La stabilizzazione delle "carceri-fortezza": modifiche in tema di ordinamento penitenziario', in Oliviero Mazza and Francesco Viganò (eds), *Il 'pacchetto sicurezza'* (Giappichelli, 2009) 395–421. On the developments in and after 2009, see Paola Corvi, *Trattamento penitenziario e criminalità organizzata* (CEDAM, 2010).

33 Della Bella (n 7) 150.

detained in special 'reserved areas' (discussed later in this chapter).[34] In 2020, 118 new 41 bis orders (20 of them re-applications) and 610 renewals were issued. 209 prisoners were serving final life sentences. In November 2019, 410 41 bis detainees had final convictions (i.e. not in remand and not under appeal). 255 persons detained under 41 bis were members of the Camorra, more than of any other mafia-style organisation.[35]

10.3 Current legal framework and rulings of the Constitutional Court

The following sections summarise the conditions and elements of the 41 bis regime as it now stands and has been in operation since the amendments made by Law No 94/2009.[36]

10.3.1 Scope of application; power to order 41 bis detention

The power to initiate the process leading to detention under Article 41 bis rests exclusively with the Executive. Article 41 bis(2) of the *Prison Administration Act* authorises the Minister of Justice, also at the request of the Minister of the Interior, to suspend, in whole or in part, for serious reasons of order and public safety, the conventional rules relating to the treatment of prisoners and to prisons under the Act if, in particular cases, these rules compromise the need to maintain order and security.

The 41 bis prison regime can be imposed on persons who are in pre-trial detention or who have been sentenced to a term of imprisonment for any of the offences stipulated in Article 4 bis of the *Prison Administration Act.* The list set out here is rather long and the offences are rather heterogeneous; for the purpose of the present chapter, it suffices to note that it encompasses crimes relating to membership of a mafia-type, terrorist, and subversive criminal organisation, relying on or aiding mafia-type criminal organisations, and offences committed for mafia, terrorist, or subversive purposes. In this context, it has to be noted that Article 4 bis serves to deny access to probation measures for persons convicted of any of the offences listed in this provision. Convicted persons may only be exempted from this rule if they agree to become a witness

34 Italy, Board of the National Guarantor for the Rights of Detainees and Persons Deprived of their Liberty, *Thematic Report on the Special Prison Regime Pursuant to Article 41-bis of the Penitentiary Act* (20 March 2023).

35 Associazione Antigone, 'Il carcere visto da dentro. XVIII rapporto di Antigone sulle condizioni di detenzione' (2022) <https://www.rapportoantigone.it/diciottesimo-rapporto-sulle-condizioni-di-detenzione/>.

36 Pierpaolo Rivello, 'Il regime dell'art. 41 bis', in Pierpaolo Rivello (ed), *Profili sistematici del diritto penitenziario* (Giappichelli, 2022) 197–208; Sebastiano Ardita, Leonardo degl'Innocenti, and Francesco Faldi, *Diritto penitenziario* (Laurus Robuffo, 2020) 131–139; Fabio Fiorentin and Carlo Fiorio, *Manuale di diritto penitenziario* (Giuffrè, 2020) 395–408.

for the State in criminal proceedings or if their collaboration with the authorities is impossible or objectively irrelevant.

The default rule under Article 4 bis has been at the centre of several cases before higher courts, such as the Italian Constitutional Court and the ECtHR, especially concerning persons serving a life sentence without the possibility to access alternative measures of detention (*ergastolo ostativo*).[37] These legal challenges resulted in the amendments made by Law No 162/2022 which is relevant for the purposes of this chapter insofar as it theoretically allowed access to probation measures, but only after any 41 bis order is either revoked or no longer renewed.[38] In combination, the result of these provisions is a 'triple crushing effect' on the affected persons, who are not only severed from the outside world by their imprisonment (serving a life sentence) but also barred from accessing probation measures, and, through Article 41 bis, are excluded from the ordinary prison treatment.[39]

The rules regarding the phase in which the imposition of the 41 bis prison regime is considered entrust both ordinary and special anti-mafia prosecution authorities with a powerful role but make no mention of the rights of the persons (and their lawyers) against whom such measures may be imposed. The prosecutor handling the detainee's investigation or trial has to be consulted and give an opinion on the dangerousness of the individual. Furthermore, any other necessary information has to be gathered from the Office of the National Anti-Mafia Prosecutor (*Direzione Nazionale Antimafia*) and central and specialised branches of the police forces.[40]

The initial order under Article 41 bis applies for a period of four years. Subsequent extensions can be made every two years without any limit as to how many times the order can be extended. Law No 279/2002 limited the first order to a period of one to two years and mandated annual renewal after the initial period. To impose or renew the order, it must be shown that the person has not relinquished their capacity to maintain ties with the mafia-type, terrorist, or subversive criminal organisation. To do so, it is required to ascertain the criminal profile of the person, their position in the criminal organisation, the continuing operation of the criminal group, the laying of new charges not previously considered, the outcome of any treatment received in prison, and the standards of living of the person's family members. The mere passing of time is not, in and by itself, a relevant factor to determine whether

37 On the interconnections between 41 bis and *ergastolo ostativo*, see Emilio Dolcini et al., *Il diritto alla speranza davanti alle corti: ergastolo ostativo e articolo 41-bis* (Giappichelli, 2020).

38 Emilio Dolcini, 'Opinioni: L'ergastolo ostativo riformato in articulo mortis', (7 November 2022) *Sistema penale* <https://www.sistemapenale.it/it/opinioni/dolcini-ergastolo-ostativo-riformato-in-articulo-mortis#>.

39 Nicola Valentino, *L'ergastolo: Dall'inizio alla fine* (Sensibili alle foglie, 2009) 98.

40 *Prison Administration Act* (Italy), Article 41 bis(2).

the person is capable of maintaining their ties to the group or to prove that the criminal group has ceased to operate.[41]

10.3.2 Content and consequences of a 41 bis order

The extensive conditions and outcomes of the order are set out in Article 41 bis of the *Prison Administration Act* and regulations issued by the Ministry of Justice, Department of Prison Administration.[42] These conditions concern, *inter alia*, room allocation, in-person conversations and phone calls, defence rights, access to money, access to mail and the ability to receive parcels, representation, social life, visits from the National Guarantor [Ombudsperson] for the Rights of Detainees and Persons Deprived of their Liberty (*Garante nazionale dei diritti delle persone private della libertà personale*), the right to appeal, daily activities, and in-prison treatment.

Generally, 41 bis prisoners must be detained in designated facilities, preferably prisons located on islands or otherwise in special sections of ordinary gaols that are logistically separated from other parts of the prison and are staffed by a specialised branch of the penitentiary police (*Polizia Penitenziaria*). This branch, the *Gruppo Operativo Mobile*, is primarily tasked with managing and monitoring 41 bis inmates. As its name suggests, for security reasons, its members rotate between locations every six to eight months.[43]

Persons detained under Article 41 bis are accommodated in solitary cells furnished with essential items, namely a bed, table, wardrobe, chair, plexiglass mirror, and a television secured within an unbreakable glass box.[44] Windows, bars, gates, and walls ought to be left free of any objects, pictures, or posters, except for a single image of a family member. Limited exceptions include images and symbols of a religious nature, as well as no more than 30 pictures, each no larger than 20 by 30 cm.[45]

In-person conversations by 41 bis detainees are limited to one hour per month, with the possibility to audio-monitor and video-record them. Alternatively, after serving six months of detention under Article 41 bis, phone calls of ten minutes are allowed. The in-person conversations can be carried out with close family members, with three people at most, and to prevent the exchange of objects and any physical contact, they must be conducted by

41 Ibid.

42 Presently, the most relevant is Circular n. 3676/6126 of 2 October 2017. See further, Alessia Meloni and Antonella Fabi, 'Conditions of detention under art. 41-bis 2nd subparagraph of the penitentiary system: its exact functionality. Some comments to the circular letter n. 3676 of 2.10.2017' (2018) 1 *Criminology and Criminal Law Review* 22–29; Carlo Fiorio, 'Le prescrizioni trattamentali e le fonti normative, dalla legge alla circolare amministrativa 2 ottobre 2017' (2020) 1-bis *Giurisprudenza penale web* 69–94.

43 *Prison Administration Act* (Italy), Article 41 bis(2quater).

44 Circular n. 3676/6126 of 2 October 2017, Article 3.

45 Ibid., Article 13.

intercom with the detainee separated by full-height thick glass.[46] In 2023, the Constitutional Court declared that the use of the said barrier is not always required in the case of in-person conversations with minors.[47] Article 41 bis used to restrict conversations and calls between detainees and their lawyers. In 2013, the Constitutional Court held that a limitation on such conversations and calls to three per week was violating the right of defence under Article 24 of the Italian Constitution.[48]

Detainees under 41 bis rules are allowed to work, study, and participate in religious activities.[49] They are permitted to receive money transfers of up to EUR 500 per month or EUR 150 per week; the transfer may be made during the in-person meetings or through mail.[50] In the same manner, detainees may receive parcels weighing up to 10 kg up to twice a month.[51] Any correspondence or other mail received by detainees is monitored and, if necessary, censored (not including mail from Members of Parliament or national or European justice authorities).[52] In 2022, a rule permitting the censoring of mail between detainees and their lawyers was declared unconstitutional by the Constitutional Court in light of Article 24.[53]

46 *Prison Administration Act* (Italy), Article 41 bis(2quater)(b); Circular n. 3676/6126 of 2 October 2017, Articles 16–16.2.

47 Corte Costituzionale, sentenza n 105/2023 (6 April 2023). See further Giovanni Caruso, 'Una nuova stagione del c.d. carcere duro nel prisma delle tecniche decisorie della Consulta? I diritti fondamentali tra "piccoli gesti di vita quotidiana", auspici e perplessità' [2024] 1 *Archivio penale* 1–37; Fabrizio Siracusano, 'Proporzionalità e congruità nella gestione dei colloqui dei detenuti al 41-bis comma 2 ord. penit. con i familiari minorenni' [2023] 3 *Giurisprudenza costituzionale* 1144–1153; Veronica Manca and Silvia Bulighin, 'Il difficile equilibrio nel giudizio di bilanciamento tra contrapposte esigenze di rango costituzionale: la disciplina dei colloqui visivi per i detenuti in regime di "carcere duro"' [2023] 3 *Rivista italiana di diritto e procedura penale* 1207–1210; Roberta Casiraghi, 'La dimensione del diritto del detenuto alle visite familiari fra atti sovranazionali, Corte di Strasburgo e Corte costituzionale' [2023] 3 *Rivista italiana di diritto e procedura penale* 1225–1229.

48 Corte Costituzionale, sentenza n 143/2013 (17 June 2013). See further Paola Corvi, 'La Corte costituzionale riafferma il diritto di difesa dei soggetti sottoposti al regime detentivo previsto dall'art. 41 bis o.p.' [2013] 10 *Diritto penale e processo* 1189–1196; Barbara Giors, 'Illegittime le limitazioni dei colloqui difensivi per i detenuti in regime di "carcere duro"' [2013] 3 *La Legislazione penale* 924–929; Vittorio Manes and Valerio Napoleoni, 'Incostituzionali le restrizioni ai colloqui difensivi dei detenuti in regime di "carcere duro": nuovi tracciati della Corte in tema di bilanciamento dei diritti fondamentali' [2013] 4 *Diritto penale contemporaneo* 336–352; Fabio Fiorentin, 'Regime speciale del "41-bis" e diritto di difesa: il difficile bilanciamento tra diritti fondamentali' [2013] 3 *Giurisprudenza costituzionale* 2180–2187; Marco Ruotolo, 'Le irragionevoli restrizioni al diritto di difesa dei detenuti in regime di 41-bis' [2013] 3 *Giurisprudenza costituzionale* 2176–2180.

49 Circular n. 3676/6126 of 2 October 2017, Articles 33, 34, 36.

50 *Prison Administration Act* (Italy), Article 41 bis(2quater)(c); Circular n. 3676/6126 of 2 October 2017, Article 7.1.

51 *Prison Administration Act* (Italy), Article 41 bis(2quater)(d).

52 Ibid., Article 41 bis(2quater)(e); Circular n. 3676/6126 of 2 October 2017, Articles 18, 18.1.

53 Corte Costituzionale, sentenza n 18/2022 (2 December 2021). See further Riccardo De Vito, 'Carcere duro e visto di censura della corrispondenza con il difensore: una incostituzionalità che conclude un percorso' [2022] 1 *Rivista italiana di diritto e procedura penale* 538–

Article 41 bis detainees may socialise for a maximum of two hours per day in a group of no more than four inmates. The number of hours was increased to up to four by the Constitutional Court in 2025[54] on account of Articles 3 (equality) and 27 (humane and reformational punishment) of the Italian Constitution. Nonetheless, the prison authority is still allowed to reduce them to two for justified reasons.The group is pre-selected by the prison authority to avoid contact between people who have previously spent time in gaol and persons who are either newly placed under the 41 bis regime or have been under it for a long time. Furthermore, prison authorities separate persons who have the same hierarchical status in their respective organised criminal group, who have affiliations with the same group, who are allies, rivals, or come from neighbouring areas.[55]

A rule prohibiting the exchange of objects between 41 bis inmates who are part of the same social group was held to be violating Articles 3 and 27 of the Italian Constitution by the Constitutional Court in 2022.[56] For similar reasons, in 2018 the Court terminated a rule prohibiting 41 bis detainees from heating up food items.[57]

Article 41 bis detainees may only receive and subscribe to newspapers and other periodicals with prior approval from the prison authority.[58] The inmate

541; Giulia Moscatelli, 'La corrispondenza con il difensore del detenuto sottoposto al 41-bis e i visti di censura' [2022] 1 *Archivio penale* 1–13; Fabio Gianfilippi, 'La Corte costituzionale e la corrispondenza intrattenuta dal detenuto in regime differenziato con il proprio difensore' [2022] 1 *Giurisprudenza costituzionale* 241–251; Marco Ruotolo, 'Visto di censura della corrispondenza e diritto di difesa. Un esito nella sostanza condivisibile, raggiunto con una discutibile tecnica decisoria' [2021] 4 *Diritto di difesa* 825–834.

54 Corte Costituzionale, sentenza n 30/2025 (25 February 2025). See further Veronica Manca, '41-bis e ore d'aria: la Corte costituzionale amplia il diritto di permanenza all'aperto anche per il carcere duro' (7 April 2025) IUS Penale <https://ius.giuffrefl.it/dettaglio/11257984/41-bis-e-ore-daria-la-corte-costituzionale-amplia-il-diritto-di-permanenza-allaperto-anche-per-il-carcere-duro?searchText=%2241%20bis%22>.

55 Circular n. 3676/6126 of 2 October 2017, Article 3.1.

56 Corte Costituzionale, sentenza n 97/2020 (5 May 2020). See further Riccardo De Vito, 'L'illegittimità costituzionale della norma che sancisce l'assoluta impossibilità di scambiare oggetti per i detenuti in 41-bis ord. penit.' [2020] 3 *Rivista italiana di diritto e procedura penale* 1577–1581; Davide Galliani, 'Incostituzionale, ma senza esagerare. Il divieto di scambiare oggetti al 41-bis' [2020] 3 *Giurisprudenza costituzionale* 1197–1206.

57 Corte Costituzionale, sentenza n 186/2018 (26 September 2018). See further Ercole Aprile, 'È illegittimo il divieto di cuocere cibi in cella previsto per i detenuti soggetti al regime dell'art. 41-'bis'' [2019] 1 *Cassazione penale* 196–200; Silvia Bernardi, 'Per la Consulta il divieto di cuocere cibi imposto ai condannati al 41-"bis" è inutile e meramente afflittivo. Verso un carcere "duro" più umano?' [2018] 4 *Rivista italiana di diritto e procedura penale* 2325–2343; Riccardo De Vito, 'L'illegittimità costituzionale dell'assoluta impossibilità di cuocere cibi per i detenuti sottoposti al regime dell'art. 41-bis ord. penit' [2018] 4 *Rivista italiana di diritto e procedura penale* 2370–2372; Andrea Bonomi, 'La Corte dichiara incostituzionale il divieto di cuocere cibi per i detenuti sottoposti al regime del "carcere duro": la conclusione persuade, ma la motivazione non convince' [2018] 5 *Giurisprudenza costituzionale* 2096–2105; Riccardo De Vito, 'L'illegittimità costituzionale del divieto di cottura dei cibi per i detenuti in 41-bis' [2018] 5 *Giurisprudenza costituzionale* 2088–2096.

58 Circular n. 3676/6126 of 2 October 2017, Article 19.

can keep at most four books at a time for no more than 40 days each.[59] In 2017, the Constitutional Court held that a rule prohibiting the transfer of books and other publications between 41 bis detainees and from the outside to them is constitutional.[60] Access to television inside the rooms is permissible, though the selection of channels and hours is limited.[61]

10.3.3 Supervision and review

The National Guarantor for the Rights of Detainees and Persons Deprived of their Liberty is allowed access to 41 bis prison sections and to meet inmates without limitations.[62] Supervisory judges are authorised to review the conditions imposed on detainees under their 41 bis order. The original order made by the Minister of Justice and any renewal can be reviewed by the Supervisory Court of Rome.

Centralising these powers in one place sought to bring about some consistency in the case law and ease the work of the Office of the National Anti-Mafia Prosecutor, which is based in Rome as well. It eliminated creative and liberal interpretations by different district supervisory courts across the country and also had the effect that the assessment of the detainees' situation was physically distanced. In some cases, this made the exercise of procedural rights of detainees more cumbersome and prolonged the duration of proceedings.[63] The decisions taken by the Supervisory Court of Rome can be appealed before the Court of Cassation on points of law only.[64]

10.4 Reserved areas

The so-called 'reserved areas' (*aree riservate*) are sections of prisons dedicated to accommodating those 41 bis inmates who are deemed to be particularly dangerous, such as leading organised crime figures. The restrictions placed on detainees in these sections are particularly tight.[65] Generally, reserved areas are designed to comprise only two single cells, a walking area, and a small room. Social interaction is usually limited to two or three inmates. In prison jargon, detainees who share time with mafia bosses in a reserved area are nicknamed

59 Ibid., Article 11.5.

60 Corte Costituzionale, sentenza n 122/2017 (8 February 2017). See further Angela Della Bella, 'Libri e riviste al 41 bis: la Consulta ritiene legittimi i divieti contenuti nelle circolari' [2018] 1 *Diritto penale e processo* 62–68; Agata Ciavola, 'Cosa si nasconde dentro un libro: Riflessioni su alcune restrizioni del regime del c.d. "carcere duro"' [2017] 3 *Giurisprudenza costituzionale* 1236–1246.

61 Circular n. 3676/6126 of 2 October 2017, Article 14.

62 *Prison Administration Act* (Italy), Article 41 bis(2 quater)(1); Circular n. 3676/6126 of 2 October 2017, Article 16.6.

63 See Della Bella (n 7) 285–290.

64 *Prison Administration Act* (Italy), Article 41 bis(2 quinquies), (2 sexies); Circular n. 3676/6126 of 2 October 2017, Article 29.1.

65 See Carlo Fiorio, 'L'Isola che non c'è: "area riservata" e art. 41-bis ord. penit.' [2014] 12 *Giurisprudenza italiana* 2862–2866.

'maids of honour'.[66] There is no limit to the time persons may spend in a reserved area; in theory, they could serve their entire prison sentence there.

The rules and rights applicable to reserved areas are not stipulated in the *Prison Administration Act* or any other statutory law or regulation; they are not present on the 'legal map'. Hence, Carlo Fiorio refers to them as 'nev-erland' (*l'isola che non c'è*), a place that does not officially exist.[67] In a 2008 decision, the ECtHR, however, held that placement in reserved areas did not constitute inhuman or degrading treatment as prohibited by the ECHR.[68] Limited insight into the conditions inside reserved areas can be gained from reports by the National Guarantor for the Rights of Detainees and Persons Deprived of their Liberty and the Council of Europe's European Committee for the Prevention of Torture and Inhuman or Degrading Treatment or Punishment.

In its *Report on the Special Prison Regime Pursuant to Article 41 bis* for the years 2016 to 2018, the National Guarantor noted that 'the application of these rules is sometimes leading to an almost substantial isolation [(*quasi sostanziale isolamento*)] of the detained person (in four cases at L'Aquila, Novara, Parma, and Opera prisons)'.[69] The report raises concerns about the consequences for the mental health of detainees as illustrated in this example:

> Particularly difficult appeared to be the conditions of P.C. who is refusing to share his room with others and to establish any form of community with facts other than his (radio, television, foodies even if packed). A situation clearly due to his psychiatric disorders … [H]e is thus prevented from any form of communication and psychiatric support.[70]

The report further recommended 'that steps be taken to dismiss the "reserved areas" within those prison establishments that have special regime units pursuant to Article 41-bis'.[71]

The Council of Europe's Committee report followed a visit to Italian prisons in March 2019.[72] In relation to reserved areas, it highlighted, *inter*

66 Della Bella (n 7) 193.

67 Fiorio (n 65) 2865.

68 *Bagarella v Italy* (ECtHR, Second Section, Application No 15625/04, 15 January 2008) [35], [43]; see further Giulio Garuti, 'Le limitazioni dovute al regime carcerario ex art. 41-bis ord. pen. non costituiscono trattamento inumano o degradante' [2008] 3 *Diritto penale e processo* 392.

69 Italy, Board of the National Guarantor for the Rights of Detainees and Persons Deprived of their Liberty, *Thematic Report on the Special Prison Regime Pursuant to Article 41-bis of the Penitentiary Act (2016–2018)* (7 January 2019) <https://www.garantenazionaleprivatiliberta.it/gnpl/resources/cms/documents/a5db4acf7c430ee2221c5453720730c2.pdf> 4.

70 Ibid., 5.

71 Ibid.

72 Council of Europe, European Committee for the Prevention of Torture and Inhuman or Degrading Treatment or Punishment (CPT), *Report to the Italian Government on the visit*

alia, issues relating to lack of natural light, privacy, the size and equipment of common rooms, and described communal courtyards as concrete boxes, especially those in the Milan Opera and the Viterbo prisons.[73] Throughout its report, the Committee made a series of recommendations to improve the conditions.

10.5 European Court of Human Rights case law

10.5.1 Prohibition of torture and inhuman or degrading treatment

The ECtHR has decided several cases concerning 41 bis inmates in relation to alleged violations of Article 3 ECHR, which prohibits torture and inhuman or degrading treatment. Some of these cases also include references to Articles 8 (respect of private and family life), 6 (fair trial), and 13 (effective remedy).[74] In sum, and similarly to the Constitutional Court of Italy,[75] the ECtHR has never found 41 bis to be *per se* incompatible with Article 3.[76]

Scholars such as Adriano Martufi have explained the ECtHR's position on Article 41 bis in relation to Article 3 ECHR by referring to the Court's argument that the limitation to contacts within and outside the prison is not absolute since 41 bis inmates are given some, albeit minimal, possibilities to meet in person with family members and to interact with some other prisoners.[77] The ECtHR made the same observation about conditions in reserved areas.[78]

In the leading case *Natoli v Italy*, decided in 1998, the ECtHR stressed that the restrictions imposed by the 41 bis prison regime are triggered by the detainees' conviction for very serious offences and serve the purpose of protecting public order and safety.[79] The Court perceived the regime to create relative rather than absolute isolation because prisoners, within the rules

to Italy carried out by the European Committee for the Prevention of Torture and Inhuman or Degrading Treatment or Punishment (CPT) from 12 to 22 March 2019, CoE Doc CPT/Inf (2020) 2 (21 January 2020).

73 Ibid., 36.

74 See also Della Bella (n 7) 342–353; Carmelo Minnella, 'La giurisprudenza della Corte europea dei diritti dell'uomo sul regime carcerario ex art. 41 bis ord. penit. e la sua applicazione nell'ordinamento italiano' [2004] 3 *Rassegna penitenziaria e criminologica* 197–235.

75 See Morris Marini, 'Il regime dell'art. 41-bis ord. penit. negli itinerari della giurisprudenza costituzionale' [2022] 2 *Archivio penale* 1–43.

76 See, for instance, *Enea v Italy* (ECtHR, Grand Chamber, Application No 74912/01, 17 September 2009) [67].

77 See Adriano Martufi, *Diritti dei detenuti e spazio penitenziario europeo* (Jovene, 2015) 175, 177.

78 *Bagarella v Italy* (n 68) [32]–[34], [43].

79 *Natoli v Italy* (ECtHR, Application No 26161/95, 18 May 1998) [1]. See further Giuseppe La Greca, 'Diritti dell'uomo e regime dell'art. 41 bis ord. penit.' [1998] 9 *Foro italiano* 321–324.

of their specific circumstances, are permitted to receive family visitors, engage with other inmates, and make some phone calls.[80]

The ECtHR has been criticised for adopting the same position indiscriminately across multiple cases, thus failing to sufficiently examine the individual situations of and different restrictions imposed on detainees and, consequently, for making hasty decisions.[81] The Court has also been accused of ignoring humanitarian grounds, such as ill health, presented by the applicants.[82]

On the other hand, the ECtHR's approach may be explained by its doctrine of positive obligations, demanding that States adopt adequate measures for the protection of the community from people deemed to be dangerous,[83] which is particularly relevant in the organised crime context. In relation to special prison regimes in other States, the ECtHR's requests have mostly centred on solitary confinement and on calls on States to find alternative arrangements.[84]

10.5.2 Provenzano v Italy

A slightly different position crystallises from the 2018 case of *Provenzano v Italy* where the ECtHR indeed found a violation of Article 3 ECHR by the 41 bis prison regime.[85] The case involves Bernardo Provenzano who was the *de facto* leader of the Cosa Nostra following the arrests of his predecessors, Salvatore Riina in 1993 and Leoluca Bagarella in 1995, until Provenzano's capture in 2006. Provenzano was sentenced to multiple terms of life imprisonment for serious crimes, including membership of a mafia-type organisation. During one of his criminal proceedings in Palermo in 2012, experts were appointed to assess his mental capacity to participate in the trial. In 2013, they concluded that his capacity was compromised and consequently the proceedings against him were suspended. A year later, his son was appointed as his legal guardian.[86]

80 *Natoli v Italy* (n 79) [1].

81 Della Bella (n 7) 326.

82 Angela Colella, 'Art. 3', in Giulio Ubertis and Francesco Viganò (eds), *Corte di Strasburgo e giustizia penale* (Giappichelli, 2022) 108.

83 See, *inter alia, Maiorano and others v Italy* (ECtHR, Second Section, Application No 28634/06, 15 December 2009) [103]–[109].

84 See, *inter alia, Piechowicz v Poland* (ECtHR, Fourth Section, Application No 20071/07, 17 April 2012) [164].

85 *Provenzano v Italy* (ECtHR, First Section, Application No 55080/13, 25 October 2018) [158]. See further Luca Pressacco, 'Presupposti di applicazione dell'art. 41-bis ord. penit. e condizioni di salute del detenuto' [2019] 1 *Rivista italiana di diritto e procedura penale* 669–673; Raffaello Magi, 'L'incidenza delle condizioni di salute ai fini della valutazione della ingiustizia del trattamento carcerario differenziato' [2019] 1 *Cassazione penale* 401–408; Giulia Colavecchio, 'Riflessioni sul 41-bis a margine della sentenza Provenzano c. Italia' (21 March 2019) *La Legislazione penale* 1–22; Adriano Martufi, 'Il "carcere duro" tra prevenzione e diritti: verso un nuovo statuto garantistico?' [2019] 2 *Diritto penale e processo* 259–269; Marina Silvia Mori, 'A Strasburgo c'è un Giudice anche per i capimafia: con Provenzano non cade ma scricchiola il 41-bis' [2018] 10 *Giurisprudenza penale web* 1–9.

86 *Provenzano v Italy* (n 84) 6–13.

Provenzano's health and cognitive abilities deteriorated in the following years, leading to his death in 2016.[87]

During Provenzano's time in gaol, his lawyers filed several requests to suspend the execution of his sentences on health grounds pursuant to Articles 146 and 147 of the *Penal Code*, and seeking less restrictive detention conditions. The Supervisory Courts in Bologna and Milan both rejected the requests, noting that in line with Article 146 he could receive adequate treatment either in prison or in a hospital. In relation to Article 147, it was noted that Provenzano was a dangerous inmate, had been a fugitive, and had been tried and convicted for extremely serious offences such that he could not be released from gaol. On appeal, the Court of Cassation upheld both decisions. In 2016, a Milan supervisory judge dismissed a similar request by Provenzano's lawyers.[88]

In 2006, soon after his capture, the Minister of Justice issued a 41 bis order against Provenzano, which was later renewed multiple times. Although the District Anti-Mafia Prosecutor offices of Palermo, Caltanissetta, and Florence did not endorse a further renewal, the Minister of Justice extended the special prison regime for a further two years in 2014, and the Court of Cassation upheld this decision. In 2016, shortly before his death, the Prosecutors Offices of Caltanissetta and Florence reiterated their view, but the regime was nevertheless extended for a further two years. An appeal to the Supervisory Court of Rome was discontinued when Provenzano died.[89] His lawyers argued that Provenzano's imprisonment was unjustifiable because of his poor health as well as his age (he was 80 years old at that time). They claimed that Italy was not properly protecting his health and well-being and that any further detention under 41 bis would amount to a violation of Article 3 ECHR.[90] Counsel for Italy countered that national authorities had evaluated Provenzano's situation on numerous occasions and found no grounds to release him and stressed that he was still deemed to be dangerous.[91]

The ECtHR separately considered the incompatibility of Provenzano's detention with his health and the continued application of 41 bis. The Court did not find that his age and poor health, whilst serious, would prevent him from remaining in prison and could not find any violation of Article 3 ECHR in this context.[92] Regarding Article 41 bis, the Court noted that it had

> already had ample opportunity to assess the Article 41 bis regime in a large number of cases before it, and [had] concluded that, in the circumstances of those cases, the imposition of the regime does not give rise to an issue under Article 3 [ECHR], even when it has been imposed for lengthy periods of time.[93]

87 Ibid., [15]–[47].
88 Ibid., [48]–[55].
89 Ibid., [56]–[80].
90 Ibid., [117]–[119], [142].
91 Ibid., [120]–[125], [143]–[146].
92 Ibid., [126]–[141].
93 Ibid., [147].

Given the crimes he had committed, the ECtHR agreed that Provenzano was a dangerous prisoner, but it did not share the authorities' justification for renewing 41 bis detention. The Court argued that whilst Provenzano's deteriorating health would not bar him from being in gaol, it would cast doubt over his continuing dangerousness and his ability to maintain ties with his organised criminal group, and thus could not justify the renewal of 41 bis detention. For these reasons the ECtHR found the use of the special prison regime beyond 2016 to be violating Article 3.[94] The Court noted that it could not 'but conclude that there [was] insufficient evidence in the reasoning of the order of a genuine reassessment having been made with regard to relevant changes in the applicant's situation, in particular his critical cognitive decline'.[95]

10.5.3 ECtHR case law, European Prison Rules, Mandela Rules, and future trends

The ECtHR case law on Article 41 bis provides some insight into the conditions experienced by persons subjected to this prison regime and into the practical reality of its application. The case law further adds to the interpretation of general principles of punishment and provides an outside perspective removed from national politics and populism on the operation of the national prison system, especially through the lens of the fundamental rights enshrined in the ECHR.

Upon closer consideration, *Provenzano v Italy* marks a milestone in the ECtHR jurisprudence on Article 41 bis. Subtly, the case brings to the surface the effect of the 41 bis prison regime on the health of detainees and brings to mind the scientific research on the detrimental results of solitary confinement on the physical and mental health of prisoners, which has also been documented by the World Medical Association.[96] The case is the first in which the health of a 41 bis detainee was assessed in connection with his continuing dangerousness.[97] The decision of the ECtHR suggests that given his physical and mental health at the time of the final renewal, the 41 bis order had no more preventative function and merely served retributative purposes.[98] *Provenzano v Italy* also highlights the importance of proper review and appeal mechanisms to safeguard fundamental rights in cases of 41 bis detention. It demonstrates that the actual or perceived dangerousness of the detainee used to justify detention under 41 bis must be weighed against human rights and compassionate factors.

94 Ibid., [147]–[158].

95 Ibid., [156].

96 World Medical Association, 'Statement on Solitary Confinement' (28 September 2019) <https://www.wma.net/policies-post/wma-statement-on-solitary-confinement/>.

97 Pressacco (n 85) 672.

98 Colavecchio (n 85) 19–20.

On the other hand, the position in *Provenzano v Italy* is, on the whole, in line with prior ECtHR case law on the 41 bis prison regime.[99] It once more signals that the Court pays close attention to the protection of Article 3 of the ECHR in the context of Article 41 bis, especially in relation to the renewal of 41 bis orders and the ability to appeal them.[100]

Looking beyond *Provenzano v Italy*, the ECtHR might in the future broaden its perspective on 41 bis detention by considering guidelines and other rules developed by the Council of Europe and the United Nations to safeguard the rights of sentenced persons. Chief among these are the *European Prison Rules* of 2020[101] and the *United Nations Standard Minimum Rules for the Treatment of Prisoners*, commonly referred to as the *Nelson Mandela Rules*, of 2015,[102] which the ECtHR has cited on previous occasions.[103]

The *European Prison Rules* contain comprehensive provisions on solitary confinement. Rule 53 concerns special high security and safety measures and requires, *inter alia*, that '[t]he nature of any such measures, their duration and the grounds on which they may be applied, as well as the procedures to be followed in imposing and implementing them, shall be determined by national law'[104] and that '[s]uch measures shall only be based on the current risk that a prisoner poses, shall be proportionate to that risk and shall not entail more restrictions than are necessary to counter that risk'.[105] Rule 53A, added in 2020, among other things stresses that 'separation shall be used for the shortest period necessary to achieve its objectives and shall be regularly reviewed in line with these objectives' (53A.c) and that 'prisoners who are separated shall not be subject to further restrictions beyond those necessary for meeting the stated purpose of such separation' (53A.d). It further affirms that 'the decision on separation shall take into account the state of health of the prisoners concerned and any disabilities they may have which may render them more vulnerable to the adverse effects of separation' (53A.b) and that 'when separation is adversely affecting a prisoner's physical or mental health, action shall be taken to suspend it or to replace it with a less restrictive measure' (53A.i). Furthermore, it states that 'any prisoner who is separated shall have a right of complaint in the terms set out in Rule 70' (53A.j).

99 Magi (n 85) 405.
100 Martufi (n 85) 659.
101 Council of Europe, Committee of Ministers, *Recommendation Rec(2006)2-rev of the Committee of Ministers to member States on the European Prison Rules* (1 July 2020) (hereafter '*European Prison Rules*').
102 UN General Assembly, *The United Nations Standard Minimum Rules for the Treatment of Prisoners (the Nelson Mandela Rules)*, UN Doc A/RES/70/175 (8 January 2016).
103 See, *inter alia*, *Muršić v Croatia* (ECtHR, Grand Chamber, Application No 7334/13, 20 October 2016) [55], [59].
104 *European Prison Rules*, Rule 53.4.
105 Ibid., Rule 53.8.

The *Nelson Mandela Rules* similarly require that solitary confinement be subject to authorisation by law or by the regulation of the competent administrative authority (Rule 37). Rule 43 states that '[i]n no circumstances may restrictions or disciplinary sanctions amount to torture or other cruel, inhuman or degrading treatment or punishment'.[106] It expressly calls for the prohibition of both indefinite and prolonged solitary confinement. Rule 44 defines solitary confinement as the 'confinement of prisoners for 22 hours or more a day without meaningful human contact',[107] and prolonged solitary confinement to mean 'solitary confinement for a time period in excess of 15 consecutive days'.[108] Rule 45 stipulates that solitary confinement 'shall be used only in exceptional cases as a last resort, for as short a time as possible and subject to independent review, and only pursuant to the authorisation by a competent authority'.[109] The second paragraph adds that solitary confinement 'should be prohibited in the case of prisoners with mental or physical disabilities when their conditions would be exacerbated by such measures'.[110]

Upon closer inspection, it is questionable whether several features of the 41 bis detention regime are truly compatible with the *European Prison Rules* and the *Nelson Mandela Rules.* For example, many restrictions imposed under the 41 bis system are not articulated in legislation but instead in circulars issued by the Ministry of Justice, Department of Prison Administration, chief among them Circular n. 3676/6126 of 2 October 2017. The 'reserved areas' used to detain 41 bis inmates are also not mentioned in prison legislation. It is moreover questionable how restrictions that are not geared towards the prevention of contact between persons and organised criminal groups (such as those relating to the preparation of food, the display of pictures in cells, the possession of books, etc.) can be justified in light of the *European Prison Rules* and the *Mandela Rules.* The case of *Provenzano v Italy* also demonstrates how health concerns are sometimes not taken into consideration although this is mandated under these provisions. Further concerns relate to the ability and scope of appeal and review mechanisms.

10.6 Conclusion

The present chapter sought to outline and assess the 41 bis prison regime in light of its stated purpose. First, it is essential to ask whether the original aim of Article 41 bis, introduced as an extraordinary measure and later converted to a permanent feature of Italy's corrections system, still holds true. Here it appears that criminal justice has been utilised to serve a symbolic function and

106 *Nelson Mandela Rules*, Rule 43.
107 Ibid., Rule 44.
108 Ibid.
109 Ibid., Rule 45.
110 Ibid.

as a retaliatory tool by the State to counter the 'war' waged by the Cosa Nostra in the early 1990s. What Franco Corleone refers to as a 'war logic',[111] was used to dehumanise *mafiosi* and pave the way for a 'criminal law of the enemy' (*diritto penale del nemico*).[112] This meant that the focus shifted to the perpetrator rather than their crimes. It all but eliminated reformation and rehabilitation from the purposes of punishment and undermined the impartiality of the judiciary.[113] In essence, it involves the segregation and neutralisation of some inmates.[114]

Second, the criteria used to determine which restrictions are imposed on prisoners should aim to prevent the inmate from having contact with members of organised criminal groups within and outside the prison system. In a negative sense, this means that additional restrictions on interactions with and visits by family members should be avoided and require special justification. This position is echoed by more recent decisions by the Constitutional Court, which demonstrate greater awareness of the significant isolation of 41 bis prisoners and tend to view unnecessary restrictions as unconstitutional. This is a welcome development that may evolve further and warrant a more holistic look at the sum of all restrictions imposed on 41 bis prisoners rather than piecemeal evaluations of individual provisions.

Third, the duration of 41 bis measures, specifically the lack of any time limit, seems excessive and unjustifiable. What is needed is much closer, more frequent, and individualised assessments of the prisoners' ongoing (or fading) contact and association with organised criminal groups and of the prisoners' continuing (or passing) dangerousness behind bars. Such assessments, importantly, also need to give due consideration to the toll prolonged detention in isolation takes on the prisoners; in medical and sociological studies, the physical and mental harm caused by solitary confinement and detention in near isolation is well documented. As seen in the case of *Provenzano v Italy*, the ECtHR has cautiously started to address this issue, but there is much work left to be done to fully confront it. The *European Prison Rules* and the *Nelson Mandela Rules* articulate clear guidelines and boundaries for solitary confinement, which should be considered not only in future ECtHR case law but also in national prison laws.

Fourth, the legal basis of Article 41 bis is not sufficient. The restrictions placed on inmates' rights are not adequately articulated in the *Prison Administration Act*; most of them are merely outlined in regulations issued

111 Franco Corleone, '41-bis, un regime detentivo senza fine ma con un fine' [2016] *Criminalia, Annuario di scienze penalistiche* 248, 260.

112 See Giunta, Ardita, and Pavarini (n 6) 272.

113 Massimo Donini, 'Diritto penale di lotta: Ciò che il dibattito sul diritto penale del nemico non deve limitarsi a esorcizzare' [2007] 2 *Studi sulla questione criminale* 55–88.

114 Luigi Manconi, Stefano Anastasia, and Valentina Calderone, 'Abolire il "carcere duro": Legittimità e limiti del 41-bis alla luce della sua applicazione' [2016] *Criminalia, Annuario di scienze penalistiche* 263, 264.

by the Ministry of Justice, Department of Prison Administration. This raises concerns over the arbitrariness placed in the hands of government departments. This is best reflected in the rules around 'reserved areas' which may be described as 'special prisons within a special prison regime'. Indeed, it is desirable to discontinue the reserved areas altogether.

Fifth, there are questions about the procedural guarantees for 41 bis detainees. The issuing and renewal of 41 bis orders are largely in the hands of government departments and not as impartial as they would be if this was vested in the judiciary.[115] Further concerns relate to the long validity of 41 bis orders (four years initially and two years upon renewal). Also, the fact that 41 bis orders can only be reviewed by the Supervisory Court of Rome rather than district supervisory courts may prevent timely assessments of individual cases and thus further erode the rights of 41 bis prisoners. It may be preferable to expand the ability to appeal to the Court of Cassation beyond matters that are merely points of law as well.

In sum, much needs to be done to ensure that the special prison regime established by Article 41 bis of Italy's *Prison Administration Act* fully complies with the requirements and safeguards set out in the Italian Constitution, the ECHR, the *European Prison Rules*, and the *Nelson Mandela Rules*. There are considerable concerns regarding the function, content, legal basis, and processes of the 41 bis system. Looking back, it appears that the original system introduced in 2002 was more appropriate than the changes made in 2009. Looking ahead, careful attention needs to be given to properly assess the inmates' dangerousness, avoid unnecessary limitations on their contacts within and beyond prison facilities, and enhance the means of review and appeal. The ECtHR's decision in *Provenzano v Italy* gives some hope that Article 41 bis may be applied and interpreted more carefully and fairly in the future.

115 See further Angela Della Bella, 'Carcere e 41 bis: tra poteri del Ministro della Giustizia e opportunità di affermare la riserva di giurisdizione; note a margine del caso Cospito e di una recente decisione della Cassazione' [2023] 3 *Sistema penale* 81–87.

Index

Note: Page number followed by 'n' indicates note numbers.

FSC
www.fsc.org
MIX
Papier | Fördert gute Waldnutzung
FSC® C083411

Kolibri 360 GmbH
Ferdinand-Jühlke-Straße 7
99095 Erfurt, Deutschland
produktsicherheit@kolibri360.de